# Object-Oriented Metrics

PRENTICE HALL
OBJECT-ORIENTED
SERIES

# OBJECT-ORIENTED METRICS

## METRICS

## Measures of Complexity

Brian Henderson-Sellers

For book and bookstore information

http://www.prenhall.com

Learning Resources
Centre

Prentice Hall PTR
Upper Saddle River, New Jersey 07458

**Library of Congress Cataloging-in-Publication Data**

Henderson-Sellers, Brian.
    Object-oriented metrics : measures of complexity / B. Henderson
-Sellers
        p.    cm. — (Object-oriented series)
    Includes bibliographical references and index.
    ISBN 0–13–239872–9
    1. Object-oriented programming (Computer science) 2. Computer
software—Development.  I. Title.  II. Series: Prentice Hall object-
oriented series.
QA76.64.H47   1996                       95-35148
005.1'4—dc20                              CIP

Editorial/production supervision: *Kerry Reardon*
Cover design: *Design Source*
Cover design director: *Jerry Votta*
Manufacturing buyer: *Alexis R. Heydt*
Acquisitions editor: *Paul Becker*

© 1996 by Prentice Hall PTR
Prentice-Hall, Inc.
A Simon & Schuster Company
Upper Saddle River, New Jersey 07458

The publisher offers discounts on this book when ordered
in bulk quantities. For more information, contact:

        Corporate Sales Department
        Prentice Hall PTR
        One Lake Street
        Upper Saddle River, NJ 07548

        Phone: 800-382-3419
        Fax: 201-236-7141
        E-mail: corpsales@prenhall.com

Printed in the United States of America

10  9  8  7  6  5  4  3  2  1

**ISBN 0-13-239872-9**

Prentice-Hall International (UK) Limited, *London*
Prentice-Hall of Australia Pty. Limited, *Sydney*
Prentice-Hall Canada, Inc., *Toronto*
Prentice-Hall Hispanoamericana, S.A., *Mexico*
Prentice-Hall of India Private Limited, *New Delhi*
Prentice-Hall of Japan, Inc., *Tokyo*
Simon & Schuster Asia Pte. Ltd., *Singapore*
Editora Prentice-Hall do Brasil, Ltda., *Rio de Janeiro*

*To Ann,*
*without whom nothing would be worthwhile*

# CONTENTS

# PREFACE

Object-oriented metrics are an integral part of object technology and of good software engineering. Careful implementation of a metrics program can offer a significant range of advantages:

- A quantitative understanding of both the architecture and the detailed design of the system so that successes can be built on and repeats of failures avoided. Without metrics, risk levels are significantly higher
- A quantitative evaluation of the value of object technology (OT), for example, in terms of productivity, effort, time, and maintainability of systems
- An objective evaluation as to whether a particular design/program has all the hallmarks of a good object-oriented design/program or whether it is "sheep dressed as lamb"
- The basis for good cost estimation of object-oriented projects
- An integral part of a well thought out management strategy for object-oriented projects

This book presents the state-of-the-art on object-oriented (OO) metrics. The text is divided into eight chapters: moving through object-oriented concepts, measurement theory, a discussion of available metrics, and then how to implement them in an individual setting.

Chapter 1 introduces object-oriented ideas in the context of the product development life cycle. It is important to have a broad understanding of the technical aspects of object technology (OT) and, perhaps more importantly, to understand how and why OO project management issues are different from the traditional software development environment. These relate to team structures, the iterative life cycle, the incremental delivery of the software, and the library management of reusable and pluggable components.

Having laid the context from a project management viewpoint, we then move to more philosophical and technical issues. It is most important that the role of quantitative evaluation of software (via metrics) is seen against the backdrop of traditional science, engineering, and mathematics; as well as from a social science viewpoint. It is too easily forgotten that we are not just measuring artifacts but also people's interaction with them. Consequently, unlike science and engineering, it is difficult to derive hard and fast rules. The data are much more fuzzy when grossed up across the software engineering profession. How do we interpret these data and how do we validate the underlying metrics? Chapter 2 discusses all these issues before we discuss the metrics themselves.

Chapter 3 presents different categorizations of metrics. We discuss product versus process metrics and complexity in its many guises; and then draw these ideas together in the multidimensional framework. Chapter 4 formalizes the preceding discussion. It is important that measurement theory is seen to underly the metrics we use. Some basic understanding is therefore needed. Measurement theory provides not only the underlying rigor but also offers stability, utility, and confidence to the metrics user. Also included in this chapter is a presentation of some axiomatic approaches.

The next two chapters focus on structural complexity metrics, first in a non-OO environment (Chapter 5). Here we discriminate between intra-module and inter-module metrics and discuss the attributes of size, complexity, and control flow. The corresponding metrics are then evaluated against the measurement theory and axiomatic approaches of Chapter 4. Chapter 6 follows the format of Chapter 5, but now in an OO environment, drawing heavily on the material in Chapter 5 and assessing its usefulness for OT. In addition to a presentation and evaluation of OO structural complexity metrics, we also include a discussion of the currently proposed suites of OO metrics (rather than individual metrics) since it is clear that no one metric can give us all the information we need to measure a project (Fenton, 1994). The project manager has to choose the most appropriate metrics or suite(s) of metrics from those available.

Most of the current work on metrics ignores the programmer. Yet it is repeatedly pointed out (e.g., Curtis, 1981) that the productivities of two programmers from the same school, with ostensibly the same training and level of skill, may in fact be a factor of more than twenty times different. It is therefore critical that the programmer be brought into metrics. Chapter 7 lays the groundwork for this by introducing the cognitive complexity model.

Finally, in Chapter 8, we round off the text by an overview of current industrial applications—in terms of data availability and some ideas regarding the introduction of a measurement program into your OO environment. This last chapter focuses on how to introduce these ideas into your organization. While there are many useful lessons here, we should note that each organization is an individual. So, the way these ideas are implemented will probably require some on-site tailoring, at least at the detailed level. With careful and thoughtful introduction of a metrics program, all the benefits we identified above are attainable.

In this present volume on object-oriented metrics, the focus is on OO *complexity* metrics. Process and reuse metrics will be the topic of a future volume. The book offers insights to both technical readers and to managers. The material has been presented at conferences such as TOOLS, ECOOP, and OOPSLA over the last few years and has benefited greatly from audience feedback. As well as members of those audiences, I wish to thank, in alphabetical order, those friends and colleagues who have given of their time freely to read through preliminary drafts of this text. I am particularly grateful to Ishbel Duncan, Ian Graham, Simon Moser, and Horst Zuse; and also to the series editor, Bertrand Meyer, for his advice and continuing support.

In addition, I wish to acknowledge the following copyright holders for permission to reprint copyright material:

ACM for Tables 6.7, 6.10, 6.11, 8.3; Figures 1.1, 5.11, 6.1
American Meteorological Society for Figure 3.4
Barry Boehm for Figure 1.1
Cambridge University Press for Tables 4.2, 4.3
Chapman and Hall for Table 5.1, Figures 5.3–5.5, 6.20, 8.5
David Tegarden for Table 6.13; Figure 6.9
Elsevier for Tables 2.1, 7.1; Figures 3.8, 6.10, 7.2, 7.3, 8.3(b)
IEAust for Table 2.2(a)
IEEE for Tables 2.2(b), 4.5, 6.2; Figures 3.2, 3.5, 5.6, 5.7, 6.6, 8.1
Macmillan Publishing Company for Table 8.4
Miller Freeman Publishing for Figures 6.4, 6.18
Norman Fenton and Chapman & Hall for Figure 5.8
Robert Grady for Table 8.6
SIGS for Figures 1.2, 1.3, 1.4, 1.5, 1.11, 7.4–7.13
Walter de Gruyter for Figure 4.2
Watts Humphrey for Table 3.1

The following trademarks are used in the text:

Actor is a trademark of Symantec
Borland C++ is a trademark of Borland International, Inc.
C++ and Unix are trademarks of AT&T
C++/Views is a trademark of CNS, Inc.
Eiffel is a trademark of the Non-Profit International Consortium for Eiffel
Eiffel/S is a trademark of SIG Computer
OOMetric is a trademark of Hatteras Software, Inc.
Smalltalk and ObjectWorks are trademarks of ParcPlace Systems, Inc.
Smalltalk/V is a trademark of Digitalk, Inc.

Last, but by no means least, I wish to thank Ann for her ever-continuing support, in the midst of her own ever-expanding career as an internationally renowned scientist.

# GLOSSARY OF TECHNICAL TERMS

ADT: a description of the external characteristics of the object class. An ADT represents the concept with no implementation.

class: the ADT plus the implementation; although also loosely used to mean the collective notion of abstract data types (i.e., a grouping as opposed to an individual).

cohesion: "the degree to which the tasks performed by a single program module are functionally related" (IEEE, 1983).

complexity: the difficulty of comprehension/maintainability. Resources expended.

coupling: connection between two or more object classes.

implementation inheritance: inheritance that does not conform to the notion of is-a-kind-of.

interface inheritance: *see* specification inheritance.

object: an individual or an instance.

O/C: object/class = generic term to mean either objects (individuals) or classes (groupings or templates or concepts) within the context of the particular life-cycle stage.

OO (object-orientation): a way of thinking and modeling the business/real-world domain that focuses on encapsulation and modularization, semantic cohesion and classification, polymorphism and inheritance.

SDLC: the process underlying the delivery of a piece of software. The software development life-cycle describes all the temporal attributes from initiation of the project to delivery to the user and then to future maintenance and support for the product.

size: numbers of lines, extent of functionality.

specification or interface inheritance: inheritance that adheres to the is-a-kind-of relationship that supports substitutability.

subsystem: a semantic grouping of a number of O/Cs. These O/Cs collaborate to provide high-level functionality and are often associated with specific aspects of the system, such as the user interface or the data storage and retrieval.

type: *see* ADT.

# LIST OF ACRONYMS

| | | | |
|---|---|---|---|
| ADT | abstract data type | I/O | input/output |
| AMC | average method coupling | IDP | iterative development process |
| AMI | application of metrics to industry (program) | ISO | International Standards Organization |
| API | application programming interface | LCOM | lack of cohesion of methods |
| | | LGC | library of generalized components |
| CBO | coupling between objects | LOC | lines of code |
| CC | class coupling | LPRC | library of potentially reusable components |
| CMM | cognitive complexity model | | |
| CIC | class inheritance-related coupling | MC | method coupling |
| CLOS | common LISP object system | MDF | multidimensional framework |
| CCM | capability maturity model | MIS | management information system |
| CNIC | class noninheritance-related coupling | MIT | Massachusetts Institute of Technology |
| CPC | class path coupling | MOOD | metrics for object-oriented design |
| DAC | data abstract coupling | MOSES | methodology for object-oriented software engineering of systems |
| DAGs | direct acyclic graphs | | |
| DDD | data-driven design | | |
| DIT | depth of inheritance tree | | |
| DoD | Department of Defense | MPC | message-passing coupling |
| DSS | decision support system | MS | method size |
| | | MTTR | measured mean time to repair |
| FP | function point | | |
| FPA | function point analysis | NCV | number of class variables |
| | | NEM | number of external methods |
| GQM | goal/question/metric (paradigm) | NHM | number of hidden methods |
| GUI | graphical user interface | NIH | National Institutes of Health |

| | | | |
|---|---|---|---|
| NIV | number of instance variables | RDD | responsibility-driven design |
| NLM | number of local methods | RFC | response for a class |
| NOA | number of attributes | ROI | return on investment |
| NOC | number of children | RS | response set |
| NOM | number of methods | | |
| NORM | number of overridden methods | SC | size/complexity |
| | | SDLC | software development life cycle |
| NOT | number of tramps | | |
| NRM | number of remote methods | SEI | Software Engineering Institute |
| O/Cs | objects/classes | SLOC | source lines of code |
| OO | object-oriented | SOMA | semantic object modeling approach |
| OOPL | object-oriented programming language | | |
| OOSE | object-oriented software engineering | TQM | total quality management |
| | | UoD | universe of discourse |
| OT | object technology | UTS | University of Technology, Sydney |
| PC-CMM | people management capability maturity model | | |
| | | VOD | violations of the law of Demeter |
| PPM | parameters per method | | |
| QA | quality assurance | WAC | weighted attributes per class |
| RAD | rapid applications development | WMC | weighted methods per class |

# 1

# AN OBJECT-ORIENTED
# PRODUCT DEVELOPMENT

Object-oriented information systems are becoming increasingly popular in industrial software development environments. Object technology (OT) offers support to deliver products to market more quickly and to provide higher-quality products with lower maintenance costs. OT provides a close link between technology and business, offering the possibility of business object modeling and business process reengineering with objects (e.g., Taylor, 1995; Jacobson *et al.,* 1995).

Managing any development project requires adequate measurements to be taken and used as feedback to construct better strategies and techniques for future projects, initially in the same domain and, after further, more extensive validation, in different domains. As expertise in managing object-oriented (OO) projects grows, such a body of OO metrics knowledge will become increasingly usable across the industry. There is no doubt that there is currently an intense interest in and demand for good OO metrics for both process and product management.

The questions to be posed, and answered in detail in this book, are given in Table 1.1. The first focus (discussed shortly) is on why we need a book on *object-oriented* metrics in addition to those excellent ones of, for example, Fenton (1991) and Card and Glass (1990) on traditional metrics: Are OO systems different in ways that affect measurements of them? Of course, I believe that the answer to that is "Yes"—and presumably so do you since you are reading the book. Specifically, I would suggest that major differences lie in the newer life cycles used in developing OO systems, in the system structuring, and in the focus on objects/classes, or O/Cs (Henderson-Sellers and Edwards, 1994). The second set of questions raised in Table 1.1 relate to project management, focusing on new team structures, managing the life cycle, the role of libraries, and the new "product culture" (Meyer, 1989) and the

**TABLE 1.1   Four question areas
to be addressed**

---

1. Are OO systems any different?
   Life cycles
   System structuring
   Objects and classes
2. Project management
   Team structure
   Life-cycle phases
   Library management
   Quality and the new "product culture"
   The need for metrics
3. Applicability of traditional metrics?
4. New metrics?
   ROI
   Inheritance measures

---

overall need for metrics. We must then ask if traditional metrics are applicable in the "brave new world" of object technology and what new metrics are needed.

We answer these questions in this chapter. In Section 1.1 we clarify OO terminology, focusing particularly on the project management context, and in Section 1.2 we expand on those management aspects of direct relevance to the topic of metrics. In Section 1.3 we introduce reuse, and in Section 1.4 we confirm the need for metrics.

## 1.1 WHAT ARE THE DIFFERENCES?

While there are, of course, many similarities between OO projects and projects undertaken in a traditional environment, there are some differences that must be recognized (Table 1.2). These include the more iterative/recursive life cycle (e.g., Henderson-Sellers and Edwards, 1993), which imposes the need for a framework for the methodological steps and activities, as well as an emphasis on reuse and quality. The architectural differences between OO systems and traditional systems are also significant. These differences include a focus on peer-to-peer relationships rather than hierarchical decomposition for control flow, the enhanced number of abstraction levels utilized (e.g., system, subsystem, class, method), and the utilization of inheritance structures to interrelate classes. For instance, the presence of inheritance structures cannot be described by any existing metrics or modifications thereof, thus leading to the need to develop totally original measures. On the other hand, the peer-to-peer interactions can probably be described by some form of fan-in/fan-out measures. Size may be derivable from a weighted sum of attributes and methods, but the size of subclasses is highly problematical, especially where multiple inheritance structures are involved. Finally, it becomes even more important than in traditional systems to clarify to what abstraction level and to what life-cycle stage any particular metric applies.

**TABLE 1.2.  Why are OO systems different?**

- Recursive/iterative life cycle
- Reuse
- System structuring: subsystem, classes, methods
- Peer-to-peer message passing (with respect to fan-in/fan-out)
- More abstraction levels
- Inheritance structures
- Internal features (with respect to McCabe and fan-in/fan-out)

### 1.1.1 The Basic Concepts of Object Technology

OO systems development emphasizes three software design fundamentals that have been purported to be useful in controlling software complexity: modularity/identity, abstraction by classification, and polymorphism/inheritance (Henderson-Sellers, 1995b).

Modularity is closely associated with encapsulation and information hiding, which allow a modification to be made to the internal operations of an object (with its own unique and immutable identity) by hiding the implementation detail behind a public interface. As long as the modifications do not affect the public interface, the modifications should not have any unwanted side effects in other objects. This reduces complexity by ensuring that changes to the internal operations of an object are contained within that object.

Abstraction refers to the consideration of only those characteristics pertinent to your present purpose. Another word often used is granularity. Using abstraction permits selective information hiding based on scale issues. Classification is one particular form of abstraction by which individuals (objects) of similar/identical characteristics are grouped together in a common class. Together, the notions of abstraction and classification lead to the creation of concepts. A concept is equivalent to the programmer's abstract data type (ADT): another, more transparent, phrase would be *user-defined type* (D. McIlroy, cited in Stroustrup, 1988).

Polymorphism allows the implementation of a given operation to be dependent on the object that "contains" the operation. Thus, polymorphism can reduce the complexity of an OO system by providing highly consistent semantics across the interfaces to a set of objects. For example, the implementation of a "compute-pay" operation can be dependent on the different types of employee objects that contains it. However, if the semantic consistency across the interfaces of the objects no longer exists, polymorphism can increase the complexity of an OO system. When this occurs, a programmer may no longer assume that all operations with the same name perform the same generic function. The semantics of each individual implementation of an operation must be determined. This increases the difficulty of understanding the objects in a system. The key to controlling an OO system's complexity through the use of polymorphism is to ensure that all operations with the same name are semantically consistent.

Inheritance allows programmers to define classes incrementally by reusing previously defined classes as the basis for new objects. There are two approaches to classifying inheritance: single versus multiple inheritance and specification versus implementation inheritance. Each is described in the paragraphs that follow.

Single inheritance allows a subclass to have only a single parent class. Existing OO programming languages and methodologies permit extending the parent's definition, including redefining some or all of the properties of the parent class. With redefinition capabilities, it is possible to introduce an inheritance conflict, that is, a property of a subclass with the same name as a property of an ancestor class (a class one or more levels "higher" in the inheritance tree/lattice). Multiple inheritance occurs when a subclass may inherit from more than one parent class. In this situation, the types of inheritance conflicts are multiplied. In addition to the possibility of having an inheritance conflict between the subclass and one (or more) of its parent classes, it is now possible to have conflicts between two (or more) of the parent classes of the subclass. Inheritance conflicts tend to increase the difficulty of understanding an inheritance structure and individual objects in the structure. Another concern related to using inheritance occurs when a subclass does not utilize all the properties of its superclass(es). It has been suggested that this may indicate a subclass that has been misclassified in the inheritance structure (Coad and Yourdon, 1991). Thus, like polymorphism, there is a risk of actually increasing the complexity of an OO system, instead of decreasing it, through the use of inheritance.

Specification, or essential, inheritance represents the semantic relationships of generalization and/or specialization, that is, the a-kind-of relationship (Sakkinen, 1989). It emphasizes the semantics of the problem domain. This approach to inheritance also has been described as "strict inheritance" (Borgida *et al.*, 1984). In contrast, implementation, or incidental, inheritance deals primarily with code reuse (Sakkinen, 1989). There is no semantic interpretation associated with this type of inheritance. This type of inheritance "can lead to incorrect behavior" from a semantic point of view (Rumbaugh *et al.*, 1991), a point also elaborated upon by Armstrong and Mitchell (1994). Thus, again, inheritance can increase the complexity of both an individual object and an object system.

We should also note that our use of the terminology—object and class—follows the methodology for object-oriented software engineering of systems (MOSES) use of object/class or O/C (Henderson-Sellers and Edwards, 1994) wherein little distinction is made as to whether specific relationships are object/object or class/class on the grounds that in analysis/design classes are the focus of attention; on the other hand in coding, with a seamless transition those conceptual classes smoothly become our actual coded classes which at runtime are objects. Thus in analysis, and to a lesser extent design (using those terms very loosely; see, for example, Henderson-Sellers, 1995c), we deal mostly with classes but also keep referring to individual objects in the real or business world, and even at the code level we deal primarily with classes (coding the abstract data type into an implementable "template," i.e., the class). Yet, concurrently, in coding a class we are likely to make reference to individual objects, especially in terms of client/server relationships. Thus, the two concepts of classes and objects, while distinct themselves (a class is a collection or template, whereas an object is an instance in the real-world or a location in memory), are often merged during the processes of building software. Consequently it seems futile to try to discriminate at every stage whether we are really focusing on classes or objects (see also Graham, 1995a). We have found that in practice, context makes everything crystal clear.

### 1.1.2 Life-Cycle Models

In an OO life cycle, there is significant merging between various stages of the life cycle and a high degree of iteration. So rather than the waterfall model, the spiral (Boehm, 1986), the fountain (Henderson-Sellers and Edwards, 1990), and the pinball (Ambler, 1994) models have been proposed.

**1.1.2.1 The Spiral Model.**    Figure 1.1 illustrates the risk-driven "spiral" model (Boehm, 1986) in which iterative and incremental development revolves through four basic "activities." These are (1) assessment of objectives, (2) risk assessment, (3) product development, and (4) planning. The first phase in each circuit of the spiral, progressing from a system-level viewpoint on through to coding, is an assessment of objectives, constraints, and so on for this next "circuit." A cost-effective strategy is identified, which may involve prototyping, simulation, and user questionnaires. Next, risks are identified explicitly. Dependent upon this risk evaluation, the next stage of this may be evolutionary development, a more detailed prototype, or a traditional waterfall progression. Planning may include partitioning of the system, as well as system reviews including walkthroughs. Roughly, each circuit corresponds to a phase of the waterfall model, for example, feasibility, requirements analysis, and so on.

Williams (1988) notes that this model also subsumes other process-driven development approaches, including prototyping and specification driven, while Boehm (1986) notes its shortcomings with respect to its applicability for software developments undertaken under external contract.

The applicability of the spiral model to object-oriented developments is being increasingly explored (Wirfs-Brock *et al.*, 1990), although a number of concerns (e.g., Berard, 1992, Chapter 4) have been raised regarding its truly iterative and recursive nature. For example, although depicted as a spiral, it is in fact a linear description (Henderson-Sellers and Edwards, 1994) in which some activities are returned to. However, these are *prescribed:* while in a truly iterative/recursive OO development, one could anticipate the need for more flexibility in decisions taken on when to iterate back to an early stage (e.g., Graham, 1995b). Nevertheless, it provides a significant improvement on a linear waterfall model. This approach has also been embodied in the proposals of Iivari (1990) for an "hierarchical spiral model" and Rumbaugh (1992) for a whirlpool-like development.

**1.1.2.2 The Fountain Model.**    The fountain model is a graphic image (Figure 1.2) to remind us that although some activities cannot start before others (for example, coding must follow design, and design should not commence before the

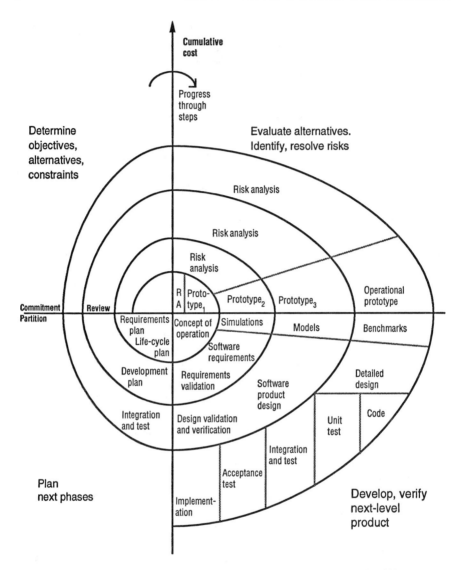

**Figure 1.1**   The spiral model (after Boehm, 1986, 1988; Boehm and Belz, 1988).

elicitation of requirements from the user), there is a considerable overlap and merging of activities. In a fountain, water rises up the middle and falls back, to the ground, or is reentrained at an intermediate level. Just so in an object-oriented software development where the general flow from analysis through design to implementation is overlaid with iterative cycles across two (or all three) of these "phases."

Figure 1.2 outlines the general characteristics of the systems-level perception of an object-oriented development. However, as we have noted elsewhere (Henderson-

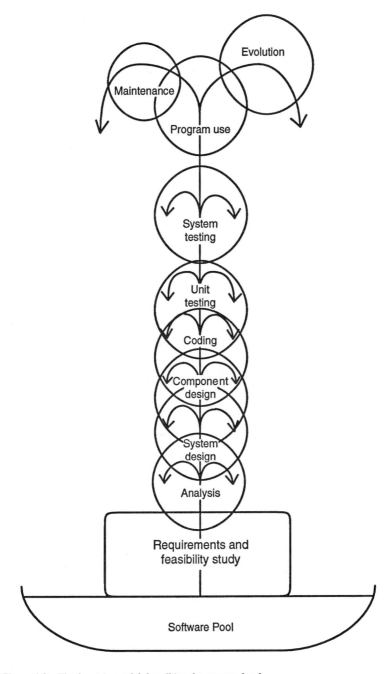

**Figure 1.2**   The fountain model describing the systems level.
*Source:* Henderson-Sellers, B. and Edwards, J. M., 1993. The fountain model for object-oriented systems development, *Object Magazine,* 3(2) 71–79.

Sellers and Edwards, 1990), development of an object-oriented system is much more likely to lead us to focus on sections of the whole such as subsystems (Wirfs-Brock *et al.,* 1990). In other words, it is more appropriate not to consider the system in toto at each stage of the life cycle, but rather to identify that individual classes or individual subsystems of classes go through their own *subsystem life cycles.* Each subsystem is a small collection of classes that work closely together. Some of these can be identified fairly early in the analysis and design; others appear much later in the design. The stage of development of each of the classes in one subsystem proceed at the same rate as each other, yet the life-cycle stage of different subsystems within the software system being developed or modified could be very different; for example, while subsystem 4 is beginning specification, subsystem 3 may already have completed this phase.

Figure 1.3 shows how the fountain model can be adapted for this subsystem development approach. There is an analysis stage and then a design stage (going from a high level through to full detail) followed by coding (implementation) followed by maintenance at the systems level (Figure 1.2). Finally, superimposed on these steps is the concept of iteration: a return from a "higher" to a "lower" phase, sometimes contiguous, sometimes further removed.

Even within a single subsystem, however, there are likely to be discrepancies in that some individual classes may reach detailed design while others are still at a low level of detail. Once the full details of the classes have each been specified in the detailed design, the class can be implemented (coded and tested), and then, in one school of thinking, additional effort to turn this *project-specific* class into a generally applicable *library* class is undertaken. However, it should be noted that with increasing experience, software developers will be able to identify potentially reusable classes ₋ignificantly earlier in the life cycle so that additional generalization effort is no longer seen as an "added extra" tacked on to the end of the life cycle by as an integral part of that life-cycle development process (Menzies *et al.,* 1992; Henderson-Sellers and Pant, 1993). Classes are coded individually (actually often in subsystem groupings) and then put together as a prelude to system testing. Following system acceptance, it is anticipated that maintenance costs will be less and extensibility significantly more feasible.

### 1.1.2.3 The Pinball Model.

A more recent proposal for an OO life cycle is that of the pinball software development life cycle (SDLC) (Figure 1.4). Here the bumpers and paddles are the various necessary activities of an OO life cycle: finding classes, attributes, methods, object relationships; defining collaborations, inheritance, aggregation, and subsystems; and converting the design to code, testing, and on-site implementation. The analogy is that of a ball moving around the pinball machine in an iterative and stochastically repetitive fashion. The ordering of transition between the sites of activity can differ from project to project. Its developer (Ambler, 1994) characterizes its weirdness as being one of its attractive features. Certainly the notion of nondeterminism and project-to-project differences in the

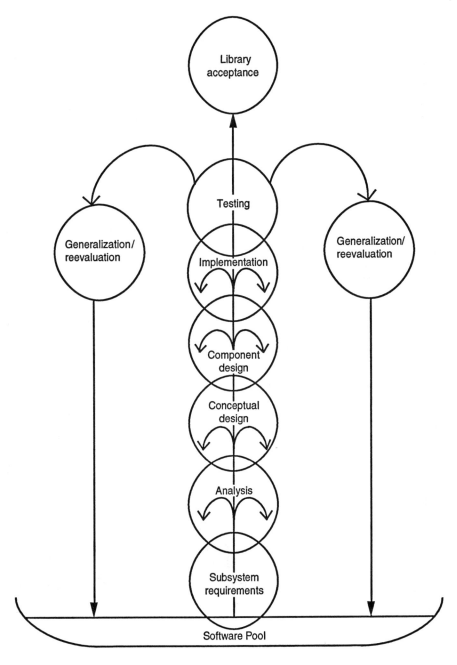

**Figure 1.3**   The fountain model applied to the subsystem level.
*Source:* Henderson-Sellers, B. and Edwards, J. M., 1993. The fountain model for object-oriented systems development, *Object Magazine,* 3(2) 71–79.

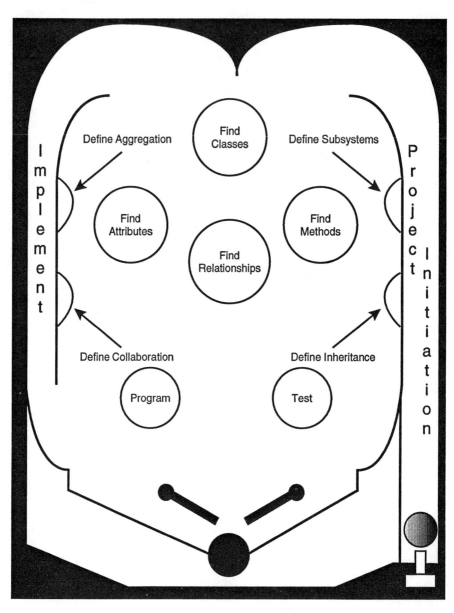

**Figure 1.4**  The pinball model.
*Source:* Ambler, S. W., 1994, In search of a generic SDLC for object systems, *Object Magazine* 4(6), 76–78.

ordering of activities is appealing. Perhaps its deficiency is its lack of enforcement for *all* necessary activities; that is, it would be possible to do only "find classes," find attributes, and program.

**1.1.2.4 The SOMA OO Model.**    In a similar vein, yet much more formally derived, is the object model–based life cycle of semantic object modeling approach (SOMA, Graham, 1995b) (Figure 1.5). In this diagram, each box represents an activity, those with sharp corners being activities bounded by an elapsed time. Each activity has an output that is tested, and the ordering is represented by a message-passing sequence of the object model in which entry to each activity is controlled by a set of preconditions. Activities at the left-hand side of Figure 1.5 are intraproject, and those on the right are extraproject activities. Evolutionary prototyping and rapid development are encouraged, and much use is made of rapid applications development (RAD) workshops and timebox-stamped deliverables. In essence, this SDLC model "objectifies" the phases of the fountain life cycle described earlier.

### 1.1.3 Architectural Issues

System architectures in an OO development reflect the strong support by the OO paradigm for the notions of abstraction. There tend to be a larger number of conceptual (abstraction) levels at which a system can be evaluated.

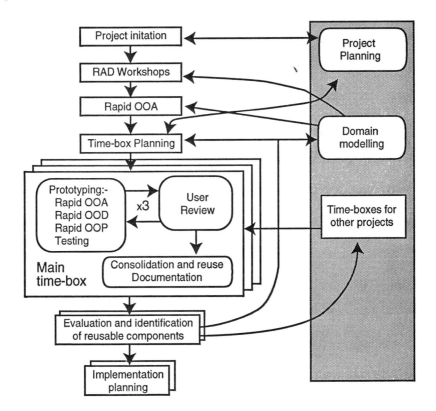

**Figure 1.5**    The object-oriented SOMA life-cycle model.
*Source:* Graham, I. M., 1995. A non-procedural process model for object-oriented software development, *Report on Object Analysis and Design,* 1(5), 10–11.

Subsystems (Wirfs-Brock *et al.,* 1990) are much in evidence. They are cohesive collections of classes that can be thought of as a single entity or single subsystem to fulfil a set of high-level responsibilities. As an example in Figure 1.6, the two subsystems of APPLICATION and MODEL form distinct domains of interest within the information system. The responsibilities of each of these subsystems are listed, and the directional arrow indicates that one or more classes in the APPLICATION subsystem use the services of one or more classes in the MODEL subsystem.

Within any one subsystem, we can describe the objects/classes as individual O/Cs interacting with each other. This gives the static picture of the system showing *potential* message-passing routes. When we then examine individual object classes we see (1) the external interface which represents the specification of the O/C and (2) the internal coded details. Methods are the control flow descriptors and can thus be described in terms of directed acyclic graphs (DAGs); the dynamics are reflected either separately in terms of objectcharts (Coleman *et al.,* 1992) or petri nets or as interactions between the methods and the datastores.

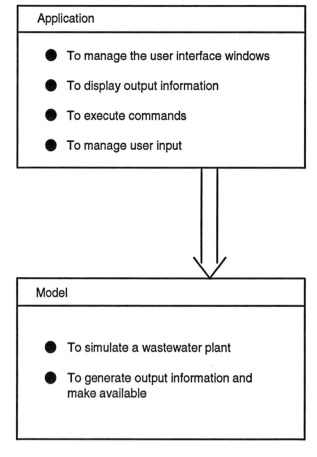

**Figure 1.6**   Interaction between two example subsystems.

Relationships between object classes are (1) associations, (2) aggregations, and (3) inheritance and, at the code level, (4) client/server links (e.g., Henderson-Sellers and Edwards, 1994). From a metrics point of view, we can represent associations and aggregations similarly as potential message-passing paths (Figure 1.7) and treat inheritance separately. These collaboration diagrams thus represent outgoing (fan-out) and ingoing (fan-in) message paths and can thus potentially be treated using traditional coupling metrics (see Section 5.1). The various types of inheritance have already been discussed (Section 1.1.1). Obviously, inheritance is what makes an OO system intrinsically different at the code stage from an object-based or traditional system.

### 1.1.4 Internal Structure

Figure 1.8 shows the internal methods of an O/C. Each external service (here $S_1$ to $S_4$ and $S_6$ are coded as a control flow represented by a DAG. Thus, a McCabe cyclomatic complexity could easily be attributed to the method control flow com-

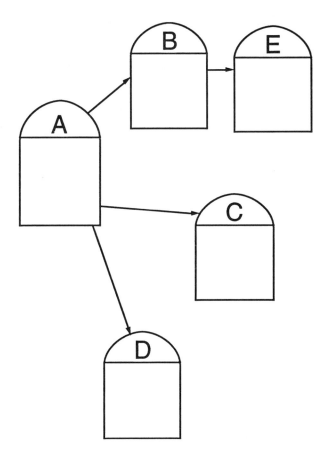

**Figure 1.7**    Interactions between classes represented by potential message passing paths.

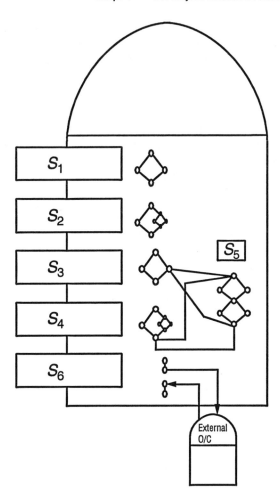

**Figure 1.8**   The internal structure of an O/C. Each public service ($S_1$–$S_4$, $S_6$) is implemented by a piece of procedural code, and there may be additional private services contained within the class ($S_5$).

plexity (assuming here and throughout the book the use of a standard OOPL such as
C++, Eiffel, and Smalltalk, which is essentially procedural at the lowest level). Differences here are that methods implementing external services may also call internal
methods (here $S_5$), often not on a one-to-one basis. Also many methods will make
external calls for services (seen here in EXTERNAL O/C). These topics are discussed in detail in Chapters 5 and 6.

## 1.2  OO PROJECT MANAGEMENT

Project management relies on various metrics being collected in order to ascertain
the degree of progress within the project. Some specific OO issues which must be

taken into account (outlined briefly in the paragraphs that follow) are the appropriate team structure, the phases of the life-cycle model being used and the specific methodological support, how the libraries of the organization are to be managed, the overall goal of quality and the move from a project to a product culture in software engineering, and the implicit need for metrics.

### 1.2.1 Team Structure

In one much favored approach (e.g., Henderson-Sellers and Edwards, 1990; Booch, 1991; Meyer, 1992c), one project team might develop the retail banking classes, another the wholesale banking classes, and a third the personnel system classes from the initial specification all the way through to final coding (Figure 1.9). In other words, there would be a "horizontal stratification" rather than a "vertical division" between analysts, designers, and programmers. In addition, this figure shows the close cooperation between subsystem teams as well as the necessary iteration across the full extent of the life cycle. This cooperation is underlined by Thomsett's (1990) introduction of the notion of a person with a linchpin role—with responsibilities to two teams so that he or she will ensure that one does not profit at the expense of the other. Thomsett (1990) also stresses that we should regard the object-oriented development paradigm as an *organizational* paradigm first and a technical development paradigm second.

### 1.2.2 Life-Cycle Phases

Since there are, as noted in Section 1.1.2, several life-cycle models in use for object-oriented development, especially the spiral and fountain models, possibly

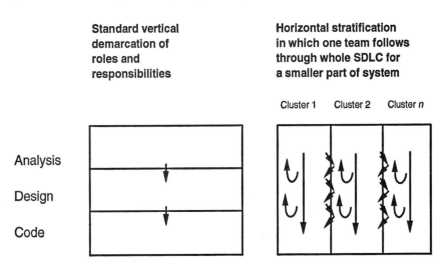

**Figure 1.9**   Two approaches to project management and team composition in an object-oriented development environment: (left-hand side) standard demarcations based on life-cycle phase and (right-hand side) division along project lines rather than life-cycle phases (after Henderson-Sellers and Edwards, 1994).

expressed using phrases such as "analyze a little, design a little, code a little" or as encapsulated in the iterative development process (IDP) of Lorenz (1993), this will lead to the identification of different life-cycle phases. Since these will likely form the "backbone" of any project management schedule, it is crucial to identify the phases being used. One example is shown in Figure 1.10, where the fountain model is overlaid with some indication of a selection of the deliverables associated with a given phase.

However, it is important to stress, first, that while these deliverables occur at the life-cycle phases, they are actually not created by the phases themselves but by the activities that occur within those phases. In a life-cycle methodology such as MOSES (Henderson-Sellers and Edwards, 1994), this is formalized in terms of a two-dimensional matrix between activities and phases. Second, deliverables are per iteration. This means that the project manager is responsible for identifying subsystems, allocating them to teams, planning the number of iterations, and being in charge of the "latest working demo" in an incremental delivery framework. Consequently, this project manager needs metrics that permit him or her to fulfill their management responsibilities.

It should be noted that, in an object-oriented development environment, not only is effort required to learn about the new technology but also, in a mature development team, the effort required in the "specification" phase (analysis and especially design) is significantly more than in a traditional development environment. Coding effort is less for a well-specified, bounded OO system, testing decreased as a result of incremental modifications of existing library classes, which are themselves well tested, and integration testing becomes in OT a natural component throughout a significant portion of the incremental delivery style of life cycle (e.g., Goldberg, 1993). Overall, this leads to increased costs for the first release (Kandibur, 1992) but lower maintenance costs and an overall decrease in total system costs.

### 1.2.3 Methodology Support

As has been indicated, specific methodologies will support these ideas in slightly different ways. However, one can say that in all cases they should offer a clear set of deliverables (both textual and graphical). MOSES lists five graphical deliverables and eight textual deliverables. Such clarity is a necessity for the project manager and one concern delaying the entry of some managers into the object technology arena.

As well as clear identification of deliverables, it is vital that reuse be factored in and supported by the methodology chosen by the project manager. Many methodologies pay "lip service" to reuse. Others discuss only "for reuse" and not "with reuse" or vice versa. Choose a methodology that fully supports

- The creation of new library classes for use in future projects ("for reuse")
- Techniques to locate and reuse existing library classes and thus capitalize on previous investment ("with reuse")
- The use of metrics and their full integration into the methodology and life-cycle model

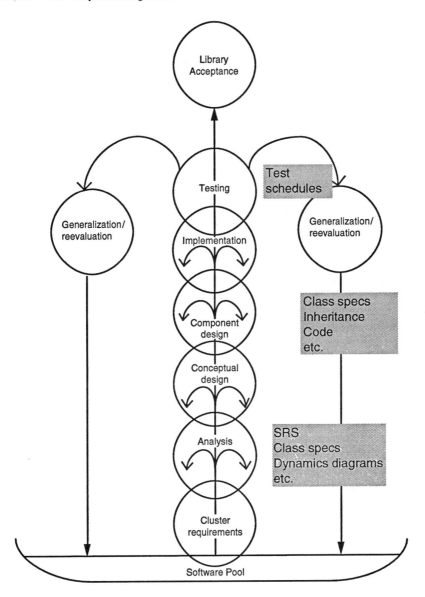

**Figure 1.10**   The fountain model with a few example deliverables superimposed.

We offer, as examples, the MOSES methodology of Henderson-Sellers and Edwards (1994) and the SOMA methodology of Graham (1995a), which were both[1] created with the intention of providing such project management support, lacking in many other popular OO methodologies.

[1]Indeed, as a consequence of their sharing of objectives and underlying structure, work has begun to create a new, third-generation methodology based on the two (MOSES + SOMA) together.

### 1.2.4 Library Management

Library management is intrinsically linked with reuse. A number of viewpoints are possible (Table 1.3). Ideally, many of the classes to be developed for a specific design will already exist as library classes prior to the commencement of the specific project (e.g., Meyer, 1990). Since the project will consist of teams, as the OO system is developed, the classes created by small teams of developers will form a set of team-specific libraries. As the project progresses, these then become released by team members to members of other teams, thus beginning to create a project-specific library. This should create few problems if good procedures are in place to control versioning and to ensure quality.

Industry-specific classes, say, for the insurance industry or the banking industry, raise the question of competitiveness. However, this is really a win-win situation in that the use of already coded classes must improve productivity and permit the exploitation of creative ideas and niche marketing to create competitive advantage. Indeed, in several industries, for example, some of the U.S. banks and in the international telecommunications industry, a trade in classes is already under way.

At the global, cross-industry scale, the only success to date is really the vending of low-level library classes to do routine jobs across a large number of problem domains, for example, time classes (e.g., Nerson, 1992), although other projects are developing to encompass wider domains. Generally available class libraries are also, at present, programming language specific, and until more general frameworks and reusable designs are developed, this is a constraint. Incompatibilities between class library vendors also exist, although there are discussions under way, for example, within the Object Management Group, to rationalize and "standardize" class library models.

From the organizational cultural viewpoint, management of class libraries needs to be addressed not simply at the project level but also in the development of an organization commitment to an integrated set of libraries. Particularly for transnational organizations, but also for industry groups and the software engineering profession more globally, this leads to concerns of class management not only at the corporate level (e.g., Chan and Henderson-Sellers, 1990) but also at the national and international level (Gibbs *et al.,* 1990).

One of the problems associated with the supply of reusable components is highlighted by Cox (1992) as that of copyright and royalty payments. Unless soft-

**TABLE 1.3   Five types of library**
**(technical viewpoint)**

1. Team-specific components
2. Project-specific components
3. Third-party domain-specific components
4. General components
5. Language-specific components

ware is distributed free, as some people believe, software has to be purchased from third-party vendors. However, software is intangible and easily copied illegally, unlike a traditional manufacturing environment in which multiple copies are tangible and a sales policy is easy to implement and enforce. Cox (1992) proposes that instead of selling copies of software packages, royalties should be paid on a usage basis. He draws on the succinct precedent of the broadcast of recorded music, which works very successfully in this framework. He also notes that a Japanese initiative (Mori, 1989; Mori and Kawahara, 1990) along these lines proposes a technique called "superdistribution," which allows free dissemination of software designed to run only on computers equipped with an appropriate hardware monitoring device. The software is thus paid for, by the user to the developer, on a "user-pays" principle analogous to that used for services such as water, electricity, gas, and telephone in many countries. Cox (1992) observes the potential importance of this idea while noting its potential ramifications for information privacy—a political issue.

## 1.3 REUSE

In procedural libraries, code modules are well tested and then frozen in libraries for future use by others. Although this certainly provides some reuse, such modules are limited to highly specific applications areas insofar as the module has to be "perfect" as-is or is essentially unreusable. However, in OO reuse, the "open/closed principle" can be applied: a principle that says that once a class is tested and accepted into a library, it should *not* need to be "opened up" (the "closed principle") while remaining "open" to further extendibility by inheritance (Meyer, 1988, 1990). Thus, the ease and extent of reuse in an OO environment is significantly enhanced (e.g., Wegner, 1990, pp. 15–16; Cox, 1990; Griss, 1991; Graham, 1991, p. 7; Lewis *et al.*, 1992; Pratap, 1992; Meyer, 1992e).

Graham (1991) notes that industrial observers suggest that a reuse strategy could save up to 20% of development costs; and this in an industry where even a 1% saving could give a competitor a major advantage. Many of the benefits of reuse are realized by generalization of coded classes for storage in libraries and subsequent reuse—either directly or via extension using inheritance. Class specialization using inheritance becomes a powerful, robust, and safe way of extending existing modular code without fear of "breaking" existing working modules—Meyer's (1988) open/closed principle. In this way, a new class that is semantically just like its parent class, but with slight differences, is created. In other words, reuse is enhanced by the capability of building on and extending existing modules and "personalizing" them for the specific task in hand. It should be noted that important levels of reuse also occur through the use of previous classes by instantiation and by new uses in aggregation and association configurations. Reusability in the long term requires the development of a library of classes from both commercially available classes and in-house developments (e.g., Goldberg and Rubin, 1990).

In commencing a new project, commonalities with past projects are first identified and then the experience of those past projects is "reused" in terms of library classes either directly or in terms of slight modifications, usually through inheritance. Costs associated with reuse include (1) the cost of finding and understanding any class in a library, (2) the cost of modifications to existing classes, as compared to (3) the cost of building a class "from scratch" (Henderson-Sellers, 1993). Then, if the library is to grow, the effort required to fully generalize an existing "one-off" class to turn it into a genuinely reusable class has to be incorporated into the economics (Bollinger and Pfleeger, 1990). This leads to an evaluation of the return on investment (ROI) given as

$$
\begin{aligned}
ROI &= \frac{\text{reuse savings}}{\text{generalization costs}} \\
&= \frac{\text{cost of project without reuse} - \text{cost of project with reuse}}{\text{cost of generalization}}
\end{aligned}
\tag{1.1}
$$

In other words, reuse is beneficial if the reuse savings are greater than the generalization costs. Note that in the case of generalization but no reuse, the numerator becomes equal to − cost of generalization; that is, the ROI is equal to minus one.

Another component of the cost/benefit equation is how an organization views its software. Many companies treat software as a capital cost, which depreciates over time (Adams and Burbeck, 1992). Consequently, the role of maintenance (ongoing short-term investments) only delays the obsolescence of the asset value of the software. It does *not* increase the value of the asset. If reusable software is viewed in such terms, it will be extremely difficult to argue a case for reuse from an economic standpoint. Rather, Adams and Burbeck (1992) argue, reusable business software components should be viewed as personnel assets that accrue over time. In personnel terms, an inexperienced employee matures within the organization so that his or her worth to the company grows over time. Software assets, too, can appreciate in value over time as they are honed to higher quality, are increasingly reused, and play a more significant role in the day-to-day business of the company. Consequently, a long-term investment strategy is called for to achieve maximum return on investment (Adams and Burbeck, 1992).

So far, the analysis has focused on *project* costs and savings, essentially assuming that the company is employing a reuse strategy. However, it should be noted that on an individual project basis, equation (1.1) implies that the maximum benefit is to be gained by minimizing generalization costs, in other words, by using classes from the library but not contributing classes to the library. It is therefore vital that the application of the ROI calculation either include amortized generalization costs and/or be applied to long-term evaluations for assessing the viability of reuse within the organization. Hence we could average the values of the ROI over *several* projects. Henderson-Sellers (1993) ran some simulations for various values of

- Generalization unit cost
- Reuse unit cost

- Percentages of new classes useful for library
- Number of classes reusable from library per project

Balda and Gustafson (1990) note that, based on evaluations in a nonobject-oriented environment, reasonable on-costs for developing a reusable component take about 25% more effort. They also balance the costs of developing a reusable component and then reusing it $n - 1$ times against the cost of developing it from scratch $n$ times. On the other hand, Humphrys (1991) found that the initial investment was recovered after three projects and that on each subsequent application a 50% savings was made.

In a first experiment (Table 1.4), realistic industrial values were used (Henderson-Sellers, 1993). The rate of return on successive projects was positive for all projects—if there are *no* library classes available initially, then the ROI becomes greater than zero for the *third* project, thus stressing the advantage of working in a language environment where library classes already exist. Although not shown here, the size of the library increases monotonically from the initial 10 to a final value of 126 at the end of the 20th project.

A third simulation represented a significantly more pessimistic calculation in that the costs of reuse were substantially greater; namely generalization was assumed to *double* the cost per class. Nevertheless, the simulations still support an ROI $> 0$ after the completion of the sixth project (Table 1.4).

Finally, a scenario in which only 10% of required classes were available in the library, such that more investment in generalization was needed (a value of 50% was assumed). Retaining as well the pessimistic costs of the third simulation, it was found that the period to "profit" required more than the 20 simulated projects (it actually required 33 projects). The conclusion, therefore, is that if such peculiar constraints exist, then management should revise its decision to adopt an object-oriented reuse strategy. These calculations also stress the need for library holdings of relevance to projects being developed.

Reuse does not just "happen" (even using object technology!) but must be planned for and managed. Griss *et al.* (1991) suggest that one of the main inhibitors to reuse is the not-invented-here (NIH) syndrome, making software developers unwilling to pay for good-quality, third-party software. Learning how to optimize on

**TABLE 1.4    Input values and simulated ROI for four experiments using the model of Henderson-Sellers (1993)**

| Experiment | Initial Library Size | % Classes in Library | Cost | | | ROI > 0 on Project No. |
|---|---|---|---|---|---|---|
| | | | New | Generalization | Reuse | |
| 1 | 10 | 50 | 10 | 2.5 | 2 | 1 |
| 2 | 0 | 50 | 10 | 2.5 | 2 | 3 |
| *Pessimistic* | | | | | | |
| 3 | 10 | 50 | 10 | 10 | 5 | 6 |
| 4 | 10 | 10 | 10 | 10 | 5 | 33 |

reuse (Smart *et al.,* 1988) is therefore not just a technical issue but also a management concern. For example, classes should conform strictly to the notion of being an implementation of an abstract data type and not simply a collection of pieces of data and functionality in a single module "for convenience." Good metrics are also highly useful here. However, even perfectly designed and constructed classes and frameworks will need to be made readily available and "managed" (Meyer, 1990; Gibbs *et al.,* 1990). The granularity at which reuse is operated ranges across classes, frameworks, and subsystems.

Reusability on a slightly larger spatial scale, that of program portions, occurs in the development of *patterns* and *frameworks.* A framework is an application-specific class library (Winblad *et al.,* 1990), in other words, a grouping of classes tuned specifically to a single applications-oriented environment, but still general enough to be widely reusable. A pattern is a repeatedly used collaboration between a small(er) number of classes (Gamma *et al.,* 1995; Pree, 1994). Another way of viewing these techniques is as reuse of design (Johnson and Foote, 1988; Wirfs-Brock and Johnson, 1990.) It should also be noted that to use a framework, you must accept its model of the problem solution, but it is hoped, it will provide so much functionality that you are happy to accept its "structure" (Wirfs-Brock, personal commmunication, 1991). Nevertheless, the development of more frameworks is seen by many as one of the most important practical requirements in the next few years.

In the increasingly competitive world within organizations, where internal cost accounting and cost and profit centers are the order of the day, managing the costs of object-oriented projects can cause a significant problem. Although they reduce costs to the organization in the long term, these benefits may be accrued by a different department from the one that produced them. For example, if a business line pays for an initial development, the benefits from reduced testing through reuse may actually be felt by a competing business line in later projects. While the organization as a whole benefits, these benefits may not be evenly distributed throughout the business lines. A number of alternative business models may therefore be required to be implemented, depending on the internal accounting structure of an organization.

The incorporation of reuse into the business plan requires insight and a corporate policy to be developed. Four models have been proposed (Henderson-Sellers and Pant, 1993) (Table 1.5). First, the "traditional" view is that generalization *for reuse* is an "add-on" to the life-cycle activities and occurs after the completion of the project (as implicit in the earlier discussion). Investment of additional effort to undertake the generalization activities necessary to create good, reusable classes has to be costed, but it is generally impossible to cost against the current project, which, after all, is ostensibly finished. Second, building in reuse as an integral part of the life cycle and encouraging a reuse *mind-set* at the corporate level is discussed by McGregor and Sykes (1992)—in conjunction with a quality focus as in TQM. For example, by bringing the generalization phase earlier in the life cycle (Menzies *et al.,* 1992), generalization is undertaken *before* the finalization of the first product so that it is then available at no additional cost for future work. This means that the generalization costs are squarely laid on the customer for whose product the class was originally developed. Consequently, although such a refocusing should indeed encourage a full life-cycle reuse mind-set, customers requesting products that have a significant component of already generalized classes are going to benefit, at the expense of the investment made by earlier customers.

Third is the two-library model, which may be useful in some industrial contexts. The first step is to put "on hold" project-specific classes from the current project by placing them in a library of potentially reusable components (LPRC) (Figure 1.11). The only additional project-specific effort is thus the identification of these classes. This adds basically nothing to the current costs. The second library is the high-quality company resource—the library of generalized components (LGC).

At the beginning of each future project, an early life-cycle activity is thus an assessment of classes currently residing in both the LPRC and the LGC repositories as to their potential value in this new project. If so, then and only then is the additional spending on generalization made. Since this is to the benefit of this new project, then it is perfectly reasonable to allocate the cost to this customer. It will still be a saving, and the developing company will then have a fully generalized class that can now undergo final quality checks and then be placed in the LGC for future reuse.

Finally, Henderson-Sellers and Pant (1993) also consider, as another option, the "alternative cost center" model in which the equivalent of an emerging technology group should be created. This would be an independent cost center that initially was funded solely to take those components of the PRC and, in parallel and not customer driven, invest in generalization. Their costs could be recovered on a longer time scale when these generalized costs were being used in projects that could therefore make a saving over a greenfield development. However, it is inevitable that such a group would run at a loss for a year or two, and this model is therefore possible only with larger companies that are able to put aside this more strategic type of investment. Its operation is thus very much akin to the role of an emerging technology group that acts as a facilitator rather than profit center. The recognition that software, and especially library classes, as company assets may require a reevaluation of accounting practices within the company (Adams and Burbeck, 1992).

TABLE 1.5    **Four reuse models for software development**
**(after Henderson-Sellers and Pant, 1993)**

1. End life-cycle model
2. G-Cl model (Menzies *et al.,* 1992)
3. Two-library model
4. Alternative cost center model

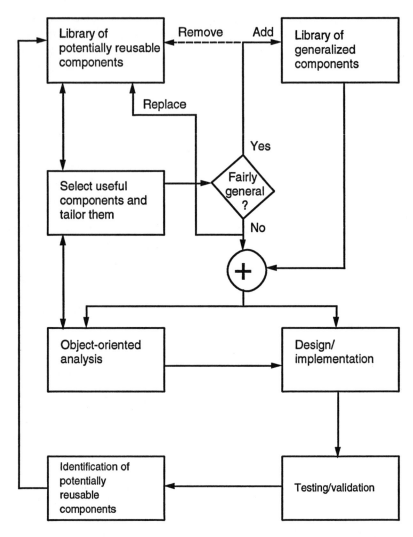

**Figure 1.11**   The two-library reuse model of Henderson-Sellers and Pant (1993).
*Source:* Henderson-Sellers, B. and Pant, Y. R. 1993. When should we generalize classes
to make them reusable? *Object Magazine,* 3(4), 73–75.

## 1.4 THE NEED FOR METRICS

There is a clear need for project managers to employ metrics to give them more information on what is happening in the project development. While these are not, of
course, absolute, there some underlying notions that are important. Several of these
have been addressed in the earlier sections of this chapter. We should also note here
that one of the consequences likely to flow from the higher quality attainable using

object-oriented techniques will be productivity gains. It is important here that productivity gains be realized only by comparing OO projects with non-OO projects and, because of the more strategic nature of OO, by comparing numbers across the full life cycle *including* maintenance, where many of the cost gains of using OO techniques are generally regarded as most likely.

## 1.5 CHAPTER SUMMARY

Understanding object technology in the context of metrics requires some small understanding of the technical details, but a greater appreciation of the way the introduction of OT impacts project management and indeed the whole organization. There are various potential life-cycle models that should underlie an OO project. Subsystems play a different role, and there is a dichotomy both between the internal and the external aspects of objects and also their statics and dynamics. Reuse and library management is perhaps the greatest impact on the corporate culture, but an impact most likely to result in vastly increased software quality, particularly flexibility and reliability (less maintenance costs).

Underscoring all these changes is the need to measure. Having laid the object-oriented foundation stone, the rest of the book focuses on measurement. In Chapter 2 we look informally at the rationale for measurement, in Chapter 3 we introduce a technical framework, and in Chapter 4 a formal framework based on measurement theory. The following two chapters introduce specific measures, first for traditional systems (Chapter 5) and then for OO systems (Chapter 6). These are essentially complexity (product) metrics, whereas a model that goes further to include the characteristics of the programmer is introduced in Chapter 7. Finally, some overview results from industrial testing and introduction of metrics programs is given in Chapter 8.

## 1.6 BIBLIOGRAPHIC DETAILS

Key papers in OO metrics are relatively sparse. For this chapter, the key issues are OO life cycles and OO project management. We suggest as background not only our own work (Henderson-Sellers, 1993, 1995a,b; Henderson-Sellers and Edwards, 1990, 1993, 1994; Dué and Henderson-Sellers, 1995) but also that of Jacobson (Jacobson *et al.,* 1992, 1995), Booch (1994, 1995), Meyer (1995), and, at a more introductory level, Taylor (1995).

# 2

# METRICS?

In this chapter we delve deeply into the question, "Why metrics?" Metrics are introduced with the background of the scientific method (Section 2.2) and the impact that that way of thinking can (and should) have on metrics (Section 2.3). Then we explore what is meant by various forms of validity in the scientific paradigm (Section 2.4) and how metrics may be used as thresholds or indicators of concern (Section 2.5). In Section 2.6 we then ask the question, "What are the desirable properties of metrics?"

## 2.1 INTO THE QUAGMIRE

Beware! The domain of metrics is deep and muddy waters.

Before we plunge into the quagmire, let us begin with a typical metrics project context statement:

> Members of a specific software development team (20 in number) have been selected to participate in an experiment. It is to be a quantitative experiment, so we begin to measure. We measure their heights, the number of lines of code they wrote last Tuesday, and what time they arrived in the office today. Management is (for some reason) interested in both personal and professional characteristics: specifically, how many are overweight, how productive this team is (their Christmas bonus depends on this!), and whether they are likely to respond to the normal pressures of impending delivery deadlines by working late (or early) in the office.

That this is an ill-conceived experiment, a set of poorly proposed objectives compounded by a nonexistent underlying model is perhaps self-evident. But this is precisely the bog that a lot of the software metrics literatii seem to wallow in. Let us look at some specific problem areas—there are a large number, and many of them will make us think hard: technically, managerially, and even philosophically.

In this "problem statement" there are many conceptual levels intermixed. For instance, I can almost certainly count the number of lines of code (LOC) written on a given day—but only if I am very careful to define what I mean by both "line of code" and "write." Do I allow for multiple statements on a single line or for comment lines, and do I permit major modifications to be equivalent to a pristine construction? I can also measure the heights of the developers. Whether a given person is overweight must have something to do with the characteristics of height and weight. Ah, but we are not measuring weight. Weight can be considered here as an orthogonal variable, that is one that is not directly measured by other variables such as height.

To represent these ideas mathematically, I have measured a set of heights, which I will denote by $H_i$, where the subscript runs from 1 to 20 (there are 20 team members) so that $H_1$ is the height of the first person and so on. If weight $W_i$ is orthogonal to height, then there is no function or mapping, $f$, that permits me to state

$$f : H_i \rightarrow W_i \qquad (2.1)$$

On the other hand, height and weight have a nature different from the concept of "overweight." Here height and weight are independent variables, and overweight is a dependent variable since it is reasonable to assume that if I know a person's weight and height then I can make a reasonable assessment of whether that person is overweight (represented by the symbol $O_i$ with binary value 0/1). Thus, in mathematical terms, it *is* valid to state that there is a mapping

$$m : H_i, W_i \rightarrow O_i \qquad (2.2)$$

or, put another way, that there is a function, $f_o$, such that

$$f_o\big(H_i, W_i\big) = \begin{cases} 0 \\ 1 \end{cases} \qquad (2.3)$$

The management may wish to define productivity in terms of LOC written per day (although this is perhaps a poor focus since a large number of LOC badly constructed[1] is of less use to the organization than a smaller number of LOC carefully crafted according to a high-quality design). If we simply use this one measure of LOC last Tuesday as a "measure" of productivity, then we are guilty of several sins. First, as we have just indicated, there is no causal connection between LOC and production of *quality* code. Partly this is a result of the lack of agreed definitions in the software industry of the terms in this discussion (e.g., quality, productivity, even LOC); partly it is because we have made a causal link simply on faith (or maybe guesswork), that is, we have gone from LOC, which we can measure on a scale because we can count LOC (once we have an agreed definition), to a more stochastic notion of productivity on an ill-defined time scale. One major difference here is between *internal* variables and *external* variables (e.g., Fenton, 1994). An internal variable such as LOC can, in

---

[1] We will discuss quality of coding later

principle, be measured objectively such that all measurers would come up with the same value for the variable of LOC. In contrast, variables such as quality, productivity, and maintainability are all external variables in the sense that they involve people, it is often not possible to define or measure them unambiguously, and they are likely to be samples from a stochastic (i.e., probabilistic) distribution.

In fact, just to complicate matters even further, this stochastic idea occurs on two levels: for an individual over time and at the population level. It is certainly possible to define unambiguously, for a specific individual, the notion of productivity. Over a long enough time, it is seen that certain people produce more code of an acceptably high quality than others—not on any given day, but averaged over time. So a variable such as productivity cannot be evaluated by a spot measurement; it has to be derived from a number of measurements, here over time. Any averaging type of measure (mean, median, mode, etc.) is of this type. The greatest difficulty comes when we try to make industry-level statements such as "code of high complexity is less maintainable than code of low complexity." Notions of maintainability, testability, and debuggability are not only external variables but are also highly dependent on the individual concerned.[2] Any statement such as these, that pertains "on average," should always be tested in this vein: not by a single experiment[3] but by a statistically valid, sufficiently large sample of experiments. Of course, a major difficulty in devising such experiments is maintaining control of all the other extraneous variables that might affect the result, such as the developer's years of experience and the software development environment, including the language used. Those metrics that survive this degree of validation should then be clearly stated as being tested in a specific environment. For instance, much of the early work in metrics was in a FORTRAN, Department of Defense (DoD), environment. Metrics tested over a large number of projects in that environment could reasonably confidently be applied to new projects *in that identical environment*, but as many authors have shown (e.g., Jeffery, 1987a), application to different technical and cultural environments of even "well-validated" metrics can be totally inappropriate and invalid.

## 2.2 THE SCIENTIFIC APPROACH

There are, in fact, two, complementary approaches of interest here. In science, attempts are made to understand our world. Tycho Brahe (1546–1601) made an extraordinary number of observations of motions within the solar system in the late sixteenth century. He simply compiled lots and lots of numbers. He could thus undertake lots of data analysis and data presentation and begin to recognize patterns. But banks of data such as these give no real explanation. Johannes Kepler (1571–1630) began to formulate mathematical models to underpin these data and,

---

[2]Bringing people into the metrics equation is the step that convolutes the whole discipline!

[3]It is frequently observed in the metrics literature that most metrics are "validated" by a single experiment, which, probably, leads to the observation that "for every positive validation there is a negative validation" (Curtis, 1979). The discussion here shows that this approach is untenable.

toward the end of the seventeenth century, Isaac Newton (1642–1727) was developing theories of how forces applied to objects could make them accelerate. Having devised a theoretical description of the process, then that theory must be tested. Boehm (1984), drawing on the same scientific parallels, notes that "the software field cannot hope to have its Kepler or its Newton until it has had its army of Tycho Brahes, carefully preparing the well-defined observational data from which a deeper set of scientific insights may be derived." In other words, neither data collection nor theorizing is self-sufficient. A scientific or engineering discipline draws on the synergy between the two.

Thus, theory and observations come together. Patterns in data might be explicable in terms of a theory—the mere existence of patterns does not necessarily do that, as tongue-in-cheek plots of telephone directory numbers has shown (Reynolds, 1978) and the well-known correlation between the birthrate and the stork population in Holland in 1951–1959. Concurrently, theories need validation with good quality data. It is important to stress "good-quality" data since using poor-quality data does not invalidate a theory. There is a tendency in some circles for people to have a total trust in data and claim that if the data do not substantiate the theory then the theory must be thrown away. While this is true for evaluations based on good-quality data, it is also critical to remember that there are many cases when, if the theory/model does not uphold the data, it is the data that could well be wrong, and it is they that should be discarded, not the theory.

Newton's theories and Kepler's observations thus came together to give us a description of the elliptical path of the Earth around the Sun, with the Sun at one of the foci of the ellipse: a "validated model" that has stood the test of time, gives us useful results, explains nature, and can be used as a stepping stone to more comprehensive or complex theories (such as galactic motions and relativity).

## 2.3 BACK TO METRICS

Metrics research has a number of responsibilities: first, to define clearly and unambiguously the population and the characteristics of software we wish to measure (e.g., Curtis and Carleton, 1994) and, second, to devise appropriate measures for these software characteristics together with "instruments" with which to measure them. This gives a sound basis for the scientific method (discussed earlier): data collection and the seeking of patterns (local, empirical, and bottom up) and, concurrently, the derivation of theories which might have more global applicability (top down, goal focused, external). Card (1991) notes that "A perfect measure" is based on an unimpeachable theory and exhibits "incredibly high correlations" with the characteristic we wish to assess.

Thus we might imagine two possibilities regarding available measurements on an internal variable, $A$ (say, LOC), and an external variable, $B$ (say, maintainability): (1) we may have measurements on both $A$ and $B$, or (2) we may only have measurements on $A$, yet wish to know values of $B$. In other words, there are two routes to $B$ (Figure 2.1): direct measurement or by use of a prognostic model that allows us to

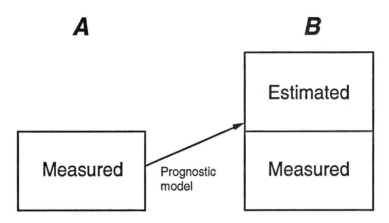

**Figure 2.1**   An internal variable (*B*) may be (1) measured or (2) estimated by the use of
a prognostic model and a measurement of another variable (*A*).

forecast a value for *B* given a value of *A*. It is often feasible to measure *B* directly;
for example, maintainability, *M*, can be calculated as

$$M = \frac{1}{1 + \text{MTTR}} \tag{2.4}$$

(Pfleeger, 1991, p. 326), where MTTR is the measured mean time to repair. The
problem here is that this is a post facto measurement, whereas generally we wish to
have an idea of the likely maintenance costs available to us when we decide whether
or not to ship a product on a given date. Measurements of *A* (an internal variable)
may be available at an earlier stage in the software development life cycle (SDLC).
Thus, a common goal is to measure characteristics of the software design or code
relatively early in the life cycle (or even *estimate* the size; see Verner and Tate, 1992)
and from these values forecast events/costs/characteristics farther down the track.
This is generally known as "estimation" (a term often used in "cost-estimation models") and is likely to give only a rough value (an estimate). This should be expressed
either as a deterministic number with error bars or in probabilistic terms. Shepperd
(1992) notes the common enthusiasm for predicting a quality parameter from a structural measure to identify "potentially troublesome [modules] from a maintenance
perspective while the project is still at a high level design stage and while changes
are still relatively inexpensive to make," while Fenton (1991, p. 151) notes that it is
widely assumed that " 'good' internal structure leads to 'good' external quality."

    This leads to a third responsibility: *not* to make unjustified leaps between ob-
jective measures and subjective, global measures. For instance, it is not appropriate
to collect data on control flow complexity and infer from that a measure of quality,
despite the assertion by Rajaraman and Lyu (1992b) that software engineers take this
as being axiomatic.

    Finally, from a software engineering perspective, there is a critical need for
measures to be *objective* and *repeatable*. In the early days of any scientific or engi-

neering discipline, unknown and unquantified factors may be introduced. Metrics that require subjective assessment, often characterized by the use of a 3- or 4-point Likert scale (e.g., Judd *et al.*, 1991), are open to question. Metrics with subjective weightings in which not only are Likert scales used, but the mapping from that scale to a numerical scale itself is fuzzy (Table 2.1), have no scientific validity and should be avoided if at all possible.

At present we might therefore argue, simplistically, that there are some "internal" metrics which are objectively measurable. Let us denote these as the set $\{M_O\}$. Indeed, we would argue that simply identifying elements of this set of "potentially useful" metrics is a valid component of the scientific method. The harder task is to see which members of the set are meaningful in the broader context—ultimately for use in prognostic models (as opposed to their more direct use for diagnosis).

A second set of metrics contains those that involve external agencies such as people and the environment. These include concepts such as maintainability, comprehensibility, and reliability and are more likely to be describable stochastically. Let us denote these as the set $\{M_E\}$. The first set, $\{M_O\}$, is typically those metrics we can devise ways of measuring relatively easily, but it is the second set, $\{M_E\}$, that most managers have most interest in. Hence, there is a pressure on metrics researchers to try to make connections between these two sets. Finding such functional relationships is the major challenge of metrics: to move from measurable characteristics quantified by a product metric, which is then used (in the role of a "predictor metric") to forecast the value of another metric, often a process metric (known as a "result metric") (Ince, 1990). It is much akin to any other forecasting system. Meteorological variables can be measured unambiguously. They can then be fed into a prognostic model (theoretically derived but empirically validated), which gives results that are interpretable as a forecast for the future behavior of the system (in that case the weather, in our case the software system and/or the software process). It is a sad indictment on much of the metrics literature that prognostic equations have been inferred where none exist

**TABLE 2.1    Operation complexity values**

| Rating | Complexity Value |
| --- | --- |
| Null | 0 |
| Very low | 1–10 |
| Low | 11–20 |
| Nominal[1] | 21–40 |
| High | 41–60 |
| Very high | 61–80 |
| Extra high | 81–100 |

[1]One dictionary definition equates *nominal* to "pertaining to name"!

*Source:* Chen, J.-Y. and Lu, J.-F., 1993, A new metric for object-oriented design, *Information and Software Technology,* 35(4), 232–240.

and that objective metrics from the set $\{M_O\}$ have been used as a direct surrogate for $\{M_E\}$ *without any intervening model, theory, or identified causality* (see, also, Troy and Zweben, 1981; Kearney *et al.*, 1986; and Fenton, 1991, p. 52). While managers might want a number as an "indicator" (Card, 1991) for the anticipated maintenance costs, if all we have as data are the numbers of LOC of each subroutine or object class, then it is our professional responsibility *not* to succumb to delivering a number that has neither empirical nor theoretical validation.

## 2.4 VALIDATION OF METRICS

Validation of new metrics is difficult and has led to much abuse in the literature of the scientific method. It is observed that many metrics are "validated" against only one data set. This does not, in itself, render the validation process invalid but *cannot* be used to justify anything other than a very restricted and careful use of the metric. A variant on this is the use of multiple regression techniques that combine a set of measures (overlapping or orthogonal, of similar or different dimensions) into that elusive single number for complexity (Chen and Lu, 1993)—a number that Fenton (1994) reminds us is an impossible and pointless "holy grail."

A second "validation" technique is that of correlation. A good inferential statistical approach demands the a priori statement of a null hypothesis. Following this statement, it then becomes clear what entities should be measured. For example, the hypothesis may be that there is no difference in average number of services per class for the same system design implemented in two different programming languages. Thus, data on service numbers per class are collected. What often happens, and is quite rightly decried by Courtney and Gustafson (1993), is (1) the collection of large amounts of data, (2) the correlation of each measure with every other measure, (3) the identification of "good" correlation (often ignoring the effects of the number of degrees of freedom), and only then (4) the identification of a research hypothesis. This (incorrect) approach they label a "shotgun" approach.

A third incorrect approach is that of correlating the new measure with an old measure. Fenton (1994) notes the widespread use of this technique (e.g., in Li and Cheung, 1987), whereby "the validation study tells us nothing of interest."

## 2.5 METRICS AS THRESHOLDS

One application of internal metrics, used frequently by software engineers during development (Verner, 1993) and which may be justifiable and pragmatically useful, even in the absence of any link to an external characteristic, is in terms of a threshold value or "alarm" (e.g., Szentes and Gras, 1986; Kitchenham and Linkman, 1990) (Table 2.2). An alarm would occur whenever the value of a specific internal metric exceeded some predetermined threshold. While it is clearly not the case that there is a discontinuity in the range of values whereby a value less than or equal to the threshold is acceptable and a value greater than the threshold indicates a problem that *must* be solved, values not in the acceptable range (Kitchenham and Linkman, 1990)

TABLE 2.2    The use of metrics as thresholds and some suggested values

| (a) Measures | Alarm Levels | | |
| --- | --- | --- | --- |
| McCabe (MCC-V) | $\leq 15$ | | |
| $N$-McCabe | $\leq 0.4$ | | |
| Effort | $\leq 300,000$ | | |

| (b) Measure | Safe | Flag | Alarm |
| --- | --- | --- | --- |
| LOC | $< 50$ | 50–100 | $> 100$ |
| Effort | $< 50,000$ | 50,000–100,000 | $> 105,000$ |
| MCC-V | $< 10$ | 11–20 | $> 20$ |

*Source:* (a) Szentes and Gras (1986). (b) Lewis, J. and Henry S., 1989, A methodology for integrating maintainability using software metrics, *Procs. Conf. on Software Maintenance,* Miami, Florida 16–19 October 1989, IEEE, 32–39. © 1989 IEEE.

should be used merely to draw attention to that particular anomalous part of the code. Another alternative (Lewis and Henry, 1989) would be to predetermine three ranges for each metric: safe, flag, and alarm. Thus, without presuming either a causality or even a high enough correlation to propose any type of model, these flags and/or alarms draw a developer's attention toward a particular program module or chunk for further evaluation (see also Lorenz and Kidd, 1994). Finally, it should be noted that such alarm levels should not be absolute (as many metricians might read into McCabe's (1976) alarm level of $V(G) = 10$) but rather relative (Kitchenham and Linkman, 1990), dependent on the particular development environment, especially the complexity of the problem itself—an area of metrics almost totally ignored.

## 2.6  DESIRABLE PROPERTIES OF SOFTWARE METRICS[4]

Many authors have proposed desirable properties of software measures. First, it should be objective; that is, the value must be computed in a precise manner (reliable) (Conte *et al.,* 1986). It must be intuitive (possess face validity) and possess some form of internal validity. To be useful, a measure must be robust; that is, it must be reliable. A measure must provide useful feedback to the user of the measure; that is, the measure must provide information that would allow the user to "gain a better understanding of improving the design" (Ejiogu, 1993, p. 71). Finally, a measure must be amenable to statistical analysis.

Schneidewind (1992) suggests that each measure should be associated with a specific quality factor (attribute) and a specific quality function (use). He also states that a measure must be consistent, repeatable, and capable of tracking changes made to the entity. All these imply that the measure should possess some form of internal validity (see Section 2.6.1) and the measure should be reliable. Useful measures also

[4]This discussion was contributed by B. Henderson-Sellers and D. P. Tegarden.

should possess sufficient discriminant power. Finally, he feels for a measure to be useful, it must be capable of prediction. This implies that a measure may not be useful if it can be used only for assessment purposes. This is really the contrast between descriptor statistics and inferential statistics. Both are useful but provide different information. It is only in mistaking the one for the other that danger lies.

Kearney *et al.* (1986) stress the need for a measure to address the human component of software development; otherwise, the measure will not be capable of really describing any useful attribute of a software entity. This is due, in part, to the fact that the analyst/programmer is always part of the development process. They also feel that "generic" measures probably are not very useful. For a measure to be useful, it should be developed for specific applications. For example, function points have proven to be useful in management information systems (MIS) applications, but not as useful in engineering applications. The authors also list four specific properties of measures: robustness, normativeness, specificity, and prescriptiveness. Robustness, as described by the authors, tends to imply internal validity. If an entity is modified, and the measure increases in value, the entity should have increased when considering the measure's attribute. Normativeness addresses issues of assessment and interpretation. It is difficult, if not impossible, to interpret an assessment of an entity on an attribute if a standard set of values for the attribute's measure has not been developed, although it should be noted that it is not possible to develop a standard until enough measurement has occurred. Specificity deals with the idea that a measure must be associated with an attribute of the entity being measured. If a measure is to be associated with multiple attributes, then it must be separately validated for each of the attributes. Finally, prescriptiveness is a property that requires that a measure have defined with it a set of procedures that describe how to "improve" a software entity along the particular attribute's dimension.

In constructing his metrics for object-oriented design (MOOD), Brito e Abreu (1994), focuses on life-cycle stages and quality assessment and recommends "extensive comparative metrics evaluation throughout the OO community to try to find evidence of best design practices." He suggests the need for the adoption of the following seven criteria:

1. Metrics determination should be formally defined.
2. Nonsize metrics should be system size independent.
3. Metrics should be dimensionless or expressed in some unit system.
4. Metrics should be obtainable early in the lifecycle.
5. Metrics should be down-scalable.
6. Metrics should be easily computable.
7. Metrics should be language independent.

He also suggests viewing metrics as probabilities to permit the application of statistical theory to software metrics.

Sheetz *et al.* (1991) summarize the recommendations of Tsai *et al.* (1986) and Zuse (1990) for properties of system design complexity metrics. They suggest that

1. A measure of both the structure of the data and process must be included.
2. The measures must demonstrate consistency (i.e., if a structure is contained within another structure, the containing structure is computed to be at least as complex as the contained structure).
3. Measures must be capable of representing at least a weak order (i.e., the measures must be at least on an ordinal scale).
4. Measures must be additive (i.e., if two independent structures are put into sequence, then the total complexity of the combined structures is simply the sum of the complexities of the independent structures).
5. It must be possible to automate the measures.[5]

For any measure to be useful, the measure must be at least valid, reliable, and practical. Generally speaking, a measure is valid if it measures what we want it to measure. A measure is reliable if the application of its algorithm consistently produces the same result given the same conditions. A measure can be reliable, but not valid. For example, SLOC (really a measure of size) could be used as a measure of complexity (Chapter 3, Section 3.3). The algorithm to count SLOC could be defined as the number of semicolons in a C program. The measure would be reliable. However, its validity should be questioned; in other words, is there an underlying conceptual model to connect size and complexity? The practicality of a measure deals with issues of economy (How much does it cost to compute?), convenience (How easy is it to compute?), and interpretability (How easy is it to interpret the results of the computation?). The validity and reliability criteria of sound measurement are discussed in the next two subsections.

### 2.6.1 Validity

There have been many different types of validity identified in the literature. In general, they can be classified into three categories: face, internal, and external. Technically speaking face validity is not a type of validity. All face validity implies is that a measure seems to be valid "on the face of it" (Mehrens and Lehmann, 1978). As such, face validity is useful only from a practicality perspective. If a measure does not possess face validity, it is doubtful that it would be adopted.

Internal validity deals with how well a measure captures real differences in the values of an attribute of the real-world entities being measured. For example, using the foregoing definition of SLOC, in comparing one C program to another based on the length/size attribute, if the number of semicolons is greater in one program, then one program is larger than the other. This measure could have some form of internal validity if it captures the "meaning" of length. Internal validity can be established through carefully constructed experiments. There have been three general forms of internal validity identified: content, criterion related, and construct.

Content validity addresses how well the measure covers the attribute being measured. Going back to our length measure (number of semicolons), how well does

---

[5]Note that this demand rules out function points (Graham, 1995, personal communication).

it address our understanding of the attribute length. Are there multiple aspects of the attribute length? What do we mean precisely by the "length" of the program? From a content validity perspective, would the number of bytes that the source code requires to be stored on a disk be a better measure of length? External attributes, such as complexity, understandability, or maintainability are more difficult to ensure content validity since we tend to measure them indirectly and they tend to be dependent on other attributes (both internal and external). One approach to determine the level of content validity is to use a "panel of experts" to judge the coverage that the measure provides of the attribute.

Criterion-related validity addresses how well a measure predicts a future event or how well a measure estimates a current condition. These two separate, but related, ideas are addressed through predictive and concurrent validity, respectively. For example, a design measure of a program's length/size, such as the number of separate modules in the structure chart, could be used to predict the size of the program as measured by the number of functions or procedures in the source code. The difficult part for criterion-related validity is the identification of the criterion used to determine whether the measure is valid or not. In this example, the measure would have good predictive validity if a causal relationship was discovered between the size of the structure chart and the size of the program.

Construct validity, in this domain, deals with the identification of the attributes of the entity, the different measures of the attributes, and the theories on which the attributes were based. For example, complexity, an external attribute, must be defined over some empirically grounded theory; otherwise, it is unclear as to what complexity means. Once the attribute has been shown to "make sense" from a theoretical perspective, then a measure, or set of measures, would be created/identified that would be used to measure the attribute. Given a previously validated measure of the attribute, the new measure simply could be correlated with the old one. This leads to convergent validity, a type of construct validity, of the new measure. (Note: It is important to point out that both measures must be theoretically sound and that the previously validated measure must have been validated for the attribute being measured. If the previous measure had only been validated on size, it could only be used to validate a new measure of size, not, for example, a new measure of complexity.) However, just because a new measure correlates with a previous measure, it may not be enough evidence to demonstrate construct validity. In these cases, discriminant validity, a second type of construct validity, is pursued. This is done by demonstrating that the new measure has a low correlation to validated measures of attributes that are theoretically unrelated to the attribute being measured by the new measure.

External validity addresses the issue of generalizability. There are two major issues when considering generalizability. First, can the measure be generalized beyond the sample entities that have been measured? For example, using either of the above (different) length/size measures (number of semicolons and number of bytes), we could attempt to generalize them beyond the original programs measured. As long as we are addressing C programs, both measures seem to be reasonable, that is, they are both valid from a population validity point of view. However, if we were to attempt to generalize beyond C programs to, say, COBOL programs, the first measure definitely would fail. (COBOL programs are not from the same population as C programs.) Second, can the measure be generalized beyond the environment in which the measurement took place? For example, many measures have been proposed that need to be "calibrated" to the specific environment (Conte *et al.*, 1986). If this is the case, then the measure is not ecologically valid. Unlike internal validity, external validity cannot be experimentally determined. In fact, it rarely can be achieved. (Note: For a complete description of validity issues, see Emory and Cooper, 1991; Kerlinger, 1964; Smith and Glass, 1987.)

### 2.6.2 Reliability

Reliability is a necessary, but not sufficient, property of a measure. As has been observed, reliability addresses whether or not a measure produces consistent results. There are two issues related to reliability: stability and equivalence.

Stability deals with the idea that the measure should produce the same results given the same entity in the same environment. Depending on the type of measure being tested, two potential problems could arise. First, if a "test/retest"-based design was used, the subject could possibly remember the answers to the "test." For example, a programmer is given a maintenance task, multiple times, to perform for the purpose of determining whether a "maintenance cost" prediction measure was reliable or not. If the programmer remembers the task from the previous times, then the measure could look as if it is unstable. Second, the actual process of measuring could modify the entity being measured. Using the same example, the programmer could learn the purpose of the measure. Knowing this, the programmer could go and read about potential approaches to maintenance. This, of course, could affect the results of the "retest" phase.

The equivalence issue addresses whether different samples or investigators impact the measure. For example, given the previously described size measures, any C program could be considered equivalent, from a size perspective, to another C program if the two programs had the same values for the measures. (Note: For a complete description of reliability issues, see Emory and Cooper, 1991; Kerlinger, 1964; or Smith and Glass, 1987.)

### 2.6.3 Robustness

Tsai *et al.*, (1986) suggest that a measure must be theoretically grounded, intuitive, and applicable to early phases of development. They also feel that a measure must be robust. Robustness, as described by the authors, relates to the measure's ability to tolerate incomplete information; that is, the measure must possess some form of internal validity and it must be reliable. The IEEE definition of robustness is the ability to recover from failure and to be able to handle incorrect input.

### 2.6.4 Practical Aspects

Card and colleagues (Card, 1991; Card and Glass, 1990) are concerned with practical issues. They believe that the data upon which the measure is based must be economical to collect; otherwise, they won't be collected. The measure must be understandable and informative; otherwise, it won't be used. All measures must also provide timely feedback to be useful. Finally, they also believe that a measure must be field tested (validated) to be of use.

Grady and colleagues (Grady and Caswell, 1987; Grady, 1992), like Card and colleagues, tend to be concerned with practical issues. They believe that a measure must be part of an overall strategy for software development process improvement. Otherwise, what is the purpose for measurement? Furthermore, the measure must be relevant to the goals of the organization. As such, specific attributes of the software entity must be associated with organizational goals and the measure must be associated with the attribute. They also feel that useful measures should be automatible. From their perspective, if the measure is not automatible, the data necessary for the computation of the measure will not be collected. Finally, like most authors, the measure must be accurate; that is, they must possess some form of internal validity.

Jones (1991), another practitioner, also focuses on practical issues. One of his desired properties is that the measure must be easy to apply and calculate. Like the previous practitioners, if it's not easy to apply and calculate, the measure won't be used. Useful measures should be applied only to visible parts of an entity. He believes that if the measure is applied to some hidden part of the entity, the user of the measure could become confused. Like most practitioners, he is interested in measures that can be used to predict. As such, he wants measures that can be computed early in the software development process. He also states that a measure must be relevant to the user of the measure. His description of this property implies that a measure should be associated with an attribute of the entity that the user feels is important and that the measure must possess face validity. Finally, useful measures are language independent. In many ways, this is based on his earlier requirement of a measure being applicable during early phases of the software development process.

## 2.7 CHAPTER SUMMARY

It is all too easy to get embroiled in the detailed level of individual metrics and lose sight of the larger, mathematical context. We urge readers to take care in applying mathematics and statistics to their measurement endeavors. In this chapter we have laid out some of the pitfalls for the unwary and tried to offer a rationalized yet reasonably simple context in which a metrics program can flourish. Qualitatively, we can describe the desirable properties we seek. These will be formalized in the next two chapters.

## 2.8 BIBLIOGRAPHIC DETAILS

I have found Norman Fenton's work (particularly Fenton, 1991, 1994) especially useful in understanding this topic. Mention must also be made of the excellent paper by Courtney and Gustafson (1993), which is a reminder of the dangers of inappropriate statistics.

# 3

# BASIC DEFINITIONS

In this chapter we lay the groundwork and context for using metrics. In Section 3.1, we will discuss the different categorizations possible with metrics, focusing particularly on the higher-level aims of metrics and then, in Section 3.2, differentiate between product and process metrics. We then give a brief overview/introduction to the notions of complexity (Section 3.3), specifically cognitive complexity (Section 3.3.1) and structural complexity (Section 3.3.2). In Section 3.4, we conclude the chapter by introducing the multidimensional framework (MDF) approach that directs our attention to the most fruitful application areas for (OO) metrics.

## 3.1 VIEWS AND CATEGORIES OF METRICS

We have already seen that one approach to discriminating between metrics is whether they are objective, internal metrics or external, less objective metrics (Fenton, 1991, p. 43). This is a crucial distinction, as we intimated in Chapter 1, because it is this categorization (or lack of it in much of the literature) that has led many organizations to give metrics "a bad name." We can quote lots of instances of poorly constructed and often misinterpreted and/or misapplied metrics, and many reviewers use such instances (which are not totally representative of the discipline) to condemn all metrics as being worthless. In other words, while an encompassing view leads the reader to believe that the subject of software engineering metrics is in disarray, that should not lead us to condemn individual, well-specified and well-tested metrics. Of course, the trick is to be able to distinguish between the wheat from the chaff.

Figure 3.1 attempts to distinguish clearly between internal and external characteristics. Internal characteristics typically describe structural complexity. Common measures of structural complexity are metrics for size, data structure, control flow

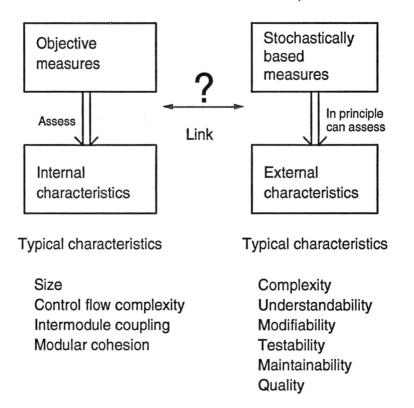

**Figure 3.1**  Internal versus external characteristics, together with some typical example characteristics.

complexity (e.g., the McCabe, 1976, cyclomatic complexity metric), and intermodule coupling (e.g., the Henry and Kafura, 1981, information flow metrics). Structural complexity is one objective, internal partial manifestation of overall system complexity. It is also influenced by the psychological characteristics of the analyst/ designer/programmer, the complexity of the problem, and complexities inherent in the selected representational medium.

Unfortunately, external characteristics are less clearly defined. Shepperd (1992), in a review of the history of software engineering metrics, focuses on a "range of quality factors, typically maintainability and reliability of the resultant software system." Pfleeger (1991), on the other hand, equates quality to reliability + availability + maintainability, to which Fenton (1991, p. 22) adds usability. Henderson-Sellers *et al.* (1993b) also include completion of the abstraction (a semantic characteristic) and reusability. Li and Cheung (1987) focus instead on maintainability (Figure 3.2), which is determined by characteristics of understandability, modifiability, and testability. (For a detailed discussion on the intricacies of these terms, we recommend Fenton,

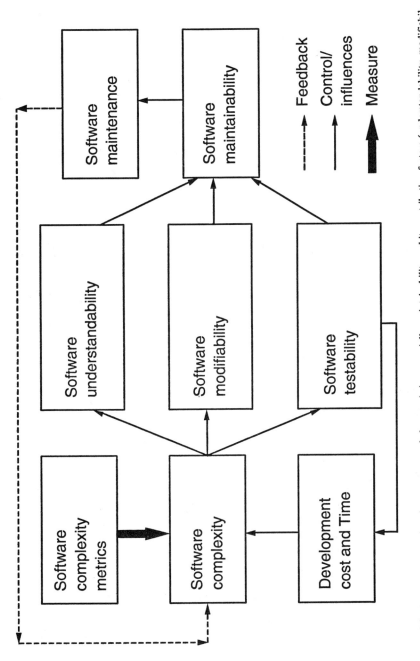

**Figure 3.2** The interconnections between external characteristics, especially maintainability and its contributing factors (understandability, modifiability, and testability) and complexity, with internal measures (of software complexity), development costs, and time.
*Source:* Li, H. F. and Cheung, W. K., 1987. An empirical study of software metrics, *IEEE Trans. Soft. Eng.*, SE-13(6), 697–708. © 1987 IEEE.

1991, Chapter 11.) Overall, this suggests an hierarchical description of quality (Figure 3.3). Thus, at the bottom level we could propose that

$$\text{quality} = \text{reliability} + \text{availability} + \text{understandability} + \text{modifiability} + \text{testability} + \text{usability} \tag{3.1}$$

where each of these components, as shown in part in Figure 3.1, is influenced by complexity.

Over the last few years, several authors have focused on the distinction between a "metric," which strictly is a function with two arguments (for example, the distance between two points), and a "measure," which is a numerical value for an attribute assessed for magnitude against an agreed scale (for example, the length of a piece of string). Although this is strictly correct, nevertheless many authors continue to use the terms measure and metric interchangeably unless they wish to be very specific. Another interpretation (Fenton, 1991) is that metrics characterize simple attributes, whereas measures are functions of metrics (Côté and St-Denis, 1992) to assess more complex attributes such as quality or complexity. Whichever definition/ rationale you prefer, it must be clearly stated that the modern trend is toward the development and use of metrics/measures[1] that can be underpinned by measurement theory.

Figure 3.1 also shows a distinction between the *characteristic* and the *measure* by which we evaluate and understand that specific characteristic. This will lead us, in Chapter 4, to an examination of the underlying principles of measurement theory and the role that this can play in helping us to both derive good-quality measures and also, more importantly, to apply them in appropriate circumstances. We should note that there is often a confusion between the characteristic and the measure. For example, many researchers talk about the complexity of code. Now complexity is one of the most important and least well-defined terms we shall use in this text. We all know what it means intuitively, but that is really as far as it goes. The problem is that complexity *must* involve a person and is, therefore, by Fenton's definition, an external concept. So, complexity, meaning perhaps difficulty of understanding or, in other circumstances, difficulty of maintaining code, is a characteristic we can use to describe a piece of code, a design, or even a problem specification—much like weight or height in our first example in Chapter 2. Confusingly, the word "complexity" is also often used to indicate the metric we use to measure the (concept of) complexity. Perhaps we should really label that the complexity measure and not the complexity. There is thus an interface (as shown in Figure 3.1) between the characteristic and a measure of the characteristic. This idea of transforming from a real-world scale (an empirical relational system) to a measurement scale as defined by a formal relational system is elaborated upon in Chapter 4. However, we should stress here that by using a single word, like quality or complexity, we are not advocating the use of a single number. Rubin's (1993) second myth of metrics is that there can be found a single best metric that will solve all management's problems—a position supported

---

[1]We shall not be pedantic and shall use these terms loosely and effectively interchangeably unless specified otherwise.

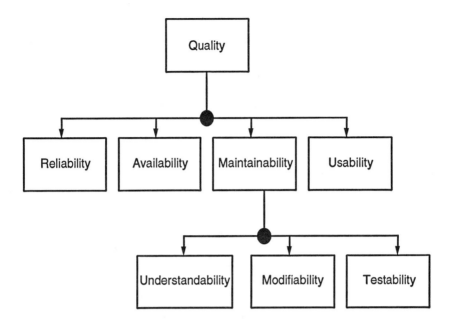

**Figure 3.3**   Quality can be considered to be a combination of reliability, availability, maintainability, and usability. In turn, maintainability comprises understandability, modifiability, and testability.

by Verner's (1993) recommended minimal set of data to be collected and by Fenton's (1994) argument that the existence of such a single number would in fact be "counter to the fundamental concepts of measurement theory."

## 3.2 PRODUCT AND PROCESS METRICS

So far we have talked of measuring internal and external characteristics, but those characteristics may be of two different natures: either product or process (e.g., Ince, 1990; Rombach, 1990; Kitchenham and Linkman, 1990). A product measure is a "snapshot" at a particular point in time. It can be a snapshot of the early design or of the code today, about which we can then derive some code metrics. It cannot therefore tell us anything about the movement from the first snapshot to the second. This occurs over a period of time. Trying to understand the process by taking only one (or possibly at best a small number) of instantaneous assessments is like trying to understand the life history of a frog by only looking at the state of the system each winter. Variables such as staffing levels or effort, both as a function of time, may be used directly or may be included in prognostic models to forecast other characteristics (see the discussion of Figure 3.4 shortly). Process contains a time rate of change (a $d/dt$ term) and requires a process model to fully understand what is happening.

Typically, as with quality assurance (QA) in manufacturing, instantaneous inspection can give only a limited insight. Not until process-based management techniques, such as total quality management (TQM), replace QA can a system be said to be fully controlled. Manufacturing insights have some applicability to software development, although the major difference between a highly repeatable and repeated mass manufacturing industry churning out identical widgets over many years and a software industry developing software that is never identical, even though there may be strong similarities between each accounting system, leads some authors to question the extent to which manufacturing statistical control (which underlies TQM, for instance) can be of use to software development.

Other process metrics include recording fault metrics (totals and fault densities) and change metrics (to record the number and nature of design and code changes) (Kitchenham and Linkman, 1990). These are not discussed further in this book, whose detailed focus is complexity metrics.

It is often argued that the complexity of a piece of code may be used to give a forecast of likely maintenance costs (e.g., Harrison *et al.,* 1982), although such a connection is conceptually tenuous. Often extreme values of *several* metrics can more reasonably be used (Kitchenham and Linkman, 1990) to draw the developer's attention to a potential problem area. Multivariate statistical evaluation techniques are also discussed by Kitchenham and Linkman (1990).

The software project manager has a variety of uses for software metrics, both for product and process (e.g., Weller, 1994). Responsibilities of a project manager range from applying (largely product metrics) to monitoring, controlling, innovating, planning, and predicting (Ince, 1990). Metrics are aimed at providing some type of quantitative information to aid in the decision-making process (e.g., Stark and Durst, 1994). They are thus "circumstantial evidence" that could be used in a decision support system (DSS), for example. The nature of software development precludes the discovery of "global verities." Second, we need to note that the decision-making process is, ideally, undertaken initially early in the project time frame. This provides a tension, since most metrics are most easily collected toward the end of the project. This leads to the attempt either to use measures of product (detailed design or code) as surrogates for process estimates or even estimates of these product measures for use in early life-cycle time and cost estimates.

The desire to forecast costs (of production or maintenance usually) is a major driving force in the derivation of a model useful for cost estimation, although frequently the emphasis in cost estimation is on production rather than maintenance costs, that is, the initial product development rather than the maturation (enhancements and bug fixes) period of the product life cycle. Since

$$\text{total costs} = \text{``tool-up'' costs} + \text{production costs} \atop + \text{maintenance costs} (+ \text{running costs}) \tag{3.2}$$

where

$$\text{production costs} = \text{investigation}^2 \text{ costs} + \text{specification costs} \atop + \text{implementation costs} + \text{integration costs} \atop + \text{testing costs} \tag{3.3}$$

---

[2]The life-cycle terminology used here is that of MOSES (Henderson-Sellers and Edwards, 1994). If you prefer, substitute investigation and specification by analysis and design, respectively.

it is possible to evaluate the likely trade-offs. For example, skimping on production costs almost inevitably leads to an increase in maintenance costs. Equation (3.2) could thus be used as a predictor of total costs for various scenarios of decreased production/increased maintenance costs or, alternatively, used in the context of fixed total budgets to allocate costs between production and maintenance.

Furthermore, it is generally accepted that the unit costs for fixing an error in maintenance are significantly larger than correction at earlier life-cycle phases (Humphrey, 1994) (Table 3.1). Running costs are related to the costs incurred by the user in utilizing the software (i.e., not borne by the developer). However, they are included in Equation (3.2), since it is frequently the case that software is developed for in-house use so that the same organization is billed for all component costs.

This concern with maintenance costs, ease of maintenance (maintainability), and other factors that could loosely be called (external) quality characteristics has led to the use of product metrics as estimators (as noted earlier). Figure 3.4 stresses these important differences in collection and use of various types of metrics. Internal characteristics, typically design or code metrics, can be collected objectively. They can be compared and perhaps used as alarms heuristically, but they can do no more than rank programs *along the scale determined by the definition of the metric itself* (see the discussion on scales in the next chapter). They *cannot* be used as surrogates or predictors for external characteristics without significant further work. This may either be in the sense of collecting voluminous amounts of data (the Tycho Brahe approach) and looking for patterns and correlations (e.g., empirical study of Troy and Zweben, 1981). In addition, the environmental constraints should be identified (for instance, these data are only from COBOL MIS environments in the United States). Then the derived relationships (unhappily sometimes called models) can be used sensibly within the constraints within which they were derived. Globally applied statements such as "Models such as McCabe's cyclomatic complexity and Halstead's software science measures have provided quantitative means of assessing the complexity, cost and reliability of coded software" must be regarded with skepticism. However, some validity may be recovered. For example, from large data

TABLE 3.1    **Hours to find a defect derived from seven independent sources**

| Inspection | Test | Use | Inspection | Test | Use |
|---|---|---|---|---|---|
| 1. 1 | 2–10 | | 5. 0.6 | 3.05 | 33 |
| 2. 0.26 | | | 6. 0.25 | 8 | |
| 3. | 20 | | 7. 0.7 | 6 | |
| 4. 1 | 2–4 | | | | |

*Source:* Adapted from Humphrey, W. S., 1994, A personal commitment to software quality, Cutter Information Corp., publishers of American Programmer, 7(12), 2–12.

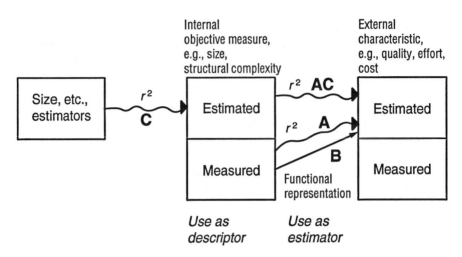

**Figure 3.4**   A model linking measurement and estimation for internal and external characteristics of software. Measurements of internal measures can be used to estimate external characteristics either by use of correlation (route A) or by use of an underlying model (route B). If internal characteristics cannot be measured directly, they may perhaps be estimated (route C) which in turn can then be used to estimate the external characteristic using correlation techniques (route labeled AC: A following C) (after Henderson-Sellers *et al.,* 1995).

volumes[3] on debugging time and structural complexity, it might be possible to derive an empirical relationship, that is, a correlation such that the measured variable can be used as an estimator of the external variable. Here, we would have

$$\text{debugging time} = \text{fn (structural complexity)} \qquad (3.4)$$

This is not the most desirable approach, but it is the most common. For example, Basili (1981) concluded that neither software science metrics nor cyclomatic complexity were any better as predictors of development effort and errors than simple lines of code counts. In other cases, such a correlative relationship may be useful (route A in Figure 3.4); for example, Card (1991) notes that cyclomatic complexity can be useful to indicate maintainability but not for development time. In part, such successes are because the connection being sought (here maintainability as a function of cyclomatic complexity) may actually exist, but has not yet been described or validated. In other words, route *B* in Figure 3.4 is being sought in which there is a scientific rationale for expecting a functional relationship to exist between the two variables, the one internal and the other an external characteristic. Using either of these two routes we might claim we have gained an *estimate* of the external characteristic from a *measurement* of an internal characteristic.

---

[3]Ince (1990) decries "the lack of good experimental design for validations." He notes that a "typical metrics project involves a few subjects with a large number of hypotheses" and that "This statistical naiveté has resulted in many research projects providing invalid results."

Another option might be simply to *measure the external characteristic*. This gives accurate and reliable data on the thing we actually want to know about; however, it is generally too late in the life cycle to be of real use. Rather, such data are vital in obtaining the ability to use internal characteristics as prognostic variables (estimators) since they can be used in validation of the models underlying the B route or in providing one of the variables for correlations using the A route in Figure 3.4.

In a process sense, it is often unacceptable to await the delivery of designs and code so that the internal variables can be measured directly and even they need to be estimated (route C). Typically, size is the internal variable of interest, which has to be estimated, perhaps by function point counts on the requirements (Verner and Tate, 1992).

Summarizing Figure 3.4, we can say that there are two possible analytical routes:

1. Take two sets of measurements (of an internal characteristic and an external characteristic) and try to relate them using correlation techniques: route A.
2. Take two sets of measurements (of an internal characteristic and an external characteristic) together with an underlying conceptual model and validate the model using the external measurements: route B.

Finally, we should note that this analysis of the relationships between internal and external characteristics has to be undertaken for (at least) each external characteristic. So, for instance, we might anticipate finding a relationship

$$\text{maintainability} = f_1 \text{ (internal measure(s))} \qquad (3.5)$$

while if we sought a connection between effort (an external characteristic) and the same or another set of internal measures, we would not expect to find the same functional relationship, but rather

$$\text{effort} = f_2 \text{ (internal measure(s))} \qquad (3.6)$$

A measurement of source lines of code (SLOC) should not be used to predict, say, quality unless intervening causality can be identified. Furthermore, an extensive data collection program of values for SLOC and quality, commonly expressed as a correlation, can be at best suggestive. Correlations only indicate the possibility of interpolation within the same data set or possibly another data set from an identical environment. As we noted earlier, correlations cannot be extrapolated to other domains unless a causal link is sought. Perhaps the most useful role of correlations is to suggest to the researcher possible causal links. At present, there are insufficient data often for those causal links to be identified. Within your own organization, you may be able, therefore, to use in-house correlations to predict, with caution (Baker *et al.*, 1990; Fenton, 1991, 1994). Sadly, many of the direct software measures in the literature have been suggested as useful predictors of external attributes without any causal links being discovered. As such, they may not reflect reality very well and potentially are misleading (e.g., SLOC being used as a predictor of understandability).

Experiments need to be extensive. Local validity does not imply global validity. Indeed, global validity may not be possible to achieve (at least in the short term); rather, acceptable values for metrics should be established locally (at the organizational level) rather than be based on industrywide averages (Kitchenham and Linkman, 1990).

This use of process metrics not merely to *measure* the software process but to extrapolate to being a predictor of cost has led to the development of "cost-estimation" techniques based on models such as COCOMO (Boehm, 1981), SLIM (Putnam, 1978), and PAMELA (Jeffery, 1987a). Other process metrics focus on performance and state of completion.

While being able to cost projects at their inception might be highly desirable, it is dubious whether there are currently *any* widely applicable and reasonably accurate cost estimation models available. Indeed, it may turn out to be an unachievable quest, certainly until more work on the psychological characteristics of the staff involved are taken into account more realistically. A further complicating factor is that since no two software projects are identical, it is inevitable that in each new project there is an element of "research" embedded within the software "engineering" process (Meyer, 1992d)—effort associated with the research process being notoriously difficult to forecast.

Assessing production costs becomes easier at later stages in the production process, since, finally, the project is ended and the costs known accurately. In other words, any cost estimate made early in the life cycle must have significant error bars, which should gradually decrease as the point of completion approaches (Figure 3.5).

Process measures thus cover the whole life cycle, either by describing the temporal (dynamic) variation of properties (e.g., staff allocation) or by integrating (sum-

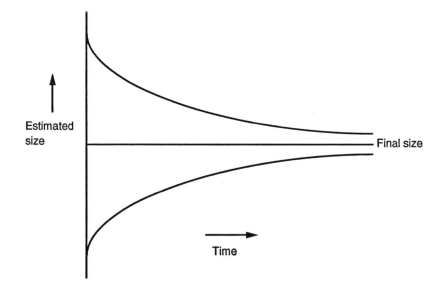

**Figure 3.5** Error bars on size estimates are initially large, but gradually decrease as the system development proceeds (adapted from Laranjeira, ©1990 IEEE).

TABLE 3.2   Lorenz and Kidd's (1994) suite of project metrics

| *Application Size* | *Staffing Size* |
|---|---|
| Number of scenario scripts | Average person-days per class |
| Number of key classes | Average number of classes per developer |
| Number of support classes | *Scheduling* |
| Average number of support classes per key class | Number of major iterations |
| Number of subsystems | Number of contracts completed |

ming) over the life-cycle phases. Suggestions, made by Lorenz and Kidd (1994), for a set of object-oriented project metrics are given in Table 3.2—these are for application size ("snapshot"), staffing size, and scheduling (integrative). In contrast, a "snapshot" taken of the process at a given instant can be used to describe the static characteristics—although Fenton (1994) warns that the reverse is untrue; that is, we should not define characteristics *purely* on the basis of what data we can collect (Figure 3.6). The static properties should be for a specific life-cycle phase. Different individual measures are appropriate for design (e.g., intermodule complexity) and code (e.g., lines of code), for example. These different measures are detailed in Chapters 5 and 6.

Static properties can be counted fairly readily; compared between systems, subsystems, subroutines, or classes; and used as "alarms" (see Section 2.5). In other words, they are used for assessment or diagnosis, *not* prognosis (or prediction). Just as in statistics, where descriptive statistics are distinct from yet basic to inferential statistics, here our focus is on the use of static metrics for assessment (or diagnosis or analysis)—a focus also taken by Lorenz and Kidd (1994). Predictive metrics are more sophisticated demanding the identification of models and extensive data collection. In addition, such approaches are necessarily stochastic (Fenton, 1994).

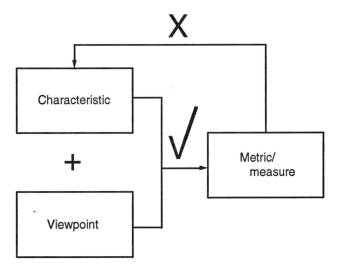

**Figure 3.6**   A good metric can be built from measuring a specific characteristic with a given viewpoint. It is *not* appropriate to collect data and then define the characteristic in which we are interested.

To estimate effort (process metric), a connection has traditionally been made to the overall "size" (product metric) of the system being developed, by means of an organization-specific value of team productivity. The use of size from the many product metrics available as input to the process model equation should not suggest that size is the "best" product measure but, rather, that it is one of the most obvious and easiest to measure, although unfortunately only available toward the end of the life cycle. Consequently, this has fed back to a focus in *product metrics* on estimating or measuring size, viewing size as in some way influenced by program modularity and structure (Figure 3.7). However, a more thorough analysis of the product metric domain suggests that "complexity" and not size may be more relevant to modern software systems. Here complexity can be loosely defined as that characteristic of software that requires effort (resources) to design, understand, or code. Such a loose definition is probably the best that can be done for the overall, generic term "complexity." Fenton (1994) stresses the uselessness of this term, which has no agreed empirical or intuitive meaning and can therefore never be used as the basis of a measure. However, if we focus in on particular types of complexity (as we do in later

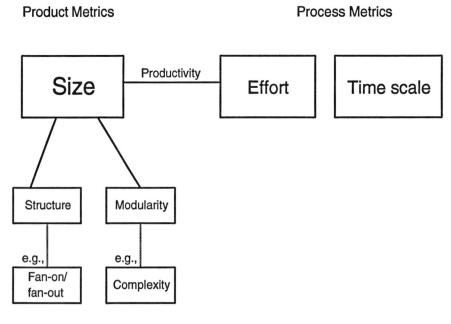

**Figure 3.7**   Product and process metrics. Product metrics relate essentially to product size, which can be measured either in terms of its structure or its modularity. Process metrics measure effort as a function of time. Size and effort are related in terms of productivity, either as a function of time or averaged over the whole life cycle of the project (after Henderson-Sellers and Edwards, 1994).

TABLE 3.3    Appropriate measures of complexity at different life-cycle stages

|  | Analysis | Systems Design | Unit Design | Code Level |
|---|---|---|---|---|
| Problem/functional complexity | Yes | No | No | No |
| Product/document complexity | Yes | Yes | Yes | Yes |
| Procedural complexity | No | Function points only | Yes | Yes |
| Semantic complexity | Yes | Yes | (Yes) | (Yes) |
| Systems design complexity (structural + data) | Yes | Yes | (Yes) | (Yes) |

chapters), then an empirical relational system (see further details in Chapter 4) becomes possible. These various views and definitions permit a composite picture of the various components of software complexity (a product measure). It should be noted that not all these facets relate to all life-cycle stages. (This is indicated in Table 3.3.)

Figure 3.8 "zooms in" on the software complexity metrics box in Figure 3.2 (relabeling it as "complexity," for simplicity). It shows that complexity, an external characteristic or attribute, has three "flavors": computational, psychological, and representational. The most important of these is psychological (e.g., Zuse, 1990), which encompasses programmer characteristics, structural complexity, and problem complexity. Programmer characteristics are hard to measure objectively (Curtis, 1979; Davis, 1984; Kearney *et al.*, 1986; Cant *et al.*, 1994), and little work has been done to date on measures of problem complexity.

Problem complexity relates strongly to design and coding. Also called functional complexity (Card and Glass, 1990, p. 44), this reflects the difficulties implicit in the problem space and is thus sometimes referred to as "difficulty" (Meyer, 1992d). The only measures are ordinal and subjective (e.g., Fenton, 1991, p. 166). It is often argued (e.g., Card and Glass, 1990, p. 46) that problem complexity cannot be controlled, and it is therefore frequently dismissed from consideration in the software engineering literature. On the other hand, it is important to realize that it should figure in terms of a comparison with design measures. In other words, the design and code complexity measures just described *do not* provide an absolute rating; rather, they should be evaluated as relative to the problem complexity. For example, a problem with a complexity of 1 unit,[4] which gives rise to a design of complexity of 100 units, leads us to believe that this is a bad design. However, if a design of 100 units complexity models a problem of complexity 100 units, then we would perceive this as a good design. In addition, there are likely to be confounding factors derivable

[4]It is not even clear that problem complexity and design complexity are independent. A seemingly simple problem, for example, the four-color map problem, may turn out to be complex but that complexity is identifiable only as such once the analysis and design have begun (T. Rout, 1994, personal communication).

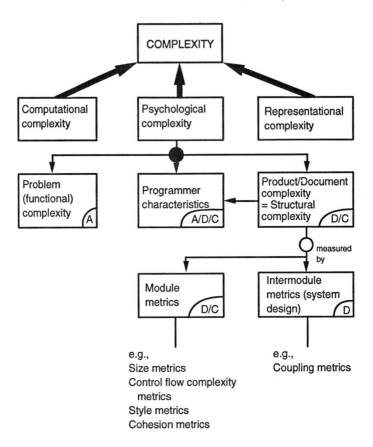

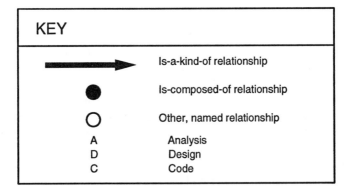

**Figure 3.8**   Classification of software complexity. There are several types of complexity that are external characteristics (or attributes) or software. The most commonly discussed is structural complexity, which is quantified by means of structural complexity metrics (or measures). These metrics may either be focused at the module (or intramodule) level or at the intermodule level and measure the internal attributes of the code or design.

from the influence of programmer characteristics. The most appropriate measures are therefore the ratios:

$$D_P = \frac{\text{design complexity}}{\text{problem complexity}} \tag{3.7}$$

and

$$C_P = \frac{\text{code complexity}}{\text{problem complexity}} \tag{3.8}$$

or

$$C_D = \frac{\text{code complexity}}{\text{design complexity}} \tag{3.9}$$

The aim would be to minimize the ratios $D_P$ $C_P$, and $C_D$ where both of these variables have a lower bound of unity. While this is an important goal, operationalizing these measures awaits an objective measure for problem complexity and agreed definitions on composite measures of complexity for the total system at each stage of the software development life cycle.

Despite these arguments, the software engineering literature is focused primarily on developing and validating structural complexity metrics (i.e., measures of internal characteristics) and then, in the context of Figure 3.4, using them to try to get some estimate (usually) of an external characteristic of interest (e.g., Harrison *et al.*, 1982; Berns, 1984)—often maintainability (Figure 3.2).

Recently, many have realized that the influence of the human programmer and analyst is of crucial importance (Curtis, 1979; Davis, 1984; Kearney *et al.*, 1986; Cant *et al.*, 1992). A combination of this, the static (product) complexity and its relation to the *problem complexity* contribute to the overall psychological complexity.

Mathematically, we thus identify three components to complexity: (1) human cognitive factors, $H$; (2) problem complexity; $P$; and (3) objective measures, which includes size, $S$, data structure, $D$, logical structure, $L$, internal cohesion, $C_h$, semantic cohesion, $C_s$, coupling, $C$. Complexity, $X$, is some (complicated) function of such objective measures *and* taking human cognitive factors into consideration, namely,

$$X = X(H, P, S, D, L, C_h, C_s, C) \tag{3.10}$$

Furthermore, the functional form of Equation (3.10) is likely to be different at different lifecycle stages. Thus, we should write

$$X_i = X_i(H, P, S, D, L, C_h, C_s, C) \qquad (i = 1 \text{ to } j) \tag{3.11}$$

where there are $j$ life-cycle phases identified in the chosen model. The particular form of equation (3.11) depends to some degree upon the (OO) life-cycle model chosen. Very roughly (Figure 3.9), we might identify some generic phases as analysis ($i = 1$), conceptual design ($i = 2$), component design ($i = 3$), coding ($i = 4$), testing ($i = 5$), and maintenance ($i = 6$). For example, the input of declared but unused variables

$$X_1 = X_1 \ (H, P, C_s, C)$$

$$X_2 = X_2 \ (H, P, D, L, C_h, C_s, C)$$

$$X_3 = X_3(H, P, S, D, L, C_h, C_s, C)$$

$$X_4 = X_4(S, D, L, C_h, C_s, C)$$

$$X_5 = X_5(H, S, D, L, C_h, C_s, C)$$

$$X_6 = X_6(H, P, S, D, L, C_h, C_s, C)$$

**Figure 3.9**  Some functional forms for complexity at various life-cycle phases.

does not affect component design ($X_3$) or coding ($X_4$) complexity, but is important for assessing complexity impacts upon maintenance ($X_6$). In a review of traditional metrics by Côté et al. (1988), this life-cycle phase applicability was considered, the majority of metrics being code focused and few appropriate for analysis and/or design (mostly process/cost-estimation assessments).

In the analysis phase, equation (3.11) is rewritten (for $i = 1$) as

$$X_1 = X_1(H, P, C_s, C) \tag{3.12}$$

since in analysis it is not possible to evaluate directly size, data structure, logical structure, or internal cohesion.

At the end of the conceptual design phase, equation (3.11) is rewritten (for $i = 2$) as

$$X_2 = X_2\left(H, P, D, L, C_h, C_s, C\right) \tag{3.13}$$

Although the independent variables are the same as those for analysis, the derived metrics will need to be modified as a result of the additional classes identified in the solution space.

As we enter the detailed design or component design phase ($i = 3$) (although we note that the discrimination between these two in an OO life-cycle phases particularly may be ephemeral or illusory), we can consider that we move into a highly granular class-level design, focusing on the design of the *interface* for each class (and ultimately the class internals as we move toward coding) when the programmer needs to know exactly what services are required to "cut the code."

The focus now is on the class module—both its interface details (external view) and its internal workings. Since this requires highly detailed design at a low level of abstraction, both the effort and the necessary documentation is more voluminous than in either the earlier analysis or conceptual design phases.

At the end of the component design phase ($i = 3$), equation (3.11) is rewritten as

$$X_3 = X_3\Big(H, P, S, D, L, C_h, C_s, C\Big) \tag{3.14}$$

since in design we not only have the attributes of analysis, but we can also now evaluate the internal logic and internal data structure as well as the internal cohesion.

Implementation ($i = 4$) follows naturally from design when using an object-oriented programming language (OOPL). With a pure OOPL, such as Eiffel or Smalltalk, this phase is almost nonexistent, again since the underlying model is transparently identical.

Appropriate code metrics focus at both the interclass level and also at the internal class level. Thus equation (3.11) is rewritten (for $i = 4$) as

$$X_4 = X_4\Big(S, D, L, C_h, C_s, C\Big) \tag{3.15}$$

since in the code itself, we can take a purely objective stance to measure its characteristics (thus, eliminating any $H$-dependency). However, in maintenance, the role of the programmer again becomes significant.

Once classes are coded, they need to be thoroughly tested; initially by class and then by cluster, where a cluster represents a set of collaborating classes (e.g., Meyer, 1988; Firesmith, 1994). Clusters have high cohesion and low coupling to the rest of the system, while typically there will be a higher coupling *between* the classes *within* the cluster.

Appropriate testing metrics focus at both the interclass level and also at the internal class level. Thus equation (3.11) is written (for $i = 5$) as

$$X_5 = X_5\Big(H, S, D, L, C_h, C_s, C\Big) \tag{3.16}$$

Maintenance ($i = 6$) involves error correction (bug fixes) and the collection of maintenance metrics (Wilde and Huitt, 1992). Appropriate metrics for assisting in the maintenance of code require recognition of both programmer comprehension to understand the piece of code (especially if it was written by someone else) as a prerequisite for attempting to fix bugs and add further capabilities. Thus, the whole gamut of possible effects is seen in this phase so that equation (3.11) retains all its independent variables for $i = 6$.

$$X_6 = X_6\Big(H, P, S, D, L, C_h, C_s, C\Big) \tag{3.17}$$

Representational complexity involves the mode of expression in visual form (textual and graphical). Finally, computational complexity (in Figure 3.10) relates to hardware considerations and is frequently not discussed with respect to software (cf. Zuse, 1990, p. 31).

It is appropriate to note also that there are other applications of metrics, notably, to quality assessment. Arthur (1985) describes the application of metrics to assess correctness, efficiency, flexibility, integrity, interoperability, maintainability, portability, reliability, testability, usability, and reusability.

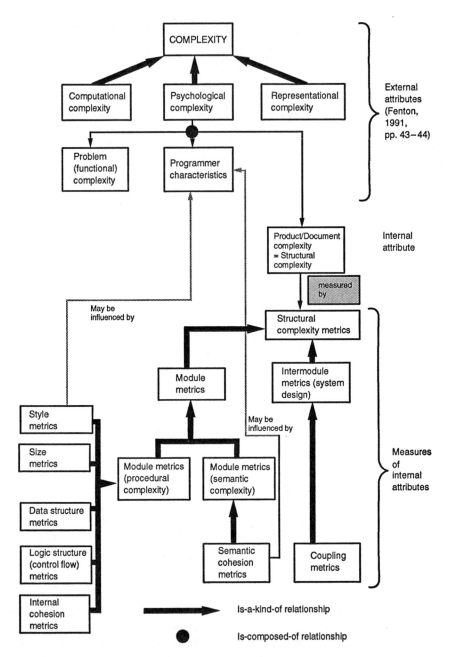

**Figure 3.10**   Classification of software complexity. There are several types of complexity that are external characteristics (or attributes) or software. The most commonly discussed is structural complexity, which is quantified by means of structural complexity metrics (or measures). These metrics may either be focused at the module (or intramodule) level or at the intermodule level and measure the internal attributes of the code or design (after Henderson-Sellers *et al.*, 1995a).

## 3.3 COMPLEXITY

Software complexity research began in the 1970s around the same time as the push for structured programming was beginning. Both were the result of an increasingly large number of poor experiences among practitioners with large systems, and as a consequence, the need for quality control for software became very strong. This quality control took two forms. First, it involved the development of new standards for programming, and, second, it required the development of measures to monitor the "complexity" of code being produced so as to provide benchmarks and to permit poor-quality sections to be modified or rewritten. The best known of the early approaches to complexity measurement were those focusing on structural complexity, such as McCabe (1976) and Halstead (1977). Despite criticisms of these metrics (e.g., Coulter, 1983; Shen *et al.,* 1983; Evangelist, 1984; Nejmeh, 1988; Shepperd, 1988), they are probably still the best known and most widely used—sometimes, as Shepperd (1988) notes, beyond their limits of validity.

At present there is no unified approach to software complexity research. Curtis (1979, pp. 96–97) examining the field lamented that "Rather than unite behind a common banner, we have attacked in all directions." He made a number of observations:

- There was an overabundance of metrics.
- Metricians defined complexity only after developing their metric.
- More time was spent developing predictors of complexity, where in fact more needed to be spent on developing criteria, such as maintainability, understandability, and operationalizing these criteria.[5]
- For every positive validation there was a negative one.

Zuse (1990, p. 3) sums up the situation as one in which "software complexity measurement is confusing and not satisfying to the user."

Cant *et al.* (1995) note that there have been some improvements in the past decade. The rate at which new structural complexity metrics are appearing has fallen. A few metrics, such as those of McCabe (1976), Halstead (1977), and Henry and Kafura (1981), have been the subject of a large amount of empirical and theoretical research. However, their dominance does not appear to be based on any impressive empirical success, but rather on the lack of any validated "rivals." Still, today there are several theoretical approaches to complexity, none of which have been successful enough to claim sole rights to the banner of software complexity research.

In contrast to this early focus on structural complexity, more recently a number of authors have been reinforcing the notion that complexity is a higher-level concept, involving people. Zuse (1990, p. 1) states that "the term software complexity is a misnomer. The true meaning of the term software complexity is the difficulty to maintain, change and understand software. It deals with the psychological complexity of programs." This notion is also seen in Evangelisti (1983) and in our earlier discussion

---

[5]Some work in this area has occurred with the most notable being McCall *et al.* (1977), Boehm *et al.* (1978), Bowen *et al.* (1984), and Kitchenham and Walker (1986).

(e.g., Figures 3.2 and 3.8). It is also supported in the definition of Sullivan (1975) that "Complexity denotes the degree of mental effort required for comprehension."

### 3.3.1 Cognitive Complexity

Cant *et al.* (1992, 1995) have proposed a theoretically based approach to complexity metrics by analyzing cognitive models for programmer comprehension of code and the coding process (including debugging and maintenance). This cognitive complexity model (CCM) can be described qualitatively in terms of a "landscape" model (described in Chapter 7) and is encapsulated quantitatively by a set of equations. The underlying rationale for the CCM is the recognition that programmers, in problem solving, use the two techniques of chunking and tracing concurrently and synergistically (e.g., Miller, 1956). In chunking, the software engineer divides up the code mentally into logically related chunks, e.g., an iterative loop or decision block; in tracing, other related chunks are located. Having found that code, programmers will once again chunk in order to comprehend it. Conversely, when programmers are primarily tracing, they will need to chunk in order to understand the effect of the identified code fragments. For example, they may need to analyze an assignment statement in order to determine its effect, or they may need to analyze a control structure to understand how it interacts with the assignment statements contained in it, to create certain effects.

### 3.3.2 Structural Complexity

As can be seen from Figure 3.8, structural complexity is one of three major components of psychological complexity (the others being programmer characteristics and problem complexity). Structural complexity is that portion of overall (psychological) complexity that can be represented and thus assessed objectively. It thus relates to the structure of the document, whether that document is the design document or the code itself.

Structural complexity is thus measured by structural complexity metrics (Figure 3.10) that offer assessment of a variety of internal attributes (also called internal characteristics). Structural metrics can be divided into intramodule (or just module) metrics and intermodule metrics (Kitchenham and Walker, 1986; Kitchenham and Linkman, 1990). These are discussed in detail in Chapters 5 (traditional) and 6 (OO) under these two headings.

Modularity metrics are focused at the individual module level (subprogram, class) and may be measures for (1) the internals of the module (procedural complexity) such as size, data structure, or logic structure (control flow complexity) or (2) the external specification of the module (semantic complexity)—typical module cohesion as viewed externally to the module. Semantic complexity metrics evaluate whether an individual class really is an abstract data type in the sense of being complete and also coherent; that is, to be semantically cohesive, a class should contain everything that one would expect a class with those responsibilities to possess but no more.

Intermodule metrics measure the structure of the interconnections between modules which comprise the system and thus characterize the system-level complexity. In an OO system this gives some assessment of how loosely or how strongly individual classes are coupled together in the final system. Since such coupling is "designed into" the system, coupling metrics can be collected at the "design" stage.

Procedural complexity metrics are perhaps best understood, although often assumed (inaccurately as we saw earlier) to give immediate information about external characteristics—for instance, Kolewe (1993) suggests that the inevitable consequence of unnecessary complexity is defective software. Maintaining a clear focus on what such procedural complexity metrics *really* measure (basically procedural complexity: an internal characteristic) is *vital*. That is not to say that they cannot be used to forecast other characteristics (internal or external), but forecasting is not the same scientific technique as measuring, and we must retain that difference clearly in mind as we use OO (and other) metrics.

Figure 3.10 shows some of these types of procedural complexity metrics. Size, data structure, and control flow metrics are most evident in the literature and will be the focus of later chapters.

## 3.4 MULTIDIMENSIONAL FRAMEWORK FOR OO METRICS[6]

Henderson-Sellers *et al.* (1993b) have undertaken some preliminary normative (theoretical) work, described in this section, that focuses on the demands of industry for measures of software characteristics such as quality, reusability, and maintainability. In this, the first step is the creation of a framework that highlights which of these characteristics are likely to be most useful, and the second step is the identification of appropriate mathematical measures. In this way, software engineers can, it is hoped, avoid wasted research effort that might otherwise develop metrics which were second order or, worse, totally inapplicable to any real software development environments. At this time, it is not possible to present the detailed entries in the full multidimensional framework, as is necessitated, but rather to illustrate the means by which one can be constructed and to give one concrete example.

There are a number of software engineering goals that an object-oriented development approach can help to attain (e.g., Henderson-Sellers and Edwards, 1994). Table 3.4 lists 14 of these. It can be seen that a number address the higher-level characteristics of software (e.g., 1–6), others address technical issues (e.g., 8, 13), and still others are more concerns of software managers (e.g., 6, 7, 11, 14). It is interesting to note that in this list quality is identified separately but described as "difficult to define" although "quality products are readily discernible by the user." A somewhat different categorization is given in Table 3.5 in which many of the attributes of Table 3.4 are listed as contributory factors to the overall characteristic of "quality." While the lists of Graham (1991), Thomsett (1990), and the International Standards Organization (1991) do not coincide precisely, they do give a flavor of some current concerns about what constitutes quality in a software development environment.

---

[6]This discussion is taken from the work of B. Henderson-Sellers, S. Moser, S. Seehusen, and B. Weinelt.

TABLE 3.4   Fourteen basic advantages of object-oriented software
engineering (after Henderson-Sellers and Edwards, 1994)

| | |
|---|---|
| 1. Correctness and verifiability | 8. Data dependency avoidance |
| 2. Robustness | 9. Better model of real world |
| 3. Extensibility | 10. Seamless transition |
| 4. Reusability | 11. Maintainability |
| 5. Integrity | 12. Ease of use |
| 6. Quality | 13. Management of complexity |
| 7. Increased productivity | 14. Competitive edge |

In the pilot proposal for an OO metrics multidimensional framework (MDF) described by Henderson-Sellers *et al.* (1993b), the major elements are (1) quality, which is itself expressible as a function of (at least and primarily) (a) degree of completion of the abstraction, (b) reusability, (c) understandability, (d) maintainability, and (e) testability; (2) estimated cost of production; and (3) functionality offered.

It is clear that the reasons for any individual using metrics in an OO development environment may vary. The motivation may be managerial or technical; it may be focused on reuse or on productivity; or it may be of concern to code maintainability or to deriving early life-cycle estimates of the whole system. Henderson-Sellers *et al.* (1993b) argue that if the most important high-level characteristics can be identified and described at (1) a life-cycle phase and (2) a level of granularity, then the matrix thus formed can identify those combinations of characteristic/life-cycle

TABLE 3.5   Attributes of software quality

(after Graham, 1991)

| | |
|---|---|
| Resilience and reliability (robustness) | Verifiability |
| Correctness | Security |
| Maintainability | Integrity |
| Reusability and generality | Friendliness |
| Interoperability | Describable |
| Efficiency | Understandability |
| Portability | |

(after Thomsett, 1990)

| | |
|---|---|
| Conformity | Portability |
| Reliability | Usability |
| Maintainability | Auditability |
| Reusability | Security |
| Efficiency | Flexibility |

(after ISO, 1991)

| | |
|---|---|
| Reliability | Maintainability |
| Security | Portability |
| Efficiency | Interoperability |
| Usability | |

phase/granularity that are most important so that researchers, both theoretical and empirical, can invest most effort of their metrics investigation in those key areas.

The three characteristics of quality, cost, and functionality form the first dimension of the MDF. The second dimension is the life-cycle phase (the details of which are methodology dependent); the third is the granularity level. In an object-oriented system, these levels might be viewed as (1) method (internal to class), (2) service (external to class), (3) class, (4) subsystem, and (5) system. The final (fourth) dimension of the framework represents actual measures, including, for instance, fan-in, fan-out, depth of inheritance tree, internal complexity measure, cohesion measure, and reuse ratio.

The relevance of each measure is then assessed for each life-cycle phase, each level of granularity, and each macroscale characteristic, thus decreasing the number of points in the four-dimensional space that require the identification or development of a quantitative, algorithmic description (a simple equation preferably). For example, in the implementation phase, the "functionality offered" is dependent upon (i.e., is a function of) the number of public services at the subsystem level, but at the class level it can be considered, in addition, to be dependent on the number of arguments passed. Thus, in this example, dependencies on the remaining measures (fan-in, complexity, depth of inheritance tree, etc.) seem not to exist.

This minimalist approach suggests retaining a focus on only three major software engineering characteristics—quality, cost, and functionality—as shown in Table 3.6. These characteristics can be considered to be orthogonal, such that other software engineering characteristics are expressible as functions of these three independent "variables." Such functions (which may be as simple as discrete tuples which therefore need to be describable in the MDF) are identifiable on one or more levels of granularity. In some cases a low granularity measure will be a simple summation of that same measure at a higher granularity; for example, lines of code at the class level is the sum of the individual LOC at the "method level" of granularity. For other measures, however, "emergent" or synergistic characteristics may be identifiable as being greater than the sum of the parts, e.g., semantic cohesion. Major effort is required to identify which measures can be summed in this way in moving between abstraction levels. This approach should lead to a minimal set of metrics.

For practical purposes, managers require a small number of metrics, such that the cross-level "grossing up" is of prime relevance to industry. Identification of this key set of metrics is possible only with the formalized MDF approach, compared to the current, more ad hoc and uncoordinated (OO) metrics research effort since the MDF permits the identification of useful metrics but also, perhaps more important, of poor and/or irrelevant metrics.

Following the procedure just described, a prototypical multidimensional framework can be devised for each phase—Henderson-Sellers *et al.* (1993b) describe only the MDF for the implementation phase. This is the phase when code is available and thus is oriented toward (1) final code measures, (2) assessing understandability, and/or (3) assessing maintainability. Table 3.6 presents the three basic characteristics. Quality is seen to be subdivided into five attributes. The entries in the

TABLE 3.6   MDF, with entries added for the implementation phase; a negative
sign implies an inverse relationship (e.g., y = –x) (after Henderson-Sellers *et al.,* 1993b)

| Measure | 1.1 | 1.2 | 1.3 | 1.4 | 1.5 | 2. | 3. |
|---|---|---|---|---|---|---|---|
| Internal size (e.g., LOC) | | | —* | —* | —* | PS | |
| Coupling: | | | | | | | |
|   fan-in | | CP | | | | | |
|   fan-out | C? | | C | * | C | | |
| ? Cohesion | CM | C | PC | * | * | | |
| Fan-down | C? | | | CPS | CPS | | |
| Number of public services: | | | | | | | |
|   new or inherited | | | —C | —C | —C | | CP |
| DIT | | | —PS | —PS | —PS | | |
| NOC | | | | —P | P | | |
| Arguments passed | | | —CV | —CP | —M | | C |
| Number of private services | | | —M | —C | —MC | | |
| Fraction of services inherited | | | C | C(—P)[1] | (—)C | | |
| Complexity (McCabe) | | | —M | —M(C) | —MC | PS | |
| Total number of classes: | | | | | | | |
|   abstract or concrete | | | —PS | —PS | —PS | PS | |
| Reuse ratio | | P | —PS | | —PS | | |
| Specialization ratio | (C) | PS | | | | | |
| Fraction of comment lines | | C | M | MC | | | |
| Number of problem reports | —VCPS | —VCPS | | —VCPS | | —PS | |
| Number of classes and | | | | | | | |
|   methods thrown away | C | | | * | | M(C) | |
| S/C | | C | M | M(C) | * | PS | |
| Function points | | | | | | VCPS | |
| ? External system size | | | | | | VCPS | |
| ? Total system size | | | —* | —* | —* | * | |
| ? Degree of coupling | | —* | —* | | —* | | |
| ? Degree of cohesion | * | * | | * | | | |

Notes: 1. The more services are inherited, the easier it is to maintain at the class level but the harder
it is to maintain at the subsystem level.

    2. Entries indicate measured *not* estimated from.

    3. Phase of SDLC is indicated by
        M = method (internal)    P = subsystem
        V = service (external)    S = system
        C = class           * = all
        ? = identified as useful in 4-D context but with no known measure
          (i.e., "yet to be developed")

    4. Characteristics are coded as follows:
        1.1 Quality: Completeness of abstraction
        1.2 Quality: Reusability
        1.3 Quality: Understandability
        1.4 Quality: Maintainability
        1.5 Quality: Testability
        2.  Estimated cost of production
        3.  Functionality offered

table indicate the level of granularity relevant to each measure (on the left-hand side) for each required macroscale characteristic (keyed in across the top). If there is no entry, it is suggested that this indicates that this combination is not worth exploring.

The *prototypical* MDF just described illustrates the approach that will, it is anticipated, focus research and empirical data collection on to the more worthwhile areas of OO metrics research rather than, for instance, offer a highly unfocused list of mere "collectibles." The framework thus offers the possibility of coordination between academic and industrial researchers and industrial practitioners. It also focuses attention on problem/unknown metrics areas marked by a "?" in the MDF and, as work progresses, on areas where answers have been found. For example, in addition to the metrics gleaned from previous research work, it is possible to propose a number of new, as yet undescribed, measures. There needs to be an OO measure of external size to enhance or replace function point counts as an early life-cycle metric—one candidate is task points (Graham, 1995a)—for overall system size to reflect the advantages of small systems. Robillard and Boloix (1989) present an "interconnectivity" metric that may form the basis for a system coupling metric beyond traditional fan-in/fan-out measures. New large-scale measures of the degree of cohesion may also be needed to enhance or replace traditional cohesion measures. The MDF is, on the other hand, intended to remain flexible as current metrics are validated or invalidated (and hence removed from the matrix) and new metrics are identified and added to the matrix "cells."

Researchers are thus encouraged to address those matrix elements indicated and industrialists to influence the refinement of this matrix and the development and consolidation of a similar matrix for earlier life-cycle phases of the OO development process. In this way, academically rigorous metrics research (in both industry and universities) that is also most readily applicable can be directed toward a common goal: of providing good-quality metrics for use in improving software quality.

## 3.5 CHAPTER SUMMARY

Product and process metrics and external and internal characteristics are all part of the foundation for later chapters. Complexity, ill defined though the word is, can form the basis for a whole family of "complexity metrics"; each of these can be described and operationalized more formally and carefully. In this chapter we have laid out these descriptors and tied them together in the form of a multidimensional framework to focus both metrics developers and metrics users on those areas of most value.

## 3.6 BIBLIOGRAPHIC DETAILS

Internal and external characteristics are best described by Fenton (1994). The work of Barbara Kitchenham in various papers is also useful. Some of the ideas on measures versus estimates were originally published in Henderson-Sellers *et al.*

# 4

# A RIGOROUS APPROACH TO METRICS

There is growing concern that metrics, both traditional and OO, should have a solid base. That base is generally regarded as measurement theory (Section 4.1). In this chapter we explore the mathematics and application of measurement theory (Section 4.2). We complement this discussion by an evaluation of an axiomatic approach (Section 4.3) as well as an overview of dimensional analysis (Section 4.4)—all vital tools in the software engineer's toolbox.

## 4.1 METRICS AND MEASURES

The laudable trend toward incorporating measurement theory into the underlying basis for all metrics leads to the identification of scales for the measures (and, hence, consideration of dimensions and units becomes paramount—a woefully neglected area in software metrics as well as some other areas of engineering and science). These scales can be of several types, the best known being nominal, ordinal, interval, ratio, and absolute (Figure 4.1). A nominal scale is a simple labeling (e.g., the numbers on the numbers on municipal bus fleets); an ordinal scale implies ordering only; an interval scale is used for ordered data such that the same interval between two pieces of data at different parts of the scale have the same meaning. Ratio scales are like interval scales except that as well as addition and averaging (Table 4.1), which is possible with data measured on an interval scale, the data have a zero point and can thus be ratioed. Hence, we can say that datum $A$ is $n$ times as big as datum $B$. (This is not possible on an interval scale, as can readily be seen by consideration of two different temperatures on the Celsius scale. Not until the ratio Kelvin scale is used can such statements be made.) Finally, an absolute scale is one used for simple

| Ordinal,  | e.g., | bus fleet numbers |
| Interval, | e.g., | degrees Celsius   |
| Ratio,    | e.g., | degrees Kelvin    |
| Absolute, | e.g., | counting entities |

**Figure 4.1**  Types of scale and some examples.

counts: values that can only be expressed in one way, for example, the number of days in a year. Ideally, we would wish our software measures to be ratio or interval scale measures so that means, standard deviations, and correlation coefficients are meaningful; sadly this is not always true in the software metrics research literature.

Metrics, or rather measures, thus measure something. They are the software equivalent of length or mass measures in the physical (i.e., nonsoftware) world. Unfortunately, as noted by Fenton (1991, p. 21), such software metrics have been "used" for many other applications. Fenton describes the use, by various authors, of the term software metrics to describe, variously,

- A number derived from product, process, or resource (e.g., LOC, effort, personnel experience)
- A scale of measurement (e.g., a proposed nominal scale for, e.g., software failure)
- An identifiable attribute (e.g., "portability" or "coupling")
- A theoretical or empirical model (e.g., "the COCOMO metric" of Boehm, 1981)

The confusion between a measure and a model is certainly widespread. A pure description of a software product or process using an appropriate measure *does not* and *cannot,* in and of itself, predict anything. Indeed, Fenton's illustrative examples of the use of a person's height (a measure) as a predictor of, say, intelligence (Fenton,

**TABLE 4.1**   Scales of measurement, admissible transformations
and appropriate statistical measures

|          | Transformation $g$ | Valid Statistics |
|----------|--------------------|------------------|
| Nominal  | Any one-to-one function $g$ | Nonparametric |
| Ordinal  | $g$: strictly increasing function | Ranking |
| Interval | $g(x) = ax + b \quad a > 0$ | As ordinal plus addition, average |
| Ratio    | $g(x) = ax \quad a > 0$ | As interval plus ratio |
| Absolute | $g(x) = x$ | All that apply above |

1991, p. 156), which, he notes, is clearly nonsensical is illuminating. As discussed in Chapter 2, correlations are suggestive—causal links are needed in order to create a valid and useful predictive model for external software characteristics. It is argued that current metrics research should aim to find good measures per se, to derive indirect measures built on these original measures and then build prognostic models once the cause-and-effect relationships have been identified.

In this book we use, predominantly, the (perhaps inaccurate) term "metrics" in describing state-of-the-art application of traditional quantitative characterization of software; first in Chapter 5, briefly in the traditional structured environment and then, second, in Chapter 6, in the object-oriented environment. This choice of the word metric as opposed to the more accurate term measure is determined by common usage, at the loss of accuracy of use of language as described by, for example, Fenton (1994, p. 203). We trust that this decision will cause no loss to the reader's understanding of the subject.

## 4.2 MEASUREMENT THEORY

One of the criticisms possible for many proposed metrics is the lack of any theoretical underpinning. Relationships may be, as we saw in Chapter 2, merely the result of correlative or regressional analysis. Dimensional inconsistencies may result especially in the construction of composite measures.

As a consequence of some of these concerns, the last few years have seen a rapid growth in the mind-set that any metric should be developed and tested in the context of measurement theory and that application of such theory will assist in clarifying whether any specific measure is appropriate in each individual situation.

From a scientific point of view, this is entirely praiseworthy and one with which we concur. Our only reservation is that this should not preclude or deny the temporary usefulness of more pragmatic metrics. In other words, the need to measure and control software developments exist *now.* That universally validated and tested metrics do not currently exist, especially for object-oriented environments, should not prevent us from using empirical metrics (see, e.g., Lorenz and Kidd, 1994). But if we do, *it is vital to remember* that any such metrics are *highly parochial,* highly limited, and highly unscientific—although they may still be useful, especially in the context of alarm triggers (Section 2.5). For instance, a measure or estimator derived on small OO projects *cannot* be transferred without further detailed evaluation to large OO projects or to non-OO systems; metrics tuned for C++ are likely to be inappropriate for Smalltalk, Eiffel, or CLOS (common LISP object system)—four languages with contrasting underlying object models and which encourage different idioms i.e., stylistic nuances in programming.

Empirical and unjustified, locally useful metrics are not our prime concern; rather we will focus on providing theoretical validity to any proposed suite of OO metrics. Hence one component of our suite of developmental tools, yet one not yet extensively employed, is measurement theory, which we will outline in this section.

Zuse and colleagues (Zuse, 1990; Zuse and Bollmann, 1989) and the Grubstake group (Baker *et al.,* 1990; Bush and Fenton, 1990; Fenton and Melton, 1990; Melton *et al.,* 1990; Fenton, 1990, 1991, 1994) are concerned with measurement theory issues (see, e.g., Roberts, 1979, or Naurens, 1985, for a complete description of measurement theory). Ejiogu (1987, 1991, 1993) has also been concerned with similar issues.

In addition to this focus on measurement theory, Zuse (1990) also introduces the idea of a viewpoint. A viewpoint is simply a way to look at something, that is, an empirical relation. He feels that measures should be based on specific viewpoints. This is nothing more than stating that a measure should be based on a specific attribute of the entity and that the attribute must be precisely defined. It is this idea of preciseness that is new. Third, a measure must address both the structure of process and data. Fourth, a useful measure must be consistent, that is, reliable. Fifth, a measure must be capable of representing at least a weak order; that is, nominal level measures are not acceptable from his perspective. Sixth, like many of the previous authors, he feels that the measure should be automatable. Otherwise, the measure could run into problems with data collection and issues of consistency.

Measurement theory involves the mathematical description of scales, measures, and methods of measuring. Other terminology that requires explanation includes homomorphism, weak order, extensive structures, meaningfulness, and atomic modification. Its application is described in Zuse (1990) and Fenton (1991). Zuse views its use as being "an essential element of all sciences" (Zuse, 1990, p. 39).

### 4.2.1 Relational Systems

The underlying notion of measurement theory is that if there exists, in our problem domain or universe of discourse (UoD), an intuitive or empirical understanding of relationships of objects within that UoD, then those relationships can be formalized in a mathematically derived *formal relational system.* For example (Figure 4.2), comparison of two wooden boards in terms of their length would result in an unambiguous ordering (as would be made by a number of observers). In other words, there is a commonly understood *empirical relation* which we might express by the phrase "equal or longer than" (denoted by Zuse and here as $\bullet \geq$). The need for an empirical or "intuitive" relation is stressed by, for example, Fenton (1994) who argues that if a term (he uses the example "complexity") means different things to different people, then there is no hope of ever transforming it toward a formal relational system. Simply portraying a number of directed acyclic graphs (DAGs) and asking the reader to rank them by complexity is subjective because there is insufficient information, particularly on the definition of "complexity." This does not mean that McCabe's cyclomatic complexity is inappropriate or invalid. Rather the reverse: given the definition of *cyclomatic* complexity, then, in fact, all assessments would be the same since cyclomatic complexity is uniquely and objectively defined.

In addition, we might (or might not) have some common understanding of one or more binary operations, such as concatenation (denoted as $\circ$). For example, for two boards of lengths $a$ and $b,$ we either have $a \bullet \geq b$ or $b \bullet \geq a$ and $a \circ b$ has meaning—two boards stuck end to end.

| Empirical Relational System | Formal Relational System |
|---|---|
| Wooden boards relation:<br>Equal or longer than: $\bullet\geq$<br><br>$\vdash\text{---}\overset{a}{\text{---}}\dashv$<br><br>$\vdash\text{-----}\overset{b}{\text{-----}}\dashv$<br><br>$b \bullet\geq a$       $<=>$ | $\Re$ (real numbers)<br><br>Equal or greater than: $\geq$<br><br><br><br>$\mu(b) \geq \mu(a)$ |
| Binary operation o:<br>Concatenation:<br><br>$\vdash\text{------}\underset{a}{+}\text{------}\underset{b}{\text{------}}\dashv$<br><br>   $a \circ b$ | Addition $+$<br><br><br><br>$\mu(a \circ b) = \mu(a) + \mu(b)$ |

**Figure 4.2** Empirical relational systems and their corresponding formal relational systems. *Source:* Zuse, H., 1990. *Software Complexity: Measures and Methods,* Walter de Gruyter, Berlin.

This "qualitative" system can be written formally as follows: an *empirical relational system,* **A,** is an ordered tuple (two definitional variants are in common use):

$$\mathbf{A} = \left(A, R_i, \circ_j\right) \qquad i = 1 \text{ to } n, \quad j = 1 \text{ to } m \tag{4.1}$$

where $A$ is a nonempty set of objects, the $R_i$ are empirical relations, such as "equal or longer than" or "equal or more complex than," and the $\circ_j$ are binary operations on the empirical objects in the set $A$ (Zuse, 1990). On the other hand, Fenton (1991, p. 22) defines an empirical relation system by

$$\mathbf{A} = \left(A, R_i\right) \qquad i = 1 \text{ to } n \tag{4.2}$$

thus omitting the need for a binary operation. Roberts (1979, p. 44) notes that a relational system (here either empirical or formal) is the $(n + m - 1)$-tuple given by equation (4.1). *However,* it may sometimes be simpler and more efficacious to regard the binary operations as relations and thus "speak of a relational system as a $(n + 1)$-tuple $(A, R_1, R_2, \ldots, R_n)$."

At this stage, we need have no measures. It is the role of a mapping function, $\mu$, from the empirical relational system, **A,** to a *formal relational system,* **B,** which provides the measure. This formal relational system is defined as

$$\mathbf{B} = \left(B, S_i, \bullet_j\right) \qquad i = 1 \text{ to } n, \quad j = 1 \text{ to } m \tag{4.3}$$

where $B$ is a nonempty set of formal objects (e.g., numbers, vectors), the $S_i$ are relations on those objects in $B$, such as "greater" or "equal or greater," and the $\bullet_j$ are the closed binary operations, such as addition or multiplication.

The formal definition of the mapping function, $\mu$, is given as a homomorphism: $\mu : A \rightarrow B$, which gives a value $\mu(a)$ in $B$ for all objects $a \in A$. We could write this as

$$\forall a \in A \; \exists \, b \in B \, | \, \mu(a) = b \tag{4.4}$$

where a homomorphism is defined formally (e.g., Fraleigh, 1969, p. 106) as a mapping $\mu$ that satisfies the condition

$$\mu(ab) = (\mu a)(\mu b) \qquad \forall a, b \in A \tag{4.5}$$

Finally, the triplet $(\mathbf{A}, \mathbf{B}, \mu)$ is known as a *scale* if the following conditions hold:

$$R_i\left(a_{ij}\right) \Leftrightarrow S_i\left(\mu(a_{ik})\right) \tag{4.6}$$

and

$$\mu\left(a \circ_j b\right) = \mu(a) \bullet_j \mu(b) \tag{4.7}$$

for all $i, j$ and for all $a_{ik} \in A$. It is also worth noting that if $B = \Re$ (the set of real numbers), then the triple $(\mathbf{A}, \mathbf{B}, \mu)$ is a real scale. (Measurement of the wooden boards in such a formal relational system is also shown in Figure 4.2.)

There are two problems specific to software measures and, in particular, software complexity that need to be addressed: (1) whether we have an agreed intuitive understanding of a term such as software size or software complexity in the sense of Figure 4.2 (left-hand side) that we can uniquely order two pieces of software on the basis of "equal or larger/more complex than" and (2) how to determine the scales appropriate for any of the commonly accepted software engineering metrics.

It is arguable that there is an agreed, common understanding of the term software size. Insofar as we can make definitions in terms of lines of code (LOC), token counts, and so on, this is probably feasible, yet less so across languages, especially if we wish to go further and try to use these size values as estimators of cost or effort (see Chapter 2).

Perhaps a more fundamental obstacle is whether all software engineers would make identical, intuitive rankings in terms of complexity. Anyone with knowledge of various available metrics (e.g., Chapter 5) might permit that knowledge to influence her or his intuitive grasp of complexity. Yet complexity is an everyday term. It is, however, important to note that it is relative to context. Complexity intuitively represents difficulty of comprehension and that comprehensibility depends on antecedent conditions. For instance, anyone new to the area of formal systems as described in this section will probably find this material "complex" and difficult. Authors of texts and holders of degrees in pure mathematics are likely to find it less daunting. In other words, it seems highly likely that we *do not have* any agreed intuitive understanding of the notion of software complexity (and to a lesser extent software size) and hence have no empirical relational system. Without the existence of such a relational system, we cannot construct a scale. This is probably the most singular difficulty facing the software metrician today.

### 4.2.2 Orders

In the literature pertaining to the application of measurement theory to software metrics (e.g., Melton *et al.*, 1990; Fenton and Melton, 1990; Baker *et al.*, 1990; Fenton, 1992), the concept of "order" is prevalent. A brief discussion only is needed here. Interested readers should consult, for example, Roberts (1979, Chapter 1.5) for further details.

Roberts (1979) gives seven types of order (Table 4.2) defined in terms of properties of relations (Table 4.3). A quasi-order or preorder is one where there is a weak preference (relation $P$) or indifference (relation $I$):

$$aWb \Leftrightarrow (aPb \text{ or } aIb) \tag{4.8}$$

An example of a quasi-order is the relation $\geq$ on the set of real numbers.

If, in addition, the relation is strongly complete (i.e., $\forall a, b \in A$ including $a = b$, either $aWb$ or $bWa$), then it is called a weak order. Thus, $\geq$ is a weak order, but $>$ is not since it is not strongly complete since if $a = 1$ and $b = 1$, $\sim aWb$ and $\sim bWa$. All weak orders are quasi-orders since completeness implies reflexivity, but a quasi-order is not necessarily a weak order. An example of a weak order that is not a simple order would be a binning of values on the real axis.

A weak order that is also antisymmetric is called a simple order (also known as linear order or total order). The relation $\geq$ is a typical example, which is used to order real numbers, laid out on the real axis.

As noted earlier, the relation $>$ is not a weak order since it is not strongly complete, but merely complete (Table 4.3). Neither is it reflexive. However, it is also transitive and asymmetric. This set of properties defines a useful set of relations known as a strict simple order (Table 4.2). The last of the weak/simple orders is the strict weak order which is asymmetric and negatively transitive (but is not of interest to us here).

**TABLE 4.2   Order relations (after Roberts, 1979)**

| Property | Relation Type | | | | | | |
|---|---|---|---|---|---|---|---|
| | Quasi Order | Weak Order | Simple Order | Strict Simple Order | Strict Weak Order | Partial Order | Strict Partial Order |
| Reflexive | X | | | | | | X | |
| Symmetric | | | | | | | |
| Transitive | X | X | X | X | | X | X |
| Asymmetric | | | | X | X | | X |
| Antisymmetric | | | X | | | X | |
| Negatively transitive | | | | | X | | |
| Strongly complete | | X | X | | | | |
| Complete | | | | X | | | |

*A given type of relation can satisfy more of these properties than those indicated. Only the defining properties are indicated.

(Reprinted with the permission of Cambridge University Press, © 1984)

TABLE 4.3    Properties of relations (after Roberts, 1979)

| A Binary Relation $(A, R)$ Is: | Provided That: |
| --- | --- |
| Reflexive | $aRa$, all $a \in A$ |
| Nonreflexive | it is not reflexive |
| Irreflexive | $\sim aRa$, all $a \in A$ |
| Symmetric | $aRb \Rightarrow bRa$, all $a, b \in A$ |
| Nonsymmetric | it is not symmetric |
| Asymmetric | $aRb \Rightarrow \sim bRa$, all $a, b \in A$ |
| Antisymmetric | $aRb$ and $bRa \Rightarrow a = b$, all $a, b, \in A$ |
| Transitive | $aRb$ and $bRc \Rightarrow aRc \Rightarrow aRc$, all $a, b, c \in A$ |
| Nontransitive | it is not transitive |
| Negatively transitive | $\sim aRb$ and $\sim bRc \Rightarrow \sim aRc$, all $a, b, c \in A$; equivalently, $xRy \Rightarrow xRz$ or $zRy$, all $x, y, z \in A$ |
| Strongly complete | for all $a, b, \in A$, $aRb$, or $bRa$ |
| Complete | for all $a, \neq b, \in A$, $aRb$, or $bRa$ |
| Equivalence relation | it is reflexive, symmetric, and transitive |

(Reprinted with the permission of Cambridge University Press, © 1984)

Two other orders (partial and strict partial) are relevant to measurement theory and software metrics. Neither exhibit completeness, for example, the relation "father-of" over the set of the world's population. A partial order is an antisymmetric quasi-order. Thus, it has reflexive, transitive, and antisymmetric properties (Table 4.3). Partial orders are often associated with stating preferences among choices with several dimensions ($i = 1$ to $n$). Thus, we have

$$aWb \text{ iff } \left[ f_i(a) \geq f_i(b) \quad \forall i \right] \tag{4.9}$$

which defines the binary relation $(A, W)$ as a partial order. A strict partial order is related to a partial order similarly to a strict simple order to a simple order; that is,

$$aSb \text{ iff } (aRb \text{ or } a = b) \tag{4.10}$$

where $(A, R)$ is a strict partial order and $(A, S)$ is a partial order.

### 4.2.3 Scale Types

Setting that difficulty on one side for the present, let us now investigate the different sorts of scales derived above, namely, the scale $(\mathbf{A}, \mathbf{B}, \mu)$. Differences in scales exist because for each scale there is a limited number of *admissible transformations* applicable to that scale. An admissible transformation is defined by a mapping $g : \mu(A) \rightarrow B$ whenever $(\mathbf{A}, \mathbf{B}, g \circ \mu)$ is a scale. Another way of saying this is that the function $g \circ \mu$ from $A$ to $B$ is a homomorphism. For example, if $\mu : \mathsf{N} \rightarrow \mathsf{Re}$ is given by $\mu(x) = 2x$, then $\mu(x)$ is a homomorphism. If $g(x) = x + 5$, then $g \circ \mu$ is also a homomorphism since $(g \circ \mu)(x) = 2x + 5$ and $x > y$ iff $2x + 5 > 2y + 5$. Thus, for this example, $g : \mu(A) \rightarrow B$ is an admissible transformation of scale. However, for $g(x) = -x$, $g \circ \mu$ is not a homomorphism so, in this case, $g : \mu(A) \rightarrow B$ is *not* an admissible transformation. For example, a mass scale in pounds can be transformed to a mass scale in kilograms by simple multiplication by a constant factor. The type of admissible transformation defines the scale type (Table 4.1).

*Nominal scales* are those in which labels are attached to objects but no ordering is possible or meaningful. Typical examples here are numbers on footballers' jerseys and numbers on metropolitan bus fleets. An admissible transformation is any one-to-one mapping. The only statistics possible are nonparametric ones. In other words, we can use only modes, frequencies, medians, and tests such as Spearman's $r_S$ and Kendall's $\tau$. We *cannot* use means, standard deviations, or the common Pearson product-moment correlation.

*Ordinal scales* are "stronger" than nominal scales in that they permit ordering. Zuse (1990) states that a weak order (see Section 4.2.2) is required for an ordinal scale (Roberts, 1979), although Fenton (1989) argues that a partial order will suffice. Consequently, an admissible transformation is any transformation that preserves this order. An example of an ordinal scale is a typical Likert scale such as "disagree, neutral, agree." Rank order statistics are possible in addition to those useful for nominal data. *However,* arithmetic operations such as means are *not* meaningful for ordinal measures. This is important to note since (1) many ordinal metrics are presented in terms of their means and (2) unless we identify scales together with the metric, we do not know if it is meaningful to calculate mean values. Another way of viewing an ordinal scale is as one in which relations are defined but not binary operations. Thus, for an ordinal scale, definitions 4.1 and 4.2 must be rewritten as

$$\mathbf{A} = \left(A, R_i\right) \qquad i = 1 \text{ to } n \tag{4.11a}$$

$$\mathbf{B} = \left(B, S_i\right) \qquad i = 1 \text{ to } n \tag{4.11b}$$

*Interval scales* are the next in order of "strength." Objects cannot simply be ordered, but the "distance between" any pair of objects has meaning, for example, temperature as measured in degrees Celsius. Consequently, admissible transformations must preserve both order and intervals. Any linear transformation of the form $g = ax + b(a > 0)$ will do this. Consequently, we are able to use arithmetic means for the first time.

*Ratio scales* permit further calculation, based on ratios and percentages. Their admissible transformations are $g = ax(a > 0)$. Examples are mass, temperature in degrees Kelvin, length, and time interval. These are all scales for which a zero value has a meaning. Simple scaling is permissible. A mass of 1 kg can equally be described as a mass of 2.20462 lb.

*Absolute scales* have the tightest constraint with respect to admissible transformations which must be of the form $g(x) = x$, that is, the identity. In other words, there is only one permissible value, however it is derived (e.g., the number of alphabetic characters in this word). Absolute scales thus represent counts and permit a full range of descriptive statistics to be applied, for example, means and standard deviations.

As examples (and based on these definitions alone), we can see that LOC is on an absolute scale, whereas $V(G)$ is on an ordinal scale since it is not additive, although Zuse and Bollmann (1989) give conditions under which it may be used on an interval and on a ratio scale.

An associated concept is that of *meaningfulness*—do mappings retain their (correct) meaning when these transformations are applied? If the transformation is admissible, then it is also meaningful, and vice versa. Thus, if we require that for a complexity measure

$$\mu\left(P_1 \circ P_2\right) > \mu\left(P_1\right) + \mu\left(P_2\right) \tag{4.12}$$

that is, that the complexity of the sum of two program parts, $P_i$, is greater than the sum of the parts (here expressed as concatenation of program parts), then we must evaluate whether this is meaningful. If we use an interval scale and apply the interval scale's admissible transformation $(g(x) = ax + b)$ to both sides of the inequality we would get

$$a\mu\left(P_1 \circ P_2\right) + b > a\mu\left(P_1\right) + b + a\mu\left(P_2\right) + b \tag{4.13}$$

which is *not* meaningful for any arbitrary $b$. Consequently we can deduce that equation (4.12) is *not meaningful* on an interval scale. However, it is meaningful if the scale is a ratio scale, since we would get

$$a\mu\left(P_1 \circ P_2\right) > a\mu\left(P_1\right) + a\mu\left(P_2\right) \tag{4.14}$$

Several authors suggest that we should aim to develop measures on a ratio scale. We saw from Table 4.1 that this allows us to take averages meaningfully as well as ratios. Indeed, Zuse (1990, p. 39) suggests that interval scales, per se, are inappropriate for metrics, although Harrison *et al.* (1982) suggest the best choice is an ordinal scale. To get a ratio scale (Figure 4.3), Zuse (1990) argues that an extensive structure is necessary, bringing with it axioms of commutativity and monotonicity. This extensive structure is the formal vehicle for adding binary operations (∘ in the empirical system and + for the formal relational system), as discussed here. In using a ratio scale, as we saw earlier, a zero is meaningful. This leads to some concern about the meaningfulness of software with a zero complexity. However, this provides no difficulties as can be seen by considering a common ratio scale such as length or mass. That a person with zero length or zero mass does not exist does not contradict the use of length or mass as ratio scales—as is normally and widely accepted (Zuse, 1995, personal communication).

### 4.2.4 Extensive Structures

An extensive structure is defined as follows.

For a nonempty set, **P,** with a defined binary relation $\bullet \geq$, and a binary operation ∘, then the relational structure $(\mathbf{P}, \bullet \geq, \circ)$ is an extensive structure if and only if the following axioms (Zuse, 1990, p. 57) hold for all $P_1 \ldots P_4 \in \mathbf{P}$:

A1: $(\mathbf{P}, \bullet \geq)$ is a weak order
A2: $P_1 \circ (P_2 \circ P_3) \approx (P_1 \circ P_2) \circ P_3$ (weak associativity)
A3: $P_1 \circ P_2 \approx P_2 \circ P_1$ (weak commutativity)

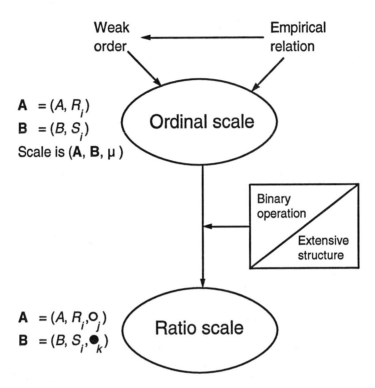

**Figure 4.3**  The relationship between a weak order, the ordinal scale, and an empirical relation. Addition of a binary operation/extensive structure permits a metric on an ordinal scale to be then used on a ratio scale.

A4: $P_1 \bullet > P_2 \Leftrightarrow P_1 \circ P_3 \bullet \geq P_2 \circ P_3 \Leftrightarrow P_3 \circ P_1 \bullet \geq P_3 \circ P_2$ (weak monotonicity)

A5: If $P_3 \bullet \geq P_4$, $\forall P_1, P_2 \, \exists$ natural number, $n$, such that $P_1 \circ nP_3 \bullet \geq P_2 \circ nP_4$ (Archimedean axiom)

Zuse (1990, p. 51) argues cogently that since there is no empirical relational system for complexity, the notion is refined to give an *empirical subrelation* $\bullet \geq_e$ which does not necessarily possess a weak order and contains only partial information about the empirical relation. This notion, together with the notion of *atomic modification*, permits greater understanding and evaluation of software metrics, especially for complexity, to be undertaken.

### 4.2.5 Atomic Modifications

An atomic modification is one of a list of prescribed changes. For instance, for a directed acyclic graph (or flow graph), as used in calculating the cyclomatic complexity, atomic modifications are addition and deletion of nodes and edges and the transferral of edges within the flow graph; for an LOC measure, atomic modifications would be the addition, removal, or transfer of a line of code.

For example, for cyclomatic complexity, $V(G)$ (see details in Chapter 5), the three atomic modifications are

$M_1$: add a node and edge (that is, a statement) at an arbitrary location in the DAG

$M_2$: transfer an edge to another location

$M_3$: add a new edge between two existing nodes

The sensitivity of the measure to these atomic modifications gives the partial properties of the measure. Since $V(G) = e - n + 2$ for a single component DAG,[1] it is clear that $M_1$ and $M_2$ result in no change in the value of $V(G)$, whereas $M_3$ increases the value. This is summarized in Table 4.4. In this case, addition of an edge increases the cyclomatic complexity, which corresponds to the intuitive notion of complexity embodied in the empirical relational system. If the results of the atomic modifications do not translate back to an acceptable statement within the empirical relational systems, then the measure should be rejected (Zuse, 1990, p. 55).

### 4.2.6 Evaluating Metrics

This approach now permits evaluation of the appropriateness of published (and new) metrics for different scales. Some examples are given in Sections 5.3.4 and 6.3.4 following the introduction of the specific metrics' definitions. (For a more detailed discussion of the use of partial properties and extensive structures, see Chapter 4 of Zuse, 1990, and for specific applications, see his Chapter 8.)

## 4.3 AN AXIOMATIC APPROACH

In a notable, but not uncriticized, paper, Weyuker (1988) proposed a set of nine axioms against which software complexity metrics could be evaluated formally. Although many authors, notably, Zuse (1990) and Fenton (1991), have observed that these nine axioms are not internally self-consistent, they *do* provide an initial framework which can be adapted and refined in an OO framework. In this section, we first present the original axioms, followed by their criticisms. Then we briefly describe the way in which these have been used in the field of object-oriented metrics.

### 4.3.1 The Original Axioms

Weyuker's (1988) first four properties addresses how sensitive and discriminative the measure is. The fifth property requires that the measure produce a value for a

TABLE 4.4    Partial properties of the McCabe cyclomatic complexity measure

| Atomic Modification | Explanation | Partial Property |
|---|---|---|
| $M_1$ | Add edge + node | = |
| $M_2$ | Transfer edge | = |
| $M_3$ | Add new edge | > |

[1]In the DAG there are $e$ edges and $n$ nodes.

component of a program that is no more than the value produced for the program. This assumes that a component is no more complex than the program itself. The sixth property addresses the interaction between two programs. It implies that the interaction between ProgramA and ProgramC can be different than the interaction between ProgramB and ProgramC (where ProgramC is called from both ProgramA and ProgramB). As such, the complexity values can be different for the two concatenations (ProgramA–ProgramC and ProgramB–ProgramC). The seventh property requires that a measure be sensitive to statement order within a program. The eighth property requires that renaming of variables not affect the value of a measure. Her last property states that the sum of the complexities of the components of a program could be less than the complexity of the program when considered as a whole.

Weyuker's proposals were couched in terms of programs rather than object classes. In this section that terminology will be maintained for consistency. The notation used is that for any program body, P, its complexity is $|P|$, where this is a nonnegative number. It is obvious therefore that for any two program elements, P, Q, then either $|P| \leq |Q|$ or $|Q| \leq |P|$, and furthermore that if $|P| \leq |Q|$ and $|Q| \leq |R|$, then $|P| \leq |R|$; that is, there is transitivity and a weak ordering.

Of the nine "axioms," several are truly axiomatic and without which there would be no discussion.

*Property 1:*    Weyuker's first property is an example. This states that

$$(\exists P)\ (\exists Q)\ (|P| \neq |Q|)$$

which ensures that any measure that rates all programs to be of the same complexity must be eliminated from consideration.

The second property extends this notion to ensure that there is sufficient resolution in the measurement scale to be useful, for example, a metric with only two values is likely to have a limited applicability.

*Property 2:*    Let $c$ be a nonnegative number. Then there are only a finite number of programs of this complexity, $c$ (Blum, 1967).

Property 2, ensuring sufficient resolution, is counterbalanced by Property 3, which requires that the metric should not be so fine that any specific value of the metric is only realized by a single program. In other words, it should be possible to find two programs that are "equally complex."

*Property 3:*    There are distinct programs, P and Q, such that $|P| = |Q|$.

Weyuker notes that these first three properties are really properties of measures and do not reflect the syntactic nor semantic nature of software complexity measures.

Property 4 suggests that it is possible for the same functionality to be encapsulated in two different programs where the identical functionality is implemented differently, for example, sorting a listing implemented as a bubble sort and a heap sort.

*Property 4:*    As before, by defining $P \equiv Q$ to mean that the two program chunks have identical behavior in that they produce identical outputs for identical inputs, we can write Property 4 as

$$(\exists P)\,(\exists Q)\,(P \equiv Q \;\&\; |P| \neq |Q|)$$

For object classes, one interpretation would be that two classes having the same message signature would respond identically and return the same object.

*Property 5:*    Property 5 expresses the notion of monotonicity. Thus, when two program chunks are concatenated (notationally the ";" operator is used here), their overall complexity should be greater than the complexity of each of the parts.

$$(\forall P)\,(\forall Q)\,(|P| \leq |P;Q| \text{ and } |Q| \leq |P;Q|)$$

For size, this is reasonable. However, it is easily seen that the psychological complexity of the whole (e.g., a loop or an O/C) may well, on occasion, be less than that of only a portion.

*Property 6:*    The next property surmises that if a program chunk R were to be concatenated with each of two chunks P and Q where $|P| = |Q|$, it is not necessarily the case that the resulting complexity would be identical. Thus

6a:    $(\exists P)(\exists Q)(\exists R)(|P| = |Q| \;\&\; |P;R| \neq |Q;R|)$

6b:    $(\exists P)(\exists Q)(\exists R)(|P| = |Q| \;\&\; |R;P| \neq |R;Q|)$

The next consideration is whether two program bodies containing the same statements have different complexities dependent upon the ordering of the statements. For example, Piwowarski (1982) argued that the depth of nesting of loops plays a critical role in software complexity of procedural code.

*Property 7:*    There are program bodies P and Q such that Q is formed by permutating the order of the statements of P but that $|P| \neq |Q|$.

*Property 8:*    Weyuker (1988) describes Property 8 in terms of psychological complexity and asks the question whether renaming should have any impact on complexity. She proposes, simply, that

If P is a renaming of Q, then $|P| = |Q|$.

However, in discussing renaming it appears that the relabeling of individual variables (object names) is meant. There are an abundance of C/C++ programs in which obfuscating names make the program virtually indecipherable (the typical example is that of a calendar program), whereas use of informative names changes the complexity of understanding (but not size in LOC, of course) dramatically.

*Property 9:*    The final axiomatic property suggests that the complexity of a program formed by concatenating two program bodies, at least in some case, can be greater than the sum of their individual component complexities such that

$$(\exists P)\,(\exists Q)\,(|P| + |Q| < |P;Q|)$$

Weyuker (1988) evaluates four traditional structured metrics using these nine axioms and finds several axioms not to be satisfied. Table 4.5 summarizes her results.

**TABLE 4.5**   **Evaluation of four traditional metrics against Weyuker's nine axioms**

| Property Number | Statement Count | Cyclomatic Number | Effort Measure | Data Flow Complexity |
|:---:|:---:|:---:|:---:|:---:|
| 1 | Y | Y | Y | Y |
| 2 | Y | N | Y | N |
| 3 | Y | Y | Y | Y |
| 4 | Y | Y | Y | Y |
| 5 | Y | Y | N | N |
| 6 | N | N | Y | Y |
| 7 | N | N | N | Y |
| 8 | Y | Y | Y | Y |
| 9 | N | N | Y | Y |

Note: Cyclomatic number is McCabe (1976), effort measure is Halstead (1977), and data flow complexity is Oviedo (1980).

*Source:* Weyuker, E. J., 1988, Evaluating software complexity measures, *IEEE Trans. Software Eng.,* 14(9), 1357–1365. © l988 IEEE.

### 4.3.2 Criticisms

Fenton (1991) notes that the underlying problem with Weyuker's (1988) nine axioms is that "complexity" is ill defined and, as we have already noted, can be interpreted to mean correctness, comprehensibility, ease of implementation, size, maintainability, and so on. Fenton's main concerns lie with Properties 5 and 6 and their mutual incompatibility. Property 5 is appropriate for complexity measures relating to size but not to those relating to comprehension (in agreement with our observations earlier). Conversely, Property 6 is violated by measures relating to size but appropriate for comprehensibility measures.

Zuse (1990) is concerned both with this mutual inconsistency and also with their related measurement scales. He notes first that these axioms are not in accord with measurement theory since they require a ratio scale in parts and reject the ratio scale in other places. For example, he notes that Property 9 is meaningful on a ratio scale but not on an interval scale. On the other hand, Properties 6 and 7 deny the ratio scale. He then discusses in turn (p. 93 et seq.) each of the properties and makes the following observations:

#### 4.3.2.1 Property 1.
This cannot apply to all software measures. The measure of KNOTS (Woodward *et al.,* 1979) measures the unstructuredness of flowgraphs and, as such, is valuable. On the other hand, for a structured program the value of KNOTS is always zero, thus violating Property 1 *for structured programs.* Weyuker's (1988) total dismissal of KNOTS as a valid measure is thus not valid for one particular subset of programs, namely, unstructured programs.

#### 4.3.2.2 Property 2.
Zuse notes that Weyuker's evaluation of McCabe's metric as not satisfying this property results from its very different properties with respect to the ordinal scale. The entry of N in Table 4.5 is therefore not surprising, and it is not appropriate to take this as a condemnation of cyclomatic complexity as a valid measure.

**4.3.2.3 Property 3.**    There is no critical discussion.

**4.3.2.4 Property 4.**    Zuse (1990, p. 93) notes that this is appropriate when measuring understandability and maintainability. We would also note that in an object-oriented program, where implementation details are at many stages of design totally irrelevant, we foresee this property being *inapplicable* to high-level designs and valid only for OO maintenance metrics.

**4.3.2.5 Property 5.**    Zuse disputes the use of the word monotonicity here, especially with respect to the axioms of extensive structures in measurement theory. He suggests that this property should be rephrased along the lines "complexity should increase when adding something." However, we would go further and dispute this in the context of psychological complexity as applied to understandability for maintenance. It has been argued (e.g., Melton *et al.,* 1990) that half a loop in a structured program is less meaningful (more complex) than the whole loop, and we foresee that this would translate to the statement that "a complete class is more understandable than an incomplete class" in object-oriented systems—once again suggesting, from a comprehension point of view, that Property 5 is likely to be inapplicable in toto to object-oriented systems.

**4.3.2.6 Property 6.**    Zuse notes that Weyuker's nonrequirement of monotonicity blocks the use of such a measure from becoming a ratio scale (as he requires) by way of the extensive structure. He does note that for some measures and goals, property 6 may be reasonable, but that it is not globally useful.

**4.3.2.7 Property 7.**    Zuse is concerned that since Weyuker does not require the axiom of commutativity, a prerequisite for the extensive structure, then again the ratio scale is unattainable.

**4.3.2.8 Property 8.**    No substantive comment.

**4.3.2.9 Property 9.**    Zuse quotes this in its stronger version:

$$(\forall P)\,(\forall Q)\,(\,|P| + |Q| \le |P;Q|\,)$$

TABLE 4.6    Evaluation of the appropriateness of the Weyuker axioms

| Property | Appropriate Measures | Inappropriate Measures |
|---|---|---|
| 1 | Structured programs | Measures of unstructuredness |
| 2 | All programs | — |
| 3 | Size related | Control flow complexity |
| 4 | Comprehension based O/C specification (interface-focussed) | — |
| 5 | Size related | Comprehension based |
| 6 | Comprehension based | Size related; ratio scale |
| 7 | Psychological complexity | Extensive structures; ratio scale |
| 8 | Size | Comprehension related |
| 9 | Ratio scale | Ordinal scale |

and proves that this property is not meaningful (see Section 4.2) for an interval scale but is meaningful for a ratio scale.

We can perhaps best summarize these criticisms in Table 4.6 by indicating to what sort of "complexity measures" each of the properties relates.

Ejiogu (1993, p. 71) suggests that any useful validated measure must possess the "power of comparison." By this, he means that the measure must support the following three principles:

1. Measurement of nothing (the empty set) should produce a value of zero.
2. Measurement of a component of a program must produce a value less than or equal to the value produced when measuring the whole program (contrast this with Weyuker's fifth axiom).
3. Measurement of a set of components of a program must produce a value less than or equal to the sum of the individual values produced when measuring the individual components (this is in direct contrast to Weyuker's ninth axiom).

Cherniavsky and Smith (1991) go further and postulate a complexity metric *solely on the basis* that it satisfies all nine axioms. That they conclude that their measure is not meaningful (despite satisfying these "axioms") is perhaps not surprising in the light of the self-contradictions noted by Fenton and Zuse. Fenton (1992) says that this newly derived "metric" is clearly not a measure. Thus, he claims, showing that it does or does not satisfy a set of axioms is of no interest; neither is the conclusion of Cherniavsky and Smith (1991) that axiomatic approaches cannot work justified since no claim was made by Weyuker of the *sufficiency* of her axioms. Fenton (1992) further notes a confusion in both Weyuker (1988) and Cherniavsky and Smith (1991) as a result of wrongly equating a numerical mapping (a metric) and a true measure, validly based on measurement theory.

A similar approach is taken by McColl and McKim (1992) who also devise a version of NPATH (Nejmeh, 1988), which they call MPath, specifically tailored to satisfy the Weyuker axioms. They then demonstrate that this new MPath measure really doesn't measure anything of any interest in software.

### 4.3.3 Utilization in OO Metrics

Chidamber and Kemerer (1991) proposed a suite of six object-oriented metrics (described in detail later in Section 6.3). Here we are concerned only with their evaluation of Weyuker's (1988) axioms as examined for their relevance to object-oriented metrics.

Property 1 is accepted, Property 2 implicitly so. Property 3 implies that two object/classes (O/Cs) can have the same complexity. Property 4 is implementation focused and therefore valid only when considering the internal code details of an O/C. Property 5, applied to object-oriented systems, suggests that the complexity of the combination of two objects can never be less than either of the component objects. Properties 6 and 9 similarly translate smoothly across. The comparison itself is deferred until Chapter 6 by which time the details of this suite of metrics will have been explained.

There have been other axiomatic approaches proposed. Prather (1984) considers only structured programs and proposes three axioms for a "proper measure (of program complexity)," $m$, such that

$$m\left(\text{begin } S_i, S_2, \ldots S_n \text{ end}\right) \geq \sum m\left(S_i\right) \tag{a}$$

$$2\left(m\left(S_1\right) + m\left(S_2\right)\right) \geq m\left(\text{if } P \text{ then } S_i \text{ else } S_2\right) > m\left(S_i\right) + m\left(S_2\right) \tag{b}$$

$$2m(S) \geq m \text{ (while } P \text{ do } S) > m(S) \tag{c}$$

where $m$ is a function from the class of structured programs to the nonnegative real numbers.

Axiom (a) states that the complexity of the (concatenated) whole is greater than the sum of the parts (equivalent to Weyuker's Axiom 9). Axioms (b) and (c) try to set some limits on this. Prather then goes on to deduce a new measure, $\mu$, useful for testing strategies. It is consistent with the intuitive assumption that "If I understand each process separately, then I understand their sequence as a whole." This notion has been challenged (as described earlier) as failing to realize that the whole may be more understandable (less complex) than the sum of the parts. Second, it should be pointed out here that it also precludes the notion of synergistic or emergent properties—highly relevant to OO applications.

These ideas of Prather were further analyzed by Fenton and Whitty (1986). They extend the metric $\mu$ to the most general of flow graphs, thus eliminating some restrictions of the applicability of the earlier work.

## 4.4 DIMENSIONAL ANALYSIS[2]

Another measurement concern is that when arithmetical manipulations are made with different measures, it is crucial that dimensional analysis arguments be applied (see also Melton *et al.*, 1990). A dimension is a generalization of a unit of measure. The fundamental dimensions identified for physical objects include length, mass, time, and temperature. Many other dimensions, such as velocity or acceleration, can be defined in terms of the fundamental dimensions. By focusing on dimensions, it is possible to convert units in one measurement system to units in another, for example, convert from mass system units in kilograms to mass system units in pounds, or vice versa. Although there are currently no generally accepted set of fundamental dimensions for software measurement, there are generally accepted attributes of software that can be defined over different units of measure. As such, dimensional analysis principles can be applied to the attributes (Langhaar, 1951; Ipsen, 1960).

Dimensional analysis is based on the principle that the dimensions of both the right-hand side and the left-hand side of an equation must match. For example, if the productivity of a programmer was defined as the number of source lines of code (SLOC) created in a month, we would expect that the unit of measure of productivity

[2]This discussion was contributed by D. P. Tegarden and B. Henderson-Sellers.

to be SLOC per person-month. However, many of the software measures in the literature, in fact, violate this simple premise. Second, the addition of measures defined on different scales is nonsensical, for example, the addition of a measure defined over an ordinal scale to one defined on a ratio scale—yet again, all too frequently we have seen this in the software measurement literature. Third, even when each datum is on the same scale type (e.g., ratio) and the operation is valid on that scale, it is important to check that we are (say) adding apples and apples and not apples and oranges. For example, if we add 100 SLOC to 13 decision points to get a value of 113, are these 113 SLOC, 113 decision points, or 113 of some other unit? Of course, the answer is that the arithmetic sum of SLOC and decision points is meaningless. Yet, again, many published software measurement papers can be criticized strongly on these grounds alone (see Melton *et al.*, 1990, and Ejiogu, 1987, 1991, 1993, for additional information). There are similar concerns when one considers "complex" measures: vectors of a number of measures. If these are dimensionally inconsistent, then vector arithmetic is inapplicable.

Dimensional analysis also raises the possibility of dimensionless numbers. For our purposes, all dimensionless numbers are dependent on other dimensions, and their computation results in the dimensions canceling themselves out. For example, the Mach number—the ratio of the speed of an object to the speed of sound—is a dimensionless number based on the dimensions of length and time (Langhaar, 1951; Ipsen, 1960). As previously stated, there are currently no generally accepted set of fundamental dimensions for software measurement. However, given the set of attributes of software entities identified, we should not ignore the possibility that some of these could be the equivalent of a dimensionless number.

There are similar concerns when one considers "complex" metrics: vectors of a number of metrics, for example, the (cyclomatic number, operator count) pair of Hansen (1978). If the individual metrics are not orthogonal, then once again vector arithmetic is inapplicable. Care is demanded!

## 4.5  CHAPTER SUMMARY

Measurement theory is being increasingly recognized as having a major contribution to make to the maturity of software engineering metrics. Axiomatic approaches are also useful, but they can be criticized in their current form. The final section introduced dimensional analysis as a third formal approach to software metrics. Each of these three aspects should be considered in the formalization and evaluation of any OO metric.

## 4.6  BIBLIOGRAPHIC DETAILS

The two main sources for measurement theory are (1) Zuse's writings (e.g., Zuse, 1990) and (2) the Grubstake group (e.g., Baker *et al.*, 1990; Melton *et al.*, 1990; Fenton, 1991, 1994). For axiomatic theory, the main reference is Weyuker (1988), although there are several criticisms of this work (again Zuse, 1990, and Fenton, 1991, 1994).

# 5

# TRADITIONAL PRODUCT METRICS FOR STRUCTURAL COMPLEXITY

In Chapter 3 we saw that the term "complexity" was often misused and that, additionally, it has been interpreted differently by different authors. Figure 3.12 (in Chapter 3), which is duplicated here as Figure 5.1 to form the basis of the discussion in this chapter, discriminates between the generic term complexity and its various (qualified) derivatives. The term "complexity" is generally used as an external characteristic (e.g., Davis and LeBlanc, 1988) and typically involves programmer characteristics via its major instantiation as "psychological complexity," which is the main focus of much of software complexity research, either implicitly or explicitly. Psychological complexity, the major concern, has components of problem complexity (also called functional complexity by some authors), programmer characteristics, and structural complexity (also known as product complexity or document complexity). Problem complexity has not been studied in any detail (see discussion in Section 3.2), the difficult topic of programmer characteristics is deferred until Chapter 7, and in this chapter we alter our focus to another component of complexity: structural complexity.

We stress that complexity, including structural complexity, is a concept that can be regarded as an external characteristic. This is thus part of the empirical relation system (Chapter 4) for which we then require a numerical relation system to form the substantial basis for a "metric" or measure. In other words, this chapter discusses the measures that may be useful for different aspects of (the concept of) structural complexity. The terms complexity (a concept) and complexity metric (the

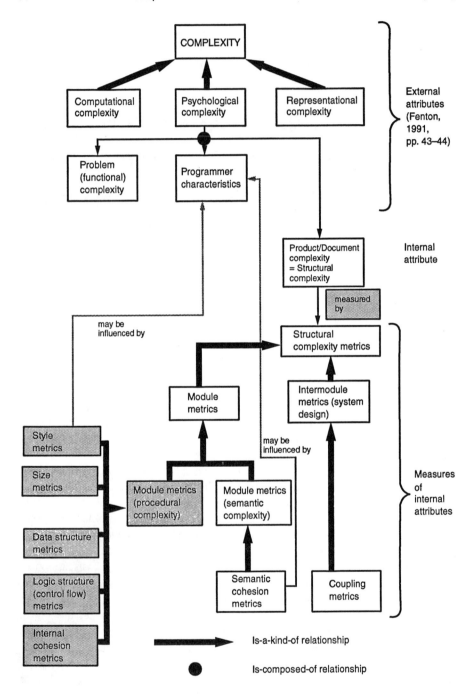

**Figure 5.1**  Classification of complexity metrics emphasizing the external attributes and the measures of internal attributes.

measure) are not interchangeable, although we are sorry to say that this equivalencing is used in much of the software metrics literature.

In this chapter we discuss, at a low level, the various possible measures (the fourth dimension of the MDF discussed in Section 3.4), without regard to whether they are prognostic of any external characteristics (the estimation process was discussed in more detail in Chapter 3). Card and Glass (1990) argue that the overall system complexity is a combination of intramodule complexity and intermodule complexity. They suggest that the system complexity, $C_S$, is given by

$$C_S = C_I + C_M \tag{5.1}$$

where $C_I$ is the intermodule complexity, and $C_M$ the intramodule complexity. Traditionally, intermodule complexity is equated to coupling in the form of subroutine CALLs or message passing and intramodule complexity to data complexity, which represents the number of I/O variables entering or leaving a module. Card and Glass (1990) suggest that the complexity components represented in equation (5.1) approximate Stevens *et al.*'s (1974) original concepts of "module complexity and cohesion."

Particularly for object-oriented systems, as can be seen in Figure 5.1, there is a third element, included as part of $C_M$ by Card and Glass (1990)—semantic cohesion—which is another form of module complexity. If we specifically exclude cohesion from the measure of intramodule complexity, $C_M$, then we can modify equation (5.1) explicitly to take into account semantic cohesion, $C_h$. Noting that increasing cohesion leads to a lower system complexity, we propose that

$$C_S = C_I + C_M + \left(C_{hmax} - C_h\right) \tag{5.2}$$

although this depends strongly on the scale used for $C_h$. ($C_{hmax}$ is the maximum cohesion possible for the module.) Thus we discriminate between (1) the objective (countable) measures such as number of I/O variables and number of control flow connections and (2) the semantic measures needed to assess the cohesiveness of a module via the interface it presents to the rest of the system.

Card and Glass's (1990) calculation of the metric for intramodule complexity (their data complexity) suggests that a module with excessive I/O is one with low cohesion. While this is grossly acceptable, it does not translate well into the object paradigm where cohesion is high, yet interconnections, via messages and services, can also be high. Indeed, it could be argued that in object-oriented systems, there is minimal data connectivity such that this notation of data complexity at the intermodule level is virtually redundant.

Finally, Card and Glass (1990) propose that a better comparative measure is the relative (per module) system complexity ($\overline{C_S} = C_S / n$, where $n$ is the number of modules in the system). This normalization allows us to compare systems of contrasting sizes. Since it gives a mean module value, it offers potential applicability to object-oriented systems as an average class metric.

In the following sections, we first describe intermodule metrics that measure the system design and focus particularly on coupling metrics useful in design (and implementation) (Section 5.1). In Sections 5.2 and 5.3 we focus on the two types of intramodule (or simply module) metrics. The literature, both traditional and OO, has focused heavily on the measurement of procedural complexity, since this can, at least in principle, be defined unambiguously and objectively and in accord with measurement theory (Chapter 4). Section 5.4 then moves from single metrics to (so-called) composite metrics, which attempt to "wrap up" a number of single metrics into a single compound measure (although this is arguably a false goal, according to Rubin, 1993).

## 5.1 INTERMODULE METRICS (FOR SYSTEM DESIGN COMPLEXITY)

An easy measure of intermodule coupling is the fan-in/fan-out metric (Henry and Kafura, 1981). Fan-in (strictly "informational fan-in") refers to the number of locations from which control is passed *into* the module (e.g., CALLs to the module being studied) plus the number of (global) data, and conversely, fan-out measures the number of other modules required plus the number of data structures that are updated by the module being studied. Since these couplings are determined in the analysis and design phases, such intermodule metrics are generally applicable across the life cycle.

While there are many measures incorporating both fan-in and fan-out (see the discussion that follows), Card and Glass (1990) present evidence that only fan-out[1] and its distribution between modules contribute significantly to systems design complexity. Thus, they propose

$$\overline{C_I} \equiv \frac{C_I}{n} = \frac{\sum^{n}(\text{fan-out})^2}{n} \qquad (5.3)$$

In contrast, Henry and Kafura (1981) propose a family of *information flow metrics:*

1. fan-in × fan-out
2. (fan-in × fan-out)$^2$
3. $S_s$ × (fan-in × fan-out)$^2$

where $S_s$ is the module size in lines of code. These metrics of Henry and Kafura's have been widely utilized and were thoroughly tested by their developers with data from the UNIX$^{TM}$ operating system.

Page-Jones (1992) recommends "eliminate any unnecessary connascence[2] and then minimize connascence across encapsulation boundaries by maximizing connascence within encapsulation boundaries." This is good advice for minimizing module complexity since (1) it acknowledges that some complexity is necessary; (2) it focuses on self-contained, semantically cohesive modules; and (3) it reflects the need for low fan-out (a point also noted by Card and Glass, 1990, equation (5.3)).

---

[1]Troy and Zweben (1981) also found fan-out and not fan-in to be positively correlated with number of faults.

[2]The connascence measure is a generalization of coupling and cohesion measures.

## 5.2 MODULE METRICS (FOR SEMANTIC COMPLEXITY)

Intermodule metrics (Section 5.1) were originally characterized by Stevens *et al.* (1974) and Yourdon and Constantine (1979) as "cohesion" and "coupling," which Card and Glass (1990, p. 31) use to provide the concept of "modularity." Cohesion or module "strength" refers to the notion of a module level "togetherness" viewed at the system abstraction level. Thus, although in one sense it can be regarded as a system design concept, we can more properly regard cohesion as a semantic concern expressed *of* a module evaluated from an external (to the module) point of view. Semantic cohesion is thus a module-focused measure, which is distinct from the *internal* module measures discussed in Section 5.3 (which includes the concept of internal or syntactic cohesion, akin to the more traditional discussions of cohesion, for example, Yourdon and Constantine, 1979, Chapter 7).

## 5.3 MODULE METRICS (FOR PROCEDURAL COMPLEXITY)

Of the five types of module metrics shown in Figure 5.1, size and logic structure account for the majority of the literature on metrics: perhaps because of their perceived relationship to cost estimation and to the difficulties of maintenance, respectively and perhaps to their ease of collection. However, it should be reiterated that these metrics can, in general, be obtained only from code and are inappropriate for the analysis and design (i.e., the specification phase).

Size metrics, notably, lines of code (LOC) or source lines of code (SLOC), Halstead's software science, and function points (FPs), and their variants will be discussed in Section 5.3.1 and their applicability to object-oriented systems evaluated in Section 6.3.1. Logic structure metrics, especially McCabe's (1976) cyclomatic complexity, are discussed in Section 5.3.2. It should be noted that the use of the term "complexity metrics" in the literature tends to infer McCabe's metric and its variants (an overloading of the phrase "complexity metric"). Data structure metrics, internal cohesion, and style metrics are discussed together in Section 5.3.3.

### 5.3.1 Size Metrics

**5.3.1.1 Lines of Code.**  The use of source lines of code as a measure of software size is one of the oldest methods of measuring software. It was first used to measure size of programs written in fixed-format assembly languages. The use of SLOC as a metric began to be problematical when free-format assembly languages were introduced (Jones, 1986) since more than one logical statement could be written per line. The problems became greater with the advent of high-level languages that describe key abstractions in the problem domain (Booch, 1991) removing some accidental complexity (Brooks, 1975). Furthermore, lines of code can be interpreted differently for different programming languages. Jones (1986) lists 11 different counting methods, 6 at the program level and 5 at the project level. With the introduction of fourth-generation languages, still more difficulties were experienced in counting source lines (Verner and Tate, 1988; Verner, 1991).

Currently the most accepted definition of SLOC is given by Conte *et al.* (1986):

> A line of code is any line of program text that is not a comment or blank line, regardless of the number of statements or fragments of statements on the line. This specifically includes all lines containing program headers, declarations, and executable and non-executable statements.

Notwithstanding their many shortcomings, SLOC counts are still one of the major tools widely used today (Côté *et al.*, 1988; Bourque and Côté, 1991). The wide acceptance of SLOC as a size/complexity metric (Weyuker, 1988) is due to its simplicity, ease of application, inertia of tradition, absence of alternative size measures (Levitin, 1986), and its intuitive appeal (Dunsmore, 1984). In addition to these properties, many empirical results also have shown the usefulness of SLOC. For example, Basili (1980) found that effort correlated better with SLOC than with Halstead's metrics (Halstead, 1977) and was at least as good as McCabe's cyclomatic complexity metric (McCabe, 1976). Similar results were also reported by Evangelist (1983) and Weyuker (1988). These empirical findings indicate that for some of the attributes of software systems, SLOC is better or at least as good as any other metric. As a result, SLOC has been used for a number of different software development activities, such as estimating, planning, tracking the progress of projects, normalizing measures of productivity and defect densities, and deriving measures and effectiveness of reuse strategies (Yu *et al.*, 1991). As a consequence, SLOC counts have also been used as a baseline for the evaluation of almost all empirical studies of metrics, including function points (Albrecht and Gaffney, 1983).

One of the features lacking in SLOC counts, reducing its usefulness as an effective size measure for understanding a piece of code (for maintenance, debugging, testing, etc.), is that it does not account for complexity of a line of code. This ambiguity of complexity between different lines of code is addressed in the new metric of S/C (size/complexity) (Figure 5.2) described by Pant *et al.* (1995a). While providing a measure that satisfies Weyuker's (1988) seventh axiom (a property *not* held by Halstead's effort measure, McCabe's cyclomatic complexity, or statement counting), this metric remains to be fully tested empirically (having been tested so far only by Pant *et al.*, 1995a, 1995b). S/C is based on the complexity and nesting level of control statements, a software size, and complexity metric—a simple, yet powerful, extension of the normal lines of code count. The measure has the potential for use in assessing the effort related to understanding software for software maintenance, debugging, and generalization in both traditional and object-oriented environments.

The S/C measure is based on the notion that, in a high-order programming language, decision making and iterative statements/keywords are normally more complex than assignment statements (e.g., Ledgard and Marcotty, 1975; Gilb, 1977; Iyengar *et al.*, 1982). The metric counts one for simple statements, one for each binder and one for each simple predicate. It also takes into account the number of mental (discriminating) paths within the control flow structure and allows for nested structures.

# S/C measure

## Counts of identified logical units, e.g.,

| | |
|---|---|
| Initialization | int i = 0 |
| Comparison | i < 10 |
| Increment | i++ |
| Binder | for ( ; ; ) { ... } |

## S/C combines logical decisions (McCabe, 1976) with " size"

## S/C differentiates "complexity" in programs of same LOC (Pant et al., 1995a)

**Figure 5.2**    The size/complexity measure of Pant *et al.* (1995a).

Pant *et al.* (1995a) conclude from their pilot study that the S/C metric appears to be highly correlated with the effort (time) for finding artificially introduced bugs in C programs (than with the source lines of code measure). A large-scale experiment is planned as a full validation of the newly proposed S/C metric.

Inclusion of reused code (e.g., code from previous projects, libraries, macros, other systems, etc.) in the SLOC measure also creates problems; for example, Jones (1986) counted all reused code modules each time they occurred in the system.

**5.3.1.2 Tokens.**    Tokens are the basic lexical units out of which a program is synthesized. A lexical analyzer, the first phase of any compilation process, converts high-level statements to tokens for further processing. Tokens are similar to words in natural languages, but the number of bytes that it takes to represent a token in one specific hardware implementation is always the same.

To solve some of the problems of SLOC measure, Halstead (1977) proposed a metric based on operator and operand as the fundamental counts. It is based on the following four counts:

$$\eta_1 = \text{the number of unique operators}$$
$$\eta_2 = \text{the number of unique operands}$$
$$N_1 = \text{the total number of operators}$$
$$N_2 = \text{the total number of operators}$$

In an algorithm or program, any symbol or keyword used to represent data is normally classified as an operand, and a keyword that is used to specify an action is considered as an operator. Thus, variable names and labels are operands, whereas most punctuation marks, arithmetic symbols (such as $+$, $-$, $*$, and $/$), keywords (such as **if, while, do,** etc.), special symbols (such as $:=$, braces, parenthesis, $==$, $!=$), function names, and so on, are counted as operators. According to Halstead, operators and operands and their sum are the key concepts of software and can be used to measure (or estimate) size of programs or algorithms. Halstead applied these four parameters to get a synthetic metric for estimating software attributes such as program length, volume, level, purity, programming effort, language level, errors, modularity, and so on, many of which, it should be noted, are ill defined.

The vocabulary of a program, $\eta$, is defined as the sum of operators and operands ($\eta = \eta_1 + \eta_2$), and the length of a program, $N$, is equal to the sum of total number of operators and operands ($N_1 + N_2$). If each line of a machine language program consists of one operator and one operand, SLOC can be defined to be equal to $N/2$ (Shen *et al.,* 1983).

Software science also defines program size in terms of volume (in bits) as $V = N \times \log_2 \eta$ (which, it should be noted, is dimensionally incorrect). Halstead mentioned that a reasonable size estimate can be made well before the program is written. The approximate size of a program, $N = \eta_1 \times \log_2 \eta_1 + \eta_2 \times \log_2 \eta_2$, is calculable from a knowledge of distinct operators and operands that are likely to be in the program. This may be converted to SLOC via the relationship $S = N/C$, where $C$ is a language-dependent constant. Conte *et al.* (1986) have proposed the value of $C$ to be equal to 2 for machine language (each line having one operator and one operand) and 7 for FORTRAN.

There have been many criticisms of software science (e.g., Lister, 1982; Shen *et al.,* 1983; Levitin, 1986). For example, there are many variations in counting and classifying operators and operands, and there is no general agreement among researchers on what is the most meaningful way to classify and count operators and operands (Shen *et al.,* 1983). Furthermore, the counting scheme is language dependent, and the software science counts are very sensitive (Elshoff, 1978). There is ambiguity in the counting of statement labels (Conte *et al.,* 1986). Originally designed with languages such as FORTRAN in mind, software science metrics are difficult to apply to more modern programming languages (Lister, 1982) that support advanced powerful concepts like data abstraction, classes, hierarchy, and so on; although some attempts have been made (e.g. Tegarden *et al.,* 1992)—see the discussion that follows. Similar problems are also experienced in counting pairs like opening and closing parentheses "( )," "begin-end," "if-then-else," and so on. Levitin (1986) suggests that counting rules for the above pairs as single operators or two operators will affect length and volume measure since they are based on the sums of operators and operands.

Most of the software science formulas were derived for algorithms (not programs) (Halstead, 1977), and it is difficult to say whether these formulas are still applicable to real-life programs. Algorithms are generally independent of programming languages. In other words, a programming language is a specific notation in which an algorithm can be expressed. Although most of the formulas are derived algebraically, several assumptions are also made without any formal justification (Shen *et al.,* 1983), and there are several errors in the derivation, especially in the use of logarithmic transformations (Card and Agresti, 1987; Shen *et al.,* 1983; Zweben, 1990) and in application of the results of cognitive complexity on human memory models and searching strategies (Coulter, 1983; Card and Glass, 1990).

Finally, there have been concerns voiced over the external validity of the experimental data used to "verify" the software science metrics (e.g., Lister, 1982; Hamer and Frewin, 1982; Shen *et al.,* 1983). Card and Glass (1990, p. 27) voice these concerns in their recommendation that *"practitioners can safely ignore software science* at present."

**5.3.1.3 Function Points.**    Function point counting (Albrecht, 1979; Albrecht and Gaffney, 1983) is a technology-independent method of estimating system size without the use of lines of code. Function points have been found useful in estimating system size early in the development life cycle and are used for measuring productivity trends (Jones, 1986) from a description of users' specifications and requirements. They are probably the sole representative of size metrics *not* restricted to code. However, Keyes (1992), quoting Rubin, argues that they are unlikely to be useful to modern-day graphical user interface (GUI) developments since they cannot include concerns of color and motion.

Albrecht argued that function points could be easily understood and evaluated even by nontechnical users. The concept has been extended more recently by Symons (1988) as the Mark II FP counting approach—a metric that the British government uses as the standard software productivity metric (Dreger, 1989).

In FP application, system size is based on the total amount of information that is processed together with a complexity factor that influences the size of the final product. It is based on the following weighted items:

  Number of external inputs
  Number of external outputs
  Number of external inquiries
  Number of internal master files
  Number of external interfaces

The weights assigned to each item depend on the characteristics of the system being developed. For example, the weights to the number of inputs can vary from 4 to 7 depending on the complexity of the system being developed, which is divided into low, medium, and high. The initial count is summed to get unadjusted function points that are later modified using 14 factors, including the use of structured programming, the use of high-level languages, the use of online development, and the use of software library, performance, ease of use, and so on, to derive a value for "adjusted function points" (Albrecht and Gaffney, 1983; Jones, 1986; Verner, 1991).

Verner (1991) groups problems of FP analysis into the following three headings:

- Problems in measuring unadjusted function point size
- Problems with the system adjustments
- Other general problems

Stathis and Jeffery (1993) evaluated the efficacy of the three levels of adjustment factors and found that (1) on theoretical grounds, there is overlap between the factors, that is, they are not orthogonal, and (2) empirically, the unadjusted values may give better results than adjusted function points. Along the same lines, Kitchenham (1993) argued that FPs were "not well-formed metrics" and that other, better formed and less complex metrics are as good as FPs for early effort prediction. She also found that unweighted counts were reasonable predictors of effort.

**5.3.1.4 Feature Points.**    Jones (1988, 1991) introduces the metric of feature points, which complements the functionality of Albrecht's (1979) function points by characterizing internal complexity in terms of a weighted algorithm count. Such a system is most useful in software containing a high degree of internal algorithmic complexity and permits the metric to be more widely applied, for example, outside the commercial MIS environment.

### 5.3.2 Logic Structure Metrics

Zuse (1990) lists over a hundred "complexity measures." However, the best established measure of module complexity is probably the cyclomatic complexity introduced by McCabe (1976). Its basis is in graph theory (e.g., Berge, 1973; Bollobás, 1979), which says that for a *connected* graph, the graph cyclomatic number,[3] $v$, is given as

$$v = e - n + 1 \qquad (5.4)$$

and for a graph with $p$ components

$$v = e - n + p \qquad (5.5)$$

(e.g., Harary, 1969, p. 39), where $e$ is the number of edges and $n$ the number of nodes. A connected graph is a graph where *all* nodes are reachable from every other node.

---

[3]Also called the first Betti number, the nullity or the cycle rank.

A disconnected graph is one with $p$ components that are disjoint, but that could, with the addition of $(p-1)$ additional edges, be turned into a connected graph (Figure 5.3). Since in a connected graph, a path from $a$ to $b$ is equivalently a path from $b$ to $a$, there is no notion of "strongly connected" until the graph becomes directed, as in software representations. This means that, for a single program or program module, the connected, directed acyclic graph (DAG) does not satisfy the definition of connectedness until an edge is added from the stop node to the start node. The resultant graph is thus known as a strongly connected graph and has one more edge than its corresponding undirected graph (or the regular DAG equivalent). Thus, the cyclomatic complexity, or cycle rank, is given for a single, strongly connected DAG by

$$V(G) = e - n + 2 \tag{5.6}$$

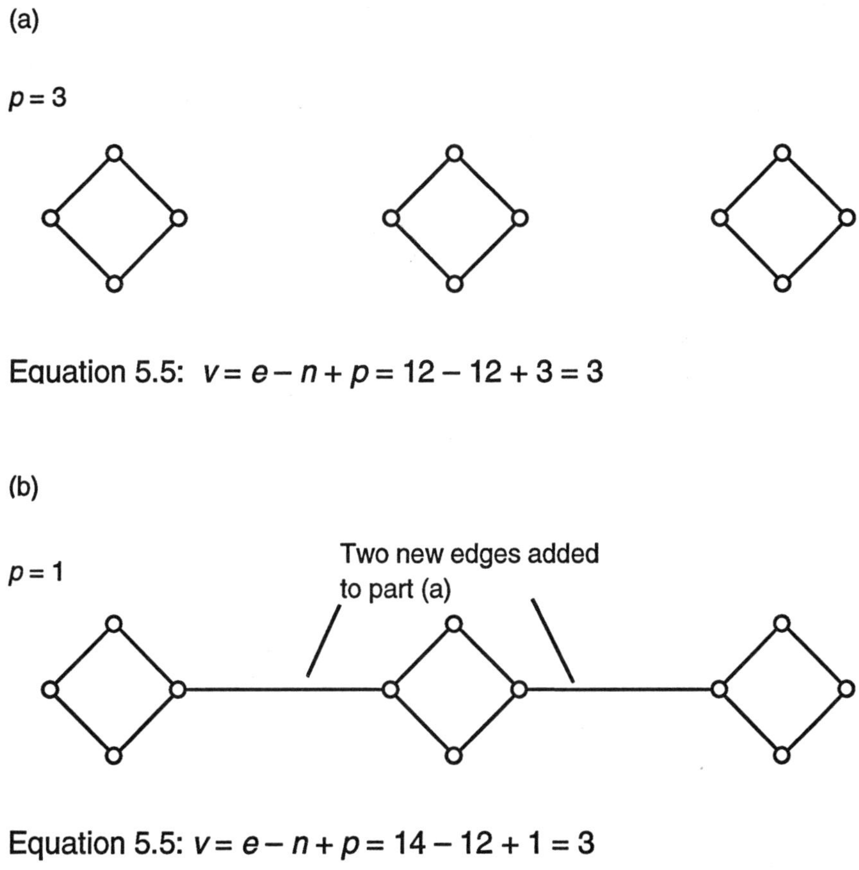

(a)

$p = 3$

Equation 5.5:  $v = e - n + p = 12 - 12 + 3 = 3$

(b)

$p = 1$

Two new edges added
to part (a)

Equation 5.5: $v = e - n + p = 14 - 12 + 1 = 3$

**Figure 5.3**  (a) Disconnected graph with three components; (b) connected graph constructed from three components by adding two edges (after Henderson-Sellers and Tegarden, 1994b).

—a form frequently quoted in the literature as representing the standard McCabe metric. McCabe's (1976) theorem 1 says that in a strongly connected graph $V(G)$ is equal to the maximum number of linearly independent circuits through the DAG and *not* the number of test paths, as it is frequently misquoted (e.g., Kearney *et al.*, 1986; Nejmeh, 1988). As McCabe (1976) himself notes, "There are often additional (to those identified by $V(G)$) paths to test." These paths can be derived from the basis set identifiable by the use of $V(G)$ or directly using, for example, the NPATH metric of Nejmeh (1988).

Equation (5.6) is useful for the cyclomatic complexity of a single-component DAG. However, with respect to the extension of $V(G)$ to more than one component, there appear to be two options. Assuming that we are trying to describe a measurement effectively for the connected graph of Figure 5.3(b) but expressed in terms of the three disjoint components of Figure 5.3(a), then the argument there is easily extended to give, inductively,

$$V_{LI}(G) = e - n + p + 1 \tag{5.7}$$

This is the form proposed by Henderson-Sellers (1992b) and relabeled here with a subscript *LI* (linearly independent) (Henderson-Sellers and Tegarden, 1994b) since we shall later show that this metric (equation (5.7)) is strongly related to the cycle rank of the graph.

Feghali and Watson (1994) point out that a different approach was taken by McCabe (1976) (although apparently rescinded in McCabe and Butler, 1989). He argued that *each* of the components needs to be converted into a strongly connected graph, thus giving

$$V(G) = e - n + 2p \tag{5.8}$$

Thus, each component is treated independently, and the value given by equation (5.8) is relevant to each component but not really to the integrated system. Indeed, Shepperd (1988) noted that this means that a program with several subroutines is "treated as unconnected components within the control graph," which has "the bizarre result of increasing overall complexity if a program is divided into more, presumably simpler, modules." Each additional subprogram isolated from the rest of the program increases the value of $V(G)$ by 1.

This concern led to Henderson-Sellers's (1992b) proposal of equation (5.7), which has the properties that

1. Modularization (prior to removal of repetitive code) has no effect on $V_{LI}(G)$.
2. The value of $V_{LI}(G)$ for the full program is equal to the total number of decisions, $D$, plus one, namely,

$$V_{LI}(G) = \sum_{i=1}^{p} d_i + 1 = D + 1 \tag{5.9}$$

3. The value of $V_{LI}(G)$ is unchanged when subroutines are merged back into the program either by nesting or sequence. This ties in with the argument that the

testing procedures (for the present limited to single calls to single-entry, single-exit components) are unchanged by modularization.

4. The value of $V_{LI}(G)$ provides a basis set for testing.

A simple example will help here to illustrate the differences between $V(G)$ and $V_{LI}(G)$. In Figure 5.4 there is a main routine and two subroutines, A1 and A2. The value of $V(G)$ is $19 - 18 + 2 * 3 = 7$, whereas the value of $V_{LI}(G)$ is $19 - 18 + 3 + 1 = 5$. In terms of testing paths, these graphs are equivalent to a single DAG, using the node-splitting technique[4] of Henderson-Sellers (1992b), as shown in Figure 5.5, for which both $V(G)$ and $V_{LI}(G)$ have the same value, given by equation (5.6), that is, $23 - 20 + 2 = 5$. In both figures, there are four decisions, while the basis set is more easily obtained from Figure 5.5. The (nonunique) basis set is

$$1\,6; 2\,4\,3\,7; 2\,5\,3\,6; 2\,5\,3\,8; 1\,7$$

All other paths (1 8; 2 4 3 6; 2 4 3 8; 2 5 3 7) are expressible as linear combinations of elements of the basis set. For example, $(1\,8) = (1\,6) + (2\,5\,3\,8) - (2\,5\,3\,6)$. Finally, both Figures 5.4 and 5.5 depict the infinite 2-D plane divided into five regions. These results are summarized in Table 5.1.

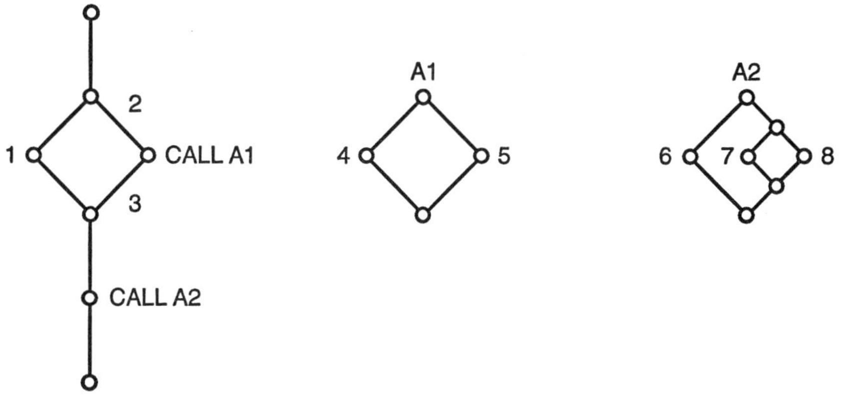

$$V(G) = e - n + 2p = 19 - 18 + 6$$
$$= 7$$
$$V_{LI}(G) = e - n + p + 1$$
$$= 19 - 18 + 4$$
$$= 5$$

**Figure 5.4**   Main routine and two subroutines (A1 and A2)—depicted as three disconnected components (after Henderson-Sellers and Tegarden, 1994b).

---

[4]A node that is actually a subroutine call is split into two: one to represent the outgoing call and one to represent the return of control.

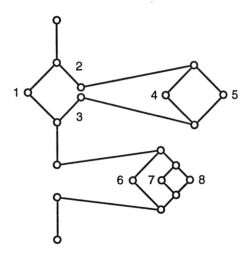

$$V(G) = V_{LI}(G)$$
$$= e - n + 2$$
$$= 23 - 20 + 2$$
$$= 5$$

**Figure 5.5**   Example of Figure 5.4 redrawn in terms of a single connected graph (after Henderson-Sellers and Tegarden, 1994b).

The relationship between the whole and the sum of the parts if also different. McCabe (1976) shows that

$$V(G) = \sum V(G_i) \tag{5.9}$$

whereas Henderson-Sellers (1992b) deduces that

$$V_{LI}(G) = \sum V_{LI}(G_i) + 1 - p \tag{5.11}$$

a form also quoted by Evangelist (1984) and discussed by Fenton and Kaposi (1987). The difference here is that Fenton and Kaposi (1987) as well as Henderson-Sellers (1992b) and Henderson-Sellers and Tegarden (1994a) are considering that summing components means merging them (by sequence or iteration), whereas the McCabe

**TABLE 5.1**   Values for $V(G)$ and $V_{LI}(G)$ for the graphs of Figures 5.4 and 5.5 (after Henderson-Sellers and Tegarden, 1994b)

|  | Main Routine | Subroutine A1 | Subroutine A2 | Whole Program | Total Decisions Plus 1 | Total in Basis Set |
|---|---|---|---|---|---|---|
| $V(G)$ | 2 | 2 | 3 | 7 |  |  |
|  |  |  |  |  | 5 | 5 |
| $V_{LI}(G)$ | 2 | 2 | 3 | 5 |  |  |

approach (Equation 5.9) sums *without* merging. Thus the focus is at the *module* level, where the most appropriate formula is equation (5.6), the former ($V_{LI}(G)$) retaining an interpretation with respect to testing paths at the program level.

The McCabe metric is in general and widespread use (Stark and Durst, 1994). Based on Ministry of Defence (MoD) data, cumulative graphs of $V(G)$ for 16 systems are plotted in Figure 5.6(a). Here the y axis gives the percentage of functions that had a $V(G)$ value less than or equal to the value on the x axis. Most systems fall within the "straightforward" or "standard" bands (Figure 5.6(b)), but systems A and B have a low percentage of modules with McCabe values less than 10. This suggests that these two particular systems should be carefully scrutinized. Thus, the metric is found to be helpful in assisting the managers in making decisions (Stark and Durst, 1994).

It should be noted that while the McCabe metric *does* describe what its author intended (control flow complexity in the context of testing), several authors have identified a "flaw" since it does not differentiate between nested and anded constructs (Figure 5.7). One important difference between the nested and the anded construct is that the execution history of the statements s1 may alter the evaluation of the second predicate, thus causing the statements s2 to be executed.

In Figure 5.7 both structures have $V(G) = 3$. Some authors argue that, intuitively, these structures are of different "complexity." That such a statement is made reflects the common (in the literature) unjustified extrapolation from a structural complexity metric to a measure of external characteristics (here complexity and, by inference, understandability). A more objective approach is taken by Davis and LeBlanc (1988) who quantify the differences between anded and nested structures using Shannon and Weaver's (1949) concept of (information) entropy, $H$, which is given as

$$H = - \sum_{i=1}^{n} P(A_i) \log P(A_i) \tag{5.12}$$

Here $P(A_i)$ is the unbiased estimate of the probability of occurrence of event $A_i$. "First-order" entropy is defined in terms of chunks (represented by nodes in the DAG) which have the same in-degree and the same out-degree. In this example, nodes are grouped into $\{a\}$, $\{b, c, e, f\}$, $\{d\}$, and $\{g\}$ (Figure 5.7(a)). Thus,

$$H = - \sum_{i=1}^{4} P(A_i) \log P(A_i)$$

$$= - \left[ \tfrac{1}{7} \log \tfrac{1}{7} + \tfrac{4}{7} \log \tfrac{4}{7} + \tfrac{1}{7} \log \tfrac{1}{7} + \tfrac{1}{7} \log \tfrac{1}{7} \right] \tag{5.13}$$

$$= 0.5011$$

(not 1.664 as stated in the original paper), whereas the value for Figure 5.7(b) is 0.641 (not 2.128 as stated in the original paper).

Thus, the entropy value differentiates between these DAGs. Davis and LeBlanc (1988) also note that there are many occasions when the first-order entropy still does not differentiate between DAGs but that the "second-order" entropy does. In this,

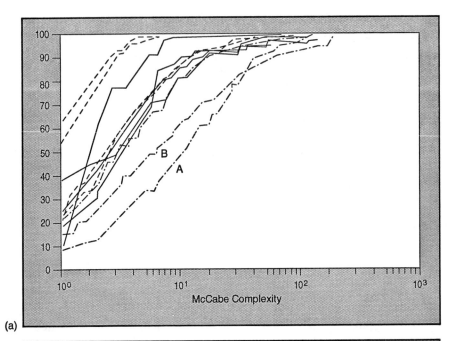

(a)

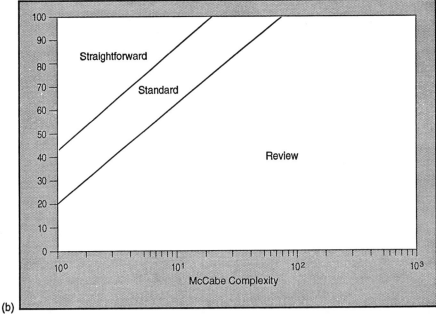

(b)

**Figure 5.6**   (a) Cumulative distribution of the McCabe complexity measure revealed systems A and B as risk areas (b) A McCabe complexity decision chart showing categories of complexity.
*Source:* Stark, G. and Durst, R. C., 1994. Using metrics in management decision making, *IEEE Computer,* 27(9), 42–48. © 1994 IEEE.

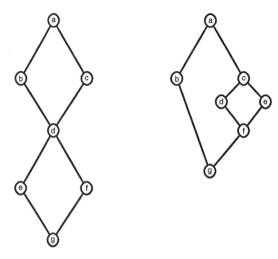

**Figure 5.7**  Two control structures, one nested, with the same cyclomatic complexity (after Davis and Leblanc, 1985). (© 1985 IEEE).

chunks are considered equivalent only if they have the same number and type of immediate neighbours. For this example, the second-order entropy values are (for Figure 5.7(a)) 2.236 and (for Figure 5.7(b)) 2.521.

### 5.3.3  Other Procedural Complexity Measures

Data structure metrics are discussed by Conte *et al.* (1986, Section 2.3). These include the number of variables, which of these are locally live, what the span of each variable is, and whether the variable is ever referenced. While the number of variables is easily extracted from compiler diagnostics, the notion of live variables and spans require a considerable amount of effort to obtain. Nevertheless, the scope of variables can be important in understanding and maintaining code. Similarly, while the existence of nonreferenced variables is not detrimental to the operation of the software, they can be misleading when trying to debug the code.

Similarly highly misleading are comments in the code that do not agree with the lines of code themselves (an all too common problem of documentation). Under the heading of style also comes the use of consistent indentation, cryptic, or exemplary naming conventions. Style metrics are seldom discussed (but see Ejiogu, 1991) and difficult to measure objectively. Lorenz (1993) suggests that, at a minimum, each method should have at least one comment line.

Internal cohesion can be best understood as syntactic cohesion evaluated by examining the code of each individual module. It is thus closely related to the way in which large programs are modularized. It is argued that the modularization can be accomplished for a variety of reasons. Crudely one could modularize a long procedural program on the guideline of "no good module should exceed one page of line printer output" (i.e., about 50 lines) and simply discretize the program into chunks arbitrarily about 50 lines each. Any cohesion here would be accidental cohesion.

More reasonably, the contents of a module should bear some relationship to each other. In a procedural language such as FORTRAN, COBOL, or C, it is most natural to arrange for the contents of each module to bear a functional cohesion to each other. In other words, decomposition into modules is undertaken on the basis of the code in a single module describing a single piece of functionality. Inevitably in such programs the data needed on which the functions operate will be stored elsewhere, that is, *outside* that module. Other types of cohesion exist; the one with which we will be most concerned here in object-oriented systems can perhaps be called data cohesion.

It should be noted that even here, in our subcategory of objective, document measures, the success of any module in attaining a high-quality cohesion (based on whatever cohesion rules are being used—data, ADT, function) relies on human assessment. This demonstrates that the idealogical description in Figure 5.1 is unlikely to be attained in practice. Cohesion is measured in a structured program by an ordinal scale as shown in Figure 5.8, although the number of fan-ins can also be used (Conte *et al.*, 1986, p. 109; Card and Glass, 1990, p. 41) where a higher number of fan-ins indicates a lower cohesion.

Finally, a system measure of cohesion can be given (e.g., Fenton, 1991, p. 200) as

$$\text{cohesion ratio} = \frac{\text{number of modules having (functional) cohesion}}{\text{total number of modules}} \quad (5.14)$$

(where we might replace "functional" by "abstract" for object-oriented systems). This, however, remains to be quantified for object-oriented systems in terms of how the success of achieving "abstract cohesion" is best measured.

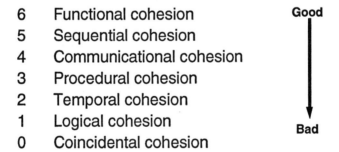

In OO systems, all services are logically (i.e., semantically) related. Hence OO rankings are different.

**Figure 5.8**   Ordinal scale for cohesion in a structured PL.
*Source:* Fenton, N. E., 1991, *Software Metrics: A Rigorous Approach,* Chapman and Hall, London.

### 5.3.4 Some Applications of Weyuker's Axioms and Measurement Theory

In the seventh property, Weyuker (1988) suggests that a good complexity measure should be responsive to the arrangement of the statements:

Property 7: There are program bodies P and Q such that Q is formed by permuting the order of the statements of P, and $|P| \neq |Q|$.

Pant *et al.*'s (1995a) S/C measure is found to satisfy this seventh axiom, whereas those of Chidamber and Kemerer (1991) do not (Chapter 6). Consider two program elements, P and Q, where

```
P: WHILE X ≥ 0 DO X ← X - Y
      ENDWHILE
      WHILE Y ≥ 10 DO X ← X + 1
            Y ← Y + 1
      ENDWHILE

Q: WHILE X ≥ 0 DO X ← X - Y
      WHILE Y ≥ 10 DO X ← X + 1
            Y ← Y + 1
      ENDWHILE
      ENDWHILE
```

In P, the two WHILE loops are sequential, whereas in Q, the WHILE loops are nested. Total lines of code in both the arrangements is equal to 5.

The two examples just given, as modified to C code, were evaluated against the S/C measure. As already discussed, in the S/C measure the following statement

```
while (x ≥ 0) {
}
```

is equal to 2 units of S/C. To give a more readable format, the program segments have been converted and written to occupy 7 lines of code in the two versions of Figure 5.9. By decomposing P and Q into primitive constructs, the S/C counts of P is 7, while that of Q is 9. However, if we rearrange the predicates as illustrated in Figure 5.10, the total number of S/C counts is 8. Thus, the S/C metric is responsive to the arrangement of statements in this case, that is, it satisfies Weyuker's (1988) property 7.

As noted earlier, McCabe's (1976) cyclomatic complexity, $V(G)$, represents a weak order but does not have full additivity with respect to a binary operation of BSEQ (concatenation of flow graphs). However, since an extensive structure can be defined, we know there is a strictly monotonic increasing function of $V(G)$. This is

$$V'(G) = e - n + 1 \equiv V(G) - 1 \qquad (5.15)$$

Since this metric is additive under the binary operation BSEQ, $V'(G)$ can be used as a ratio scale. In other words, measurement theory provides us with a means of

```
P:    while (x ≥ 0) {
            x = x - y;
      }
      while (y ≥ 10) {
            x = x + 1;
            y = y - 1;
      }

Q:    while (x ≥ 0) {
            x = x - y;
            while (y ≥ 10) {
                  x = x + 1;
                  y = y - 1;
            }
      }
```

**Figure 5.9**   Two program segments for use in the S/C calculation (see text for details).

determining a modified functional form for cyclomatic complexity which has a more sound measurement theory base. In addition, Zuse (1994) shows how $V(G)$ can be used on an absolute scale. Here a second concatenation operator, BALT, is defined as providing concatenation with an IF-THEN-ELSE structure. In this case,

$$V'(G) = V\left(G_1\right) + V\left(G_2\right) + 1 \tag{5.16}$$

In other words, it is *not* invariant to the admissible transformation of the ratio scale ($a > 0$) unless $a = 1$, which gives the absolute scale.

Zuse (1994) shows that the structure of the COCOMO cost-estimation model (Boehm, 1981)

$$\text{effort}(P) = a\text{LOC}^b \tag{5.17}$$

is compatible with the use of LOC on a ratio scale. In other words, he suggests it provides a viable path from the size measure, LOC, to an effort estimation (i.e., a prognostic model).

```
while ((x ≥ 0) && (y ≥ 10)) {
      x = x - y;
      x = x + 1;
      y = y - 1;
}
```

**Figure 5.10**   Rearrangement of code segments of Figure 5.9 (see text for details).

Other, detailed examples of non-OO structural complexity measures are given in Zuse (1990).

## 5.4 COMPOSITE METRICS

There is a general requirement to compound these various module and intermodule metrics into the structural or document complexity. Typically, the disparate types of measures used require the development of a composite metric. Some authors try to create a single composite metric by arithmetic combination, for example, Kokol *et al.* (1988), Ramamurthy and Melton (1988), and Grover and Gill (1995), often without regard for dimensional analysis and/or measurement theory (scale) considerations. Lai and Yang (1995) normalize a wide variety of measures on to a discrete, ordinal scale, which they then treat as a ratio scale by calculating a linear combination of weighted normalized metrics. Other authors reason that no single number can encapsulate all the facets of full system complexity[5] and propose the use of vector notation (e.g., Conte *et al.*, 1986, p. 78), again frequently without due regard for orthogonality of the components. Conte *et al.* (1986) note that with a pair of metrics $(a, b)$, there is the problem of establishing a partial ordering such that for two programs, $P_i$ with complexity pair $(a_i, b_i)$ $(i = 1, 2)$, we can say that $P_1$ is more complex than $P_2$ if $a_1 \geq a_2$ and $b_1 \geq b_2$ so long as one of the pairs has a nonequality. The problem arises when $a_1 > a_2$ yet $b_2 > b_1$. This would be less of a problem if $a$ and $b$ were dimensionally consistent such that a scalar could be derived as the vector magnitude.

Pairs of metrics used in this way include two versions of cyclomatic complexity (Myers, 1977): cyclomatic number and operation count (Hansen, 1978), Software Science $E$ and $V(G)$ (Baker and Zweben, 1980), and control flow complexity and data flow complexity (Oviedo, 1980).

In this context, we reevaluate $V(G)$, $v_o$, and $v_e$ from the "McCabe family," together with "nesting complexity $(N)$" designed specifically to address the questions of nesting (Magel, 1981; Piwowarski, 1982).

In Table 5.2 are presented values for these three complexity measures and Piwowarski's (1982) $N$ for his six example DAGs (Figure 5.11). The value of $N$ is given by

$$N = V * (G) + N* \tag{5.18}$$

where $V * (G)$ is an adjusted cyclomatic complexity number, in which case/switch structures are treated as a single predicate (similar to Myers's (1977) lower bound) and $N*$ represents the effect of nested control structures and is given by

$$N* = \sum_i P * (i) \tag{5.19}$$

[5]Sometimes called the "benchmark fallacy" (Hopkins, 1991).

**TABLE 5.2**   Values for the six programs/graphs of Piwowarski (1982). (Here V(G) ≡ V*(G)). Also indicated are values of $P_1$ and $P_2$ given by equations (5.22) and (5.23).

| Piwowarski's | Sequential | | Nested | | Unstructured | |
|---|---|---|---|---|---|---|
| | A | B | C | D | E | F |
| No. of single decisions | 2 | 2 | 2 | 2 | 2 | 2 |
| $V(G) \equiv V*(G)$ | 3 | 3 | 3 | 3 | 3 | 3 |
| Operating complexity ($v_o$) | 3 | 3 | 2 | 3 | 2 | 3 |
| Essential complexity ($v_e$) | 1 | 1 | 1 | 1 | 3 | 3 |
| $N*$ | 0 | 0 | 1 | 1 | 0 | 0 |
| Piwowarski's $N$ | 3 | 3 | 4 | 4 | 5 | 5 |
| KNOTs | 0 | 0 | 0 | 0 | 1 | 1 |
| $P_1$ | 3 | 3 | 4 | 4 | 5 | 5 |
| $P_2$ | 3 | 3 | 4 | 4 | 9 | 9 |

where $P*(i)$ is the nesting depth of the $i$th predicate defined as the number of predicate node scopes overlapped or contained by the $i$th predicate node.

Piwowarski's (1982) intentions are to derive a measure that gives high values for unstructured programs, intermediate values for structured programs with nested control structures, and lowest values for sequential code with only top-level control structures embedded. As such, it penalizes programs, such as E and F in Figure 5.11, in which KNOTS exist. Thus, $N$ reflects not only the cyclomatic complexity but also the nesting levels and the degree of unstructuredness. The measure could alternatively be expressed as

$$N = V*(G) + N* + 2K \tag{5.20}$$

(where $N*$ is redefined as

$$N* = \sum_i P(i) \tag{5.21}$$

where $P(i)$ is the straightforward nesting depth of the $i$th predicate and $K$ is the knot value, that is, the sum of the adjusted cyclomatic complexity, allowing for nesting (each nesting level in each control structure adding one to $N$) and twice the KNOT value. The former provides an additional weighting to evaluate nesting complexity, whereas the latter addresses the very different issue of unstructuredness. We recommend maintaining these two descriptions of disparate characteristics as separate values:

1. $V*(G)$ modified by true nesting values ($P(i)$ not $P*(i)$)

2. KNOTS

Applying this philosophy to Sagri's (1989) graphs (Figure 5.12) gives the values shown in Table 5.3. It can be seen that the "least complex" of the four nested graphs (g4–g7) is identified, using $N$, as g5; that the two unstructured DAGs have large, non-zero values for KNOTS and a large (fractional—actually unity) value for $v_i$; and that the basic cyclomatic complexity number reflects the number of decisions.

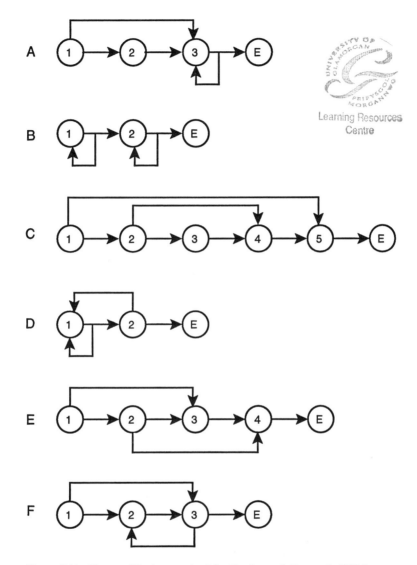

**Figure 5.11**  Piwowarski's six examples (after Henderson-Sellers *et al.*, 1993a).

As a tentative indication of one modeling approach, Henderson-Sellers *et al.* (1993a) note that the factors $v_e$, $N^*$ (equation (5.21)), and $V(G)$ all appear to be monotonic increasing functions of "complexity." Two possible models are proposed:

1. Additive model

$$P_1 = a_1 V(G) + a_2 N^* + a_3 (v_e - 1) \tag{5.22}$$

(the subtraction of 1 from $v_e$ being necessary since $v_e = 1$ is a well-structured program adding no additional complexity).

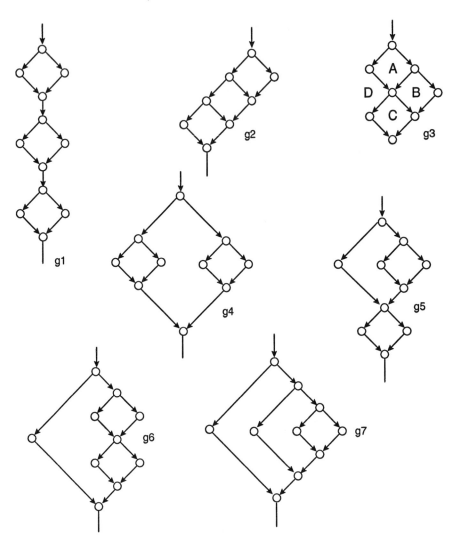

**Figure 5.12**   Sagri's graphs (after Henderson-Sellers *et al.*, 1993a).

2. Multiplicative model

$$P_2 = a_3 v_e \left[ a_1 V(G) + a_2 N^* \right] \tag{5.23}$$

where the weights, $a_1$, $a_2$, and $a_3$ will depend upon cognitive comprehension issues, as well as the task being performed. That this is a reasonable initial step (until dimensionality, meaning, and cognitive concerns can be adequately evaluated) is seen in the last two lines of Tables 5.2 and 5.3, where both "product

TABLE 5.3    Values of various complexity metrics for the seven graphs
based on Sagri's (1989) discussion

| Sagri's graph | g1 | g2 | g3 | g4 | g5 | g6(new) | g7(new) |
|---|---|---|---|---|---|---|---|
| $V(G) \equiv V^*(G)$ | 4 | 4 | 4 | 4 | 4 | 4 | 4 |
| $V^*(G) + (Pi)$ | 4 | 4 | 4 | 6 | 5 | 6 | 7 |
| KNOTs | 0 | 8–9* | 2 | 0 | 0 | 0 | 0 |
| Piwowarski's $N$ | 4 | 20–22 | 8 | 6 | 5 | 6 | 7 |
| $v_e$ | 1 | 4 | 4 | 1 | 1 | 1 | 1 |
| $v_o$ | 0 | 1 | 1 | 0 | 0 | 0 | 0 |
| $P_1$ | 4 | 7 | 7 | 6 | 5 | 6 | 7 |
| $P_2$ | 4 | 16 | 16 | 6 | 5 | 6 | 7 |

*Indicates the value is dependent on the particular coding.

complexity metrics," $P_1$ and $P_2$, are given with the (unjustified) simplistic approach that $a_1 = a_2 = a_3 = 1$. The overall distribution is seen (Table 5.4) to reflect the broad differences we might anticipate among nested, sequential, structured, and unstructured programs.

A new vector metric is proposed by Sevel and Henderson-Sellers (1995) that has three orthogonal components that represent size, control flow complexity, and nesting level. This can be represented graphically in three dimensions or the modulus of the distance from the vector point to the origin calculated as

$$C^3 = \sqrt{\left[ (C^3_{V(G)})^2 + (C^3_{size})^2 + (C^3_{nesting})^2 \right]} \tag{5.24}$$

The metric has some nice features in that the elements are orthogonal, and it appears to be fairly discriminatory, being able to distinguish between a while loop and a for loop, which other similar metrics cannot (Figure 5.13).

TABLE 5.4    Distribution of frequency of occurrence for the
three decision-structure graphs (bold) of Sagri (1989)
and the graphs (italic) of Piwowarski (1982)

| | 1 | 2 | 3 | 4 | 5 | 6 | 7 |
|---|---|---|---|---|---|---|---|
| Unstructured | | | | | 2 | | 2 |
| Nested | | | | 2 | 1 | 2 | 1 |
| Sequential | | | 2 | 1 | | | |

| | 3 | 4 | 5 | 6 | 7 | 8 | 9 | 10...16 |
|---|---|---|---|---|---|---|---|---|
| Unstructured | | | | | | 2 | | 2 |
| Nested | | | 2 | 1 | 2 | 1 | | |
| Sequential | | 2 | 1 | | | | | |

(a)

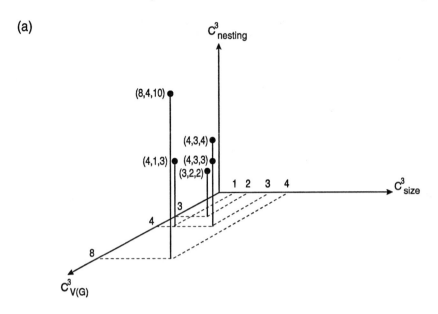

(b)

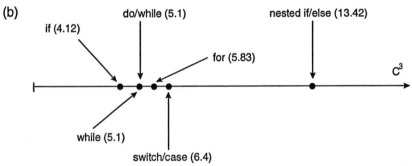

**Figure 5.13**   (a) Three-dimensional representation of six examples and (b) their 1-D representation.

## 5.5 CHAPTER SUMMARY

This chapter has described, briefly, some of the traditional approaches to software measurement of complexity and other static parameters. We have divided the discussion into intermodule metrics and module metrics. Module metrics are discussed under the headings of semantic complexity and procedural complexity. Procedural complexity is itself subdivided into size, logic structure, and "others." This pattern of subdivision is mirrored exactly in the next chapter on OO metrics.

## 5.6 BIBLIOGRAPHIC DETAILS

Traditional sources of metrics information include Yourdon and Constantine (1979), Conte *et al.* (1986), Card and Glass (1990), Zuse (1990), and Fenton (1991).

# 6

# OBJECT-ORIENTED
# PRODUCT METRICS

Having discussed traditional metrics in Chapter 5, we now follow the same format in describing object-oriented metrics. First, we consider intermodule metrics for system design complexity (Section 6.1). Then we look at a smaller scale and consider module metrics for semantic complexity (Section 6.2) and then module metrics for procedural complexity (Section 6.3). In the following section (Section 6.4) we present a number of metrics "suites" that have been proposed.

Finally, we should state that our focus in this chapter (and in fact the book) is evaluating and measuring *fully object-oriented* systems. In other words, we do not attempt to postulate, derive, or validate metrics that might be used directly to answer the question "Is this a truly object-oriented system or has it been built with a hybrid approach using partly an OO mind-set and partly a traditional mind-set?" That such a question might still be heuristically answerable will be seen; for example, the simple guideline that a C++ member function with 200 lines of code is highly unlikely to have been built with an object-oriented mind-set. The guidelines and suggested suites of OO metrics (Section 6.4) could easily form the basis for the construction of such evaluative metrics in much the same way that the "essential complexity" metric of McCabe (1976) was used as an extension of his standard cyclomatic complexity metric to discriminate between programs written with a structured approach as opposed to a nonstructured approach, evidenced by "spaghetti code."

## 6.1 INTERMODULE METRICS
## (FOR SYSTEM DESIGN COMPLEXITY)

The design guidelines of Table 6.1 express, as an objective, the need to minimize coupling and maximize cohesion. To some extent this should indeed follow accepted

TABLE 6.1   Design guidelines (modified from McGregor and Sykes, 1992)

1. The only members of the public interface of a class should be methods of the class.
2. A class should not expose its implementation details, even through public accessor operations.
3. An operator should be a member of the public class interface if and only if it is to be available to users of instances of the class.
4. Each operator that belongs to a class either accesses or modifies some data of a class.
5. A class should be dependent on as few other classes as possible.
6. The interaction between two classes should involve only explicit information passing.
7. Each subclass should be developed as a specialization of the superclass with the public interface of the superclass becoming a subset of the public interface of the subclass.
8. The root class of each inheritance structure should be an abstract model of the target concept.
9. A set of reusable classes should make maximum use of inheritance to model relationships of the problem domain.
10. The number of methods that must understand the data representation of the class must be limited.

structured heuristics. However, accepting that classes are autonomous modules with well-defined interfaces and responsibilities, in one sense the complexity added to the system by incurring an additional service connection (message passing) is likely to be less than adding a subroutine call in a procedural programming paradigm which tend to have less well-defined responsibilities.

During the analysis and design phases, and indeed in any code evaluation undertaken at the module level, intermodule coupling is measured by the number of relationships between classes or between subsystems (Lorenz, 1993). In OO systems, connectivity between classes is usually a binary state for any pair of classes. This contrasts with the later, more detailed design and implementation where a single connection of the analysis and/or conceptual design may be expanded to show multiple message paths when several services of an object/class (O/C) are used by the same "client" O/C (see detailed discussion later in this chapter).

Class coupling should be minimized, in the sense of constructing autonomous modules; yet a tension exists between this aim of a weakly coupled system and the very close coupling evident in the class/superclass relationship (Booch, 1991). Berard (1992, p. 102) differentiates between necessary and unnecessary coupling. The rationale is that without any coupling (namely, minimization of coupling), the system is useless. Consequently, for any given software solution there is a baseline or necessary coupling level—it is elimination of extraneous coupling that is the developer's goal. Such unnecessary couplings needlessly decreases the reusability of the classes—underlined by Page-Jones's (1992) introduction of the term "connascence" and its associated guidelines.

Interestingly, Sharble and Cohen (1993) showed that using a responsibility-driven methodology (e.g., Wirfs-Brock *et al.,* 1990), as opposed to a data-driven OO methodology (e.g., Coad, 1991), produces lower values of coupling and higher values of cohesion. Their method of graphing the results is useful and potentially widely applicable (Figure 6.1). They use eight metrics, one allocated to each of the compass points. The value of each metric is then displayed on a (normalized) radial scale.

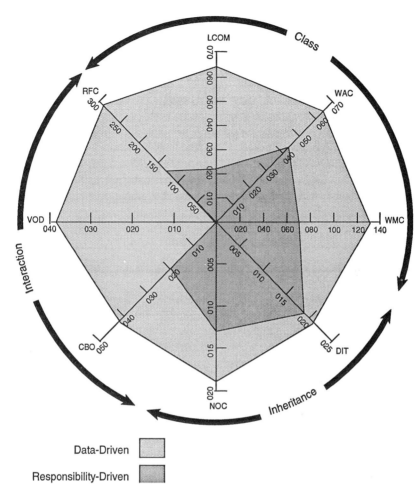

**Figure 6.1**   The use of a compass-type plot for eight metrics. The value is represented by a normalized radial distance. Here are displayed the values of eight metrics for a brewery system (after Sharble and Cohen, 1993).

Thus, not only absolute values but also patterns can be identified. Here it is seen that not only are metrics for responsibility-driven design (RDD) smaller in all cases than for a data-driven design (DDD) but that for VOD, and to some extent LCOM and CBO,[1] the ratio of RDD/DDD is also small.

Booch (1991, p. 124) also notes that coupling occurs (1) on a peer-to-peer basis or (2) within a generalization/specialization hierarchy. The former should exhibit low coupling; of necessity classes in a generalization hierarchy are more closely related. Wild (1991) discriminates between these as "interface coupling" and "internal cou-

---

[1]Violations of the law of Demeter (VOD), lack of cohesion of methods (LCOM), and coupling between objects (CBO) are defined later in this chapter.

pling." Internal coupling occurs both as "inside internal coupling," which describes the coupling of methods to their data (an intramodule metric—see Section 6.3) and the coupling of a composite class to its parts, and "outside internal coupling," which relates to relationships exemplified by the "friend" construct of C++. Lorenz and Kidd (1994, p. 77) recommend an upper limit of zero on the use of friend functions.

Some authors use the word "coupling" specifically for peer-to-peer coupling and deal with inheritance coupling separately; others use "coupling" to include both types. Yet others give an ambiguous definition. For example, Chidamber and Kemerer (1991) defined coupling between objects as "the number of non-inheritance related couples with other classes." While Li and Henry (1993) found this definition to be ambiguous, it is clear at least that it excludes inheritance coupling. Li and Henry went on to substitute their own coupling definition, data abstraction coupling (DAC), defined by them as

$$DAC = \text{number of ADTs defined in a class}$$

but perhaps more clearly expressed as the number of nonsimple attributes of a distinct type defined in a class.

Both definitions would appear to exclude inheritance and count 1 for each separate *type* referenced in a class. Coupling of multiple objects from the same class would still give an overall coupling value of unity.

Chidamber and Kemerer's (1994) definition of CBO is, however, very different from that in their 1991 paper. The earlier definition excluded inheritance but coupling only exists "if two objects act upon each other"; in other words, there must be a two-way interaction such that an object of class A references an instance of class B *and* an object of class B references an instance of class A. This seems highly restrictive and is omitted by Chidamber and Kemerer (1994). In this later paper, the definition of CBO for a class is "the number of other classes to which it is coupled." This definition now *includes* inheritance (or, more accurately, it does not preclude it, and their footnote 5 confirms this interpretation) but fails to *define* the term "coupled," although in their discussion they state that "two classes are coupled when methods declared in one class use methods or instance variables defined by the other class."

Coupling as a result of inheritance and/or polymorphism is original to object systems. While Sharble and Cohen (1993) advocate the increase of polymorphism to reduce complexity and Tegarden *et al.* (1992) show that the use of either inheritance or polymorphism reduces the counts of standard metrics, it remains true that the tight coupling of inheritance provides a potential complexity (especially in maintenance) not foreseen in the development of traditional metrics. Subclasses can essentially access their superclass's internal data and methods—a form of violation of information hiding (Wild, 1991) and a high value of connascence (Page-Jones, 1992). Complexity is also added as a result of excessive hierarchy depths, compounded when methods are overridden in descendant subclasses. Sheetz *et al.* (1991) thus define a "fan-down" metric as the number of subclasses that redefine any feature.

During analysis and design, the number of association and aggregation relationships and the argument lists can be counted. However, early in the process these will be scantily defined. In other words, if two classes are coupled in analysis, it is highly likely that in late design and implementation, this will expand to several connections as well as the addition of message arguments that would not be expected to be shown earlier. With those caveats, we can certainly evaluate the fan-in and fan-out of classes, where fan-in and fan-out here refer, respectively, to the number of other collaborating classes irrespective of the number of references made statically or dynamically; that is, for a pair of classes, the fan-in/fan-out value is either zero or one. With an analysis such as that shown in Figure 6.2, we would say that the analysis fan-out (or CBO or DAC) of class A is 3, of class B 1, and of classes C, D, and E is zero, whereas the respective fan-in numbers are 0, 1, and 1. Berard (1992, Chapter 7) confirms Card and Glass's (1990) suggestion that a low fan-out is desirable since a high fan-out is characteristic of the large number of classes needed by the particular class in question.

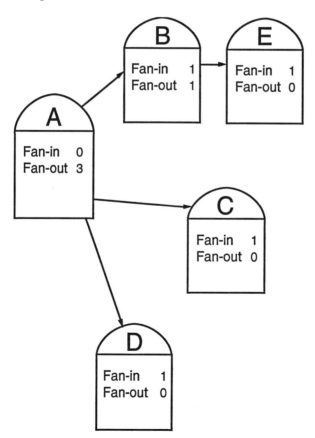

**Figure 6.2**  Fan-in and fan-out values for a small system of five classes.

Li and Henry (1993) offer a similar emphasis in their message-passing coupling (MPC) metric, which is the "number of send statements defined in a class" (a measure also proposed by Lorenz and Kidd, 1994, p. 33). The difference between fan-out (as used here in Figure 6.2) and MPC is that only one connection between any pair of classes is counted in fan-out, whereas one is added to the MPC count for each unique "send" in the class (Figure 6.3). It would thus appear that if two different methods in class A access the same method in class B, then MPC = 2 (this is in contrast to RFC; see the next discussion). A similar approach is taken by Rajaraman and Lyu (1992a,b) where they define coupling at the method level. They define method coupling (MC) as the number of nonlocal references, and then gross these values up to the class totals (CC) and class averages (AMC).

The response for a class (RFC) metric of Chidamber and Kemerer (1991) counts the number of methods, internal and external, available to (i.e., potentially used by) a class. It is given by RFC = |RS|, where RS, the response set of the class, is given by

$$RS = M_i \cup_{\text{all } j} \{R_{ij}\}$$

where $M_i$ = set of all methods in the class (total $n$) and $R_i = \{R_{ij}\}$ = set of methods called by $M_i$.

An alternative (equivalent) definition is

$$RFC = NLM + NRM \tag{6.1}$$

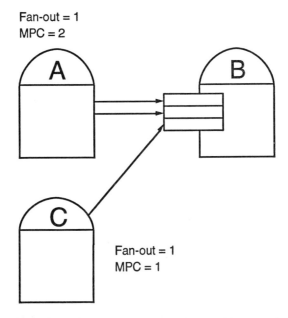

Fan-out = 1
MPC = 2

A     B

C

Fan-out = 1
MPC = 1

**Figure 6.3**  Three classes, A, B, and C, interact such that A and B are coupled (fan-out of A = 1) but where objects of class A use *two* different services of objects of class B, that is, MPC = 2.

where NLM = number of local methods = $|M_i|$ and NRM = number of remote methods = $\sum_n |R_i|$. An example is shown in Figure 6.4. It should be noted that RFC and CBO are thus not orthogonal.

Lorenz and Kidd (1994) note that there are "multiple ways to measure the coupling." They go on to discuss coupling in terms of (1) number of collaborating classes (presumably CBO or fan-out) and (2) the amount of collaboration (presumably related to MPC and/or RFC), but they do not offer any quantification or any results. It should also be noted that while their use of the term "collaborator" excludes inheritance coupling, their later discussion implies that they do intend to include inheritance in their future coupling measures.

In summary, there are various ways of counting noninheritance coupling. First, the declaration of an object of a remote ADT creates a potential collaboration. This is measurable by fan-out $\equiv$ DAC $\equiv$ CBO. If two O/Cs are collaborators, then a maximum of one is added to the fan-out count irrespective of how many messages flow between the two collaborating O/Cs.

Second, when two O/Cs collaborate, as do O/Cs A and B in Figure 6.5, for each unique service accessed, one is added to the NRM count and hence to the RFC count (since RFC = NLM + NRM).

---

Let RS = $M_i \cup R_i$

where

$M_i$ = the set of all methods in the class

$R_i$ = set of methods called by $M_i = \{R_{ij}\}$

Then RFC = $|RS|$.

For example,

Class A has four methods:

A::f1() calls B::f1(), B::f2() and C::f3()

A::f2() calls B::f1()

A::f3() calls A::f4(), B::f3(), C::f1() and C::f2()

A::f4() does not call any other methods

Then

RS = {A::f1, A::f2, A::f3, A::f4}

$\cup$ {B::f1, B::f2, C::f3}

$\cup$ {B::f1}

$\cup$ {A::f4, B::f3, C::f1, C::f2}

= {A::f1, A::f2, A::f3, A::f4, B::f1, B::f2, B::f3, C::f1, C::f2, C::f3}

giving

RFC = 10

---

**Figure 6.4**    An example RFC calculation.

*Source:* Kolewe, R. 1993. Metrics in object-oriented design and programming, *Software Development,* October 1993, 53–62.

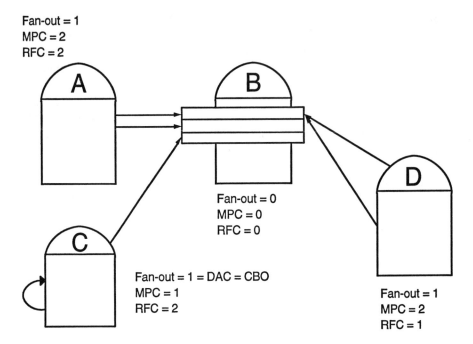

**Figure 6.5** Same as for Figure 6.3 but in which a fourth class, D, accesses one of B's services from two different places. This gives a different value for MPC and RFC, whereas for the interaction between A and B seen in Figure 6.3, the values of RFC and MPC are necessarily identical; while for class D MPC > RFC, the reverse is true for class C (RFC > MPC). This reflects the internal message coupling within class C whereby one message makes an internal call, thus adding to the value of RFC but not adding to the coupling values of MPC or fan-out.

Third, if one particular service is accessed from different parts of the "client O/C," it adds nothing to the MPC count (O/C D in Figure 6.5). Finally, class C has also one internal method call, that is, RFC = 2 (since NRM = 1 and NLM = 1).

High fan-outs represent class coupling to other O/Cs and thus an "excessively complex dependence" on other O/Cs. On the other hand, high fan-ins represent good object designs and a high level of reuse. Since these two are compensatory, it would not appear to be possible to maintain a high fan-in *and* a low fan-out across the whole system, since the cumulative values must be equal. More research is clearly needed in this crucial area.

Superimposed on these connectivity or coupling measures are different ways to describe the strength and quality of the coupling. Tegarden and Sheetz (1992) and Lorenz and Kidd (1994) propose the number of parameters per method (both at method-level and its class-level mean = PPM). Good OO designs should pass relatively few objects as parameters (or arguments) to messages—Lorenz and Kidd suggest that an upper limit of about 0.7 is appropriate. Extraneous or unused parameters are obviously a potential source of confusion. These "tramps" are evaluated by Sharble and Cohen (1993) in their NOT (number of tramps) metric (any value greater than zero is, of course, a cause for concern).

The quality of coupling is described by Lieberherr *et al.* (1988) in their law of Demeter, a component of which refers to recursive or concatenated message sends. Lorenz and Kidd (1994) give the example of myaccount.balance.print, which requires the client object using service *balance* of object Account to be knowledgeable about the internals of the myaccount object (the service *balance* calls an (external) service, *print*, from a third object). Sharble and Cohen (1993) quantify this as the measure VOD.

A similar connectivity count can be done at various stages in the design. However, unlike the structured paradigm when it is clear when the end of an activity has occurred, in the "seamless" transition of object technology, it is harder to define the completion of phases until coding is complete. This makes analysis metrics even harder to define than previously, since each analyst will tend to end the analysis at a different abstraction level, although using a specification phase (Henderson-Sellers and Edwards, 1994) rather than explicit analysis and design phases can obviate this problem.

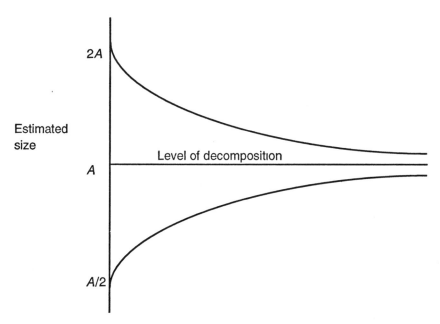

**Figure 6.6**   Estimated size ranges can be decreased in an object-oriented environment by increasing the level of decomposition.
*Source:* Laranjeira, L. A., 1990. Software size estimation of object-oriented systems, *IEEE Trans. Software Eng.*, 16(5), 510–522. © 1990 IEEE.

Laranjeira (1990) depicts this uncertainty in terms of a set of error bars (Figure 6.6) that become smaller as a function of life-cycle phase. He then develops this idea to assess to what degree of granularity a system must be decomposed to gain a required (prestated) accuracy in estimates. Although his goal is cost estimation (dynamics) rather than the product metrics addressed here, and despite the fact that the mathematics in that paper are flawed, Laranjeira's (1990) underlying *ideas* are worth investigating further.

The curves shown in Laranjeira's paper are described as exponentials, but they are plotted on log axes. Visually, these equations should therefore be straight lines (on the log axes). First, they are shown as exponentials, and second, this error then leads to an incompatability between the mathematical equations, the visual signals, and the logical development of the argument. Figure 6.6 actually shows that the error bars are multiplicative. In other words, if the upper curve has a value of $qA$, then the lower curve will have a value of $A/q$—the errors are the true value multiplied or divided by the same value. It is not surprising, therefore, that the additive confidence intervals (described as negative and positive deviations), *which are linear in nature,* are not equal. If we follow Laranjeira (1990) by assuming that the error bars are multiplicative in this sense, then we can deduce that we might increase $n$ sufficiently, where $n$ is the number of levels to which we decompose the classes, so that these multiplicative error bars (confidence interval) are smaller than some predetermined level. That level could either be stated as some absolute value (linear, additive) or as some percentage error (logarithmic, multiplicative). Laranjeira quotes a value of 25% suggesting a multiplicative value. In this case, his values of $d_1$ and $d_2$ do not apply since these give the additive error bars.

Qualitatively, this approach is appealing in its applicability to object-oriented systems. However, further research is needed (1) to establish the curves themselves (since the algebraic and graphical descriptions of Laranjeira are clearly incompatible and flawed); (2) to establish the value of the coefficient $B$, which determines the rate of convergence of the assumed decaying exponential functions; and (3) to develop criteria to establish appropriate values of acceptable accuracies, from which we can determine $N$, the level of necessary decomposition.

In a more recent study, Haynes and Menzies (1994) undertook a careful statistical analysis that suggests that there may be a linear relationship between class coupling and class size. Using several Smalltalk systems they showed that

$$\text{coupling} = (0.03 \pm 0.0006) \times \text{SLOC} + 5.5 \pm 1.7 \qquad (6.2)$$

These authors then suggest that this equation might be able to be used as the basis for "a precise size estimation schema," but take care to note that to accomplish this, the following are prerequisites:

1. Independent validation is requiring in a carefully controlled scientific manner.
2. Further study is required of classes with low coupling values, especially since most classes fall into this category.

3. Languages other than Smalltalk should be used, especially Eiffel and C++.

4. The source of experimental variation needs to be carefully scrutinized.

## 6.2 MODULE METRICS (FOR SEMANTIC COMPLEXITY)

Berard (1992, p. 101) notes that the first partial attempt at defining "object cohesion" could be traced to Myers's (1978) definition of "informational strength." A module possessing good informational strength has (1) multiple entry points, each of which perform a single specific function (service), and (2) all conceptually related, data-related, and resource-related functions hidden within the module. While focusing on an extended interface and information hiding, this is still, however, more syntactically focused than semantically focused.

Semantic cohesion cannot (at this stage) be measured objectively. It is an externally discernible concept (Berard, 1992, p. 123) that assesses whether the abstraction represented by the module (here a class) can be considered to be a "whole" semantically. Booch (1991, p. 124) describes this as embracing the behavior of this (external world) "concept," the whole concept and nothing but the concept—although his use of the term "functionally cohesive" (rather than semantically cohesive) is perhaps misleading, in the light of the discussion here and in Berard (1992). Booch (1991) also adds criteria of (1) sufficiency, (2) completeness, and (3) primitiveness. Sufficiency requires the abstraction (here, class) to capture sufficient characteristics to be identifiable and meaningful. Completeness requires the class to capture *all* meaningful characteristics. A primitive operation is one that can be efficiently implemented only if given access to the underlying representation of the abstraction (e.g., adding an item to a set). Sufficiency is thus a minimalist view, probably rendering the abstraction useful for present purposes; completeness aims at reusability by supplying a *full* specification. Primitiveness is slightly different in that it describes operations for which knowledge of the underlying representation is needed.

It is, after all, possible to have a class with high internal, syntactic cohesion but little semantic cohesion. For example, imagine a class that includes features of both a person and the car that the person owns. Assuming that each person can own only one car and that each car can only be owned by one person (a one to one association), then *person_id* ↔ *vehicle_id* (which would be equivalent to data normalization). However, classes have not only data but methods to perform various actions. They provide behavior patterns for (1) the person aspect and (2) the vehicle aspect of our proposed class. Assuming no intersecting behavior between PERSON and CAR, then what is the meaning of our class, presumably named CAR_PERSON (Figure 6.7). Such a class could be internally highly cohesive, yet semantically *as a whole class seen from outside* the notion expressed (here of a thing known as a person-car) is nonsensical. As a simple heuristic, consider the name of such classes and ask if they are meaningful within the universe of discourse (UoD) (Monarchi, 1992, personal communication).

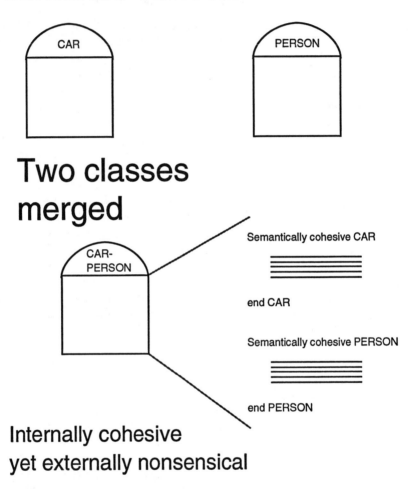

**Figure 6.7**  Individually semantically cohesive classes may be merged to give an externally semantically nonsensical class while retaining internal semantic cohesion (after Henderson-Sellers and Edwards, 1994).

## 6.3  MODULE METRICS (FOR PROCEDURAL COMPLEXITY)

### 6.3.1  Size Metrics

Tegarden *et al.* (1992) consider the applicability of several traditional procedural complexity metrics to object-oriented systems. The use of LOC as a measure of the size of a class is questioned, not only on the basic definition of a line of code, but also in respect of whether an inherited method should be counted as a contributory LOC to every class that inherits it or simply counted once in the defining class. They applied LOC, Halstead's software science, and McCabe's cyclomatic complexity to four versions of a small accounts system. These four versions were with and without inheritance, together with and without the use of polymorphism. Their results (Table 6.2), expressed for the overall system, showed that, as might be expected, the use of polymorphism and/or inheritance decreased the size measures of total SLOC and Halstead's $V$. To some extent, this must reflect the elimination of duplicate code. These results were also corroborated at the class level (Tegarden *et al.*, 1992). No comment was made by these authors regarding the additional "complexity" of an increased number of classes when using inheritance.

The applicability of function points to object-oriented systems has not been extensively evaluated. Graham (1995a) suggests that function point analylsis (FPA) is the most likely candidate from among traditional metrics for use in OO systems, perhaps based on the Mk II FPA of Symons (1985). Graham (1995a) suggests that since a "logical business transaction" (of FPA) represents a unit of functionality triggered by a single event, then it corresponds loosely to an atomic task (of SOMA, the semantic object modeling approach) or a use case (of Jacobson *et al.*'s (1992) object-oriented software engineering methodology). The utilization of use cases is also a focus of a project of Bell-Northern Research Limited (Thomson *et al.*, 1994). Graham (1995a) notes that to use FPA in OO systems, problems arise in that (1) FPA requires separate analysis of data and functions, (2) reuse cannot be accommodated clearly, and (3) FP counting is laborious and even "expert" counters may derive two different numerical values for the same system on different occasions.

In a commercial MIS study, Humphrys (1991) found that the use of object-oriented techniques resulted in an 80% reduction in code size. He further suggested

TABLE 6.2   Results of PC metrics for four versions at the system level

| Count or Metric | No Polymorphism, No Inheritance | Polymorphism, No Inheritance | No Polymorphism, Inheritance | Polymorphism Inheritance |
|---|---|---|---|---|
| Number of classes | 7 | 7 | 12 | 12 |
| Members/class | 7 | 7 | 2 | 2 |
| Number of methods | 42 | 42 | 30 | 30 |
| $n_1$ | 75 | 53 | 58 | 53 |
| $n_2$ | 58 | 56 | 56 | 56 |
| $N_1$ | 955 | 735 | 541 | 521 |
| $N_2$ | 453 | 259 | 254 | 245 |
| $N$ | 1408 | 1094 | 795 | 766 |
| $V$ | 9934 | 7404 | 5432 | 5184 |
| $V(G)$ sum | 95 | 71 | 57 | 55 |
| File $V(G)$ | 54 | 30 | 28 | 26 |
| Total SLOC | 676 | 626 | 539 | 534 |
| Executable SLOC | 202 | 181 | 126 | 124 |

*Source:* Tegarden *et al.,* 1992, Effectiveness of traditional software metrics for object-oriented systems, HICSS-92, IEEE, San Diego, pp. 359–368. © 1992 IEEE.

that a simple size decrease of this magnitude has immediate repercussions in terms of greater flexibility and a significant decrease in maintenance costs.

Other generic metrics, not discussed in the work of Tegarden *et al.* (1992), have potential, not only in the structured environments where they were first tested but also in object-oriented environments. Two examples of interest here are the cognitive complexity model (CCM) of Cant *et al.* (1995), which is described in full detail in Chapter 7, and the S/C measure of Pant *et al.* (1995a); see Section 5.3.1. Although both measures arose predominantly within a traditional, structured environment and testbed, both were designed specifically for complementary use in OO systems, and both have indeed been tested in those environments (e.g., Cant *et al.*, 1994; Pant *et al.*, 1995b).

Another commonly used, yet crude, metric is the number of classes in the sysem, $C_S$ (e.g., Tegarden and Sheetz, 1992; Lorenz and Kidd, 1994, p. 95; Figure 6.8), which could be subdivided into the numbers of abstract and concrete classes (Tegarden and Sheetz, 1992).

In addition to measures readily equivalent to standard metrics, there are some measures needed that are very specific to object-oriented systems. These include (Jacobson *et al.*, 1992)

- Width and height of inheritance hierarchies
- Number of classes inheriting a specific operation
- Number of collaborating classes (although this can be measured by an object fan-in/fan-out measure—see Section 6.1).
- A measure of the proportion of the system that consists of reused code

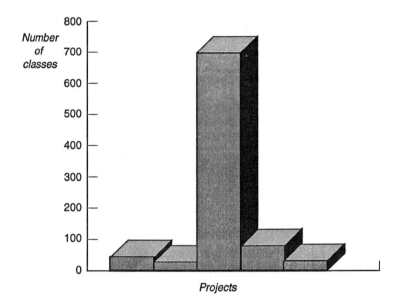

**Figure 6.8**   The number of classes in each of four projects (after Lorenz and Kidd, 1994).

Specifically, new metrics are needed to assess inheritance and reuse, to take into account the greater number of abstraction levels inherent in an OO system (Figure 6.9), and to address cost estimation and product quality across *all* life-cycle stages (Figure 6.6).

In a discussion of design metrics, Lorenz (1993) advocates measuring 11 items. Some of these coincide with Jacobson *et al.*'s list and some with the 6 recommendations of Chidamber and Kemerer (1991). Here we discuss only those metrics appropriate as size metrics; the remainder have either already been discussed in Section 6.1 (coupling) or will be discussed later in Section 6.3.3 (cohesion).

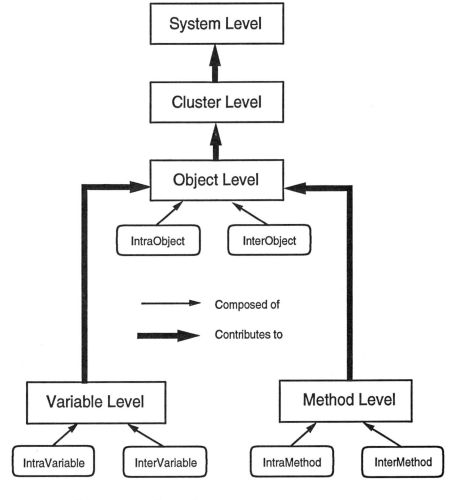

**Figure 6.9**  The various levels of abstraction found in an OO system (modified from Tegarden *et al.*, 1995).

Thomas and Jacobson (1989) suggest some of the components required in moving toward object-oriented metrics. These include lines of code reused per programmer, number of methods per class, class coupling and cohesion, and amount of reuse possible. Jacobson *et al.,* (1992, p. 460) point out that lines of code per se are not very elucidating, since the smaller the number of LOC written, the greater is the likelihood that you have reused significant code chunks and (it is hoped) the greater the quality of the final product.

There has been a natural tendency in industry to focus on easily obtained counts related to size (Table 6.3). From the range of "collectibles," useful information may be derivable from a range of size estimates, although it should be stressed that not only means but also standard deviations (where appropriate) should be collected. Kitchenham and Linkman (1990) stress the need to use "robust" descriptive statistics, such as boxplots/box-whisker diagrams (Figure 6.10).

At the lowest abstraction level, method size (measured in either LOC or number of statements) can be indicative of the "object-orientedness" of an O/C. Heuristically, method sizes should be small—around 8 lines of code in Smalltalk and fewer than 24 in C++ (Lorenz, 1993)—illustrating the language dependency implicit in this measure. Reports of method sizes of, say, 200 SLOC, sadly frequently heard in practice, simply suggest that a traditional mind-set still dominates over the object-oriented mind-set. Lorenz and Kidd (1994) give values of average method size (MS) (Figure 6.11) and indicate probabilities of poor OO design based on these values.

Similarly indicative may be the number of methods per class. A very small number may suggest class amalgamation should be undertaken; too many (say, more than 40) suggest class decomposition—although the real guidelines here should be semantic cohesiveness. Average number of methods per class is recommended to be less than 20 (see also LaLonde and Pugh, 1994), although this is perhaps better judged from a semantic cohesion viewpoint than a mere count. (Some typical values are given in Table 6.4 showing only the National Institutes of Health library exceeding this "threshold value.")

The numbers just calculated lead to estimates for class sizes, but as noted, absolute values are unlikely to be a useful goal as design criteria. Various authors have used, for instance, $\sum_{i=1}^{n}$ LOC, $\sum_{i=1}^{n}$ statements per method, and $\sum_{i=1}^{n}$ method size in tokens; all summed over the $n$ methods in the class. Li and Henry (1993) also define SIZE1 as the number of semicolons in a class (only valid for certain language grammars) or, alternatively, (Li, personal communiation, 1994), "the number of non-commented lines of source code" and SIZE2 = NOA + NEM (number of attributes plus number of external methods—see further discussion shortly). These summations, in general, imply an internal view of size, including all methods, private and public,

---

**TABLE 6.3    Current research**

Method size—mean and standard deviation
Number of methods per class—mean and standard deviation
Class size—mean and standard deviation
System—total number of classes

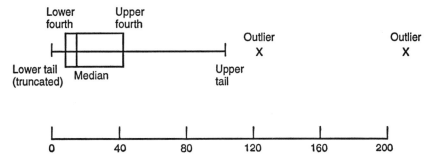

**Figure 6.10**   Box plot of design structure (17 procedures).
*Source:* Kitchenham, B. A. and Linkman, S. J., 1990, Design metrics in practice, *Information and Software Technology*, 32(4), 304–310.

although the SIZE2 metric does not include private methods. Overall number of classes in a system, also, is unlikely to do anything other than give an impression of (small, medium, large) to the project size.

At the detailed design stage, it would appear that initial metrics for size and complexity might be derived, at least as a first-order estimate, from (1) the number of attributes and (2) the number of methods per class.

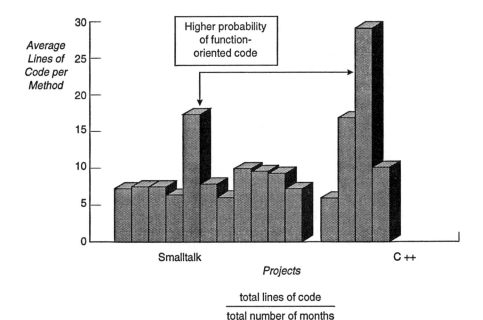

**Figure 6.11**   Average lines of code per method for several Smalltalk and C++ projects (after Lorenz and Kidd, 1994).

**TABLE 6.4   Summary of library characteristics
(adapted from Yap and Henderson-Sellers, 1993 and extended)**

| Library | Size (No. of Classes) | Total Number of Methods | Average Number of Methods |
|---|---|---|---|
| Actor 3.0 | 119 | 1,579 | 13.27 |
| Borland 2.0 | 30 | | |
| Instantiation | | 228 | 7.60 |
| Derivation | | 244 | 8.13 |
| Borland 3.0 | 166 | | |
| Instantiation | | | |
| Templates | | 1,014 | 6.11 |
| Without templates | | 1,087 | 6.55 |
| Derivation | | | |
| Templates | | 1,098 | 6.61 |
| Without templates | | 1,183 | 7.13 |
| Booch components | 32 | 340 | 10.63 |
| C++/Views | 75 | | |
| Instantiation | | 967 | 12.89 |
| Derivation | | 1,035 | 13.80 |
| Eiffel/S | 75 | | |
| Unrestricted exports | | 475 | 6.33 |
| With restricted | | 572 | 7.63 |
| NIH C++ | 66 | | |
| Instantiation | | | |
| Lower limit | | 1,683 | 25.50 |
| Upper limit | | 1,694 | 25.67 |
| Derivation | | | |
| Lower limit | | 1,823 | 27.62 |
| Upper limit | | 1,838 | 27.85 |
| Smalltalk/V—Windows | 173 | 1,825 | 10.55 |
| Smalltalk/V for PM | 139 | 1,518 | 10.92 |
| Smalltalk/Objectworks | 850 | 15,989 | 18.81 |
| Zinc interface | 54 | | |
| Instantiation | | 549 | 10.17 |
| Derivation | | 637 | 11.80 |

*Number of Attributes (or Variables) per Class, A* ≡ **NOA.**   Lorenz and Kidd (1994) discriminate between the number of instance variables, NIV, and the number of class variables, NCV, where NOA = NIV + NCV. Sharble and Cohen (1993) use "weighted attributes per class" or WAC, but it is not clear what this means in a pure object-oriented system.

The total number of attributes is easily counted using the declarations in the class. It represents the number of "data stores" in the class. However, if these "attributes" are of complex type, then they devolve to become DAC counts (see Section 6.1).

*Number of Methods per Class, $M \equiv$ NOM.*    There seems to be some termi-
nological confusion regarding NOM. Methods may be local, in that they are contained within the class under scrutiny, or remote because they belong to another
class—this is the realm of coupling and the RFC definition, given in Section 6.1. But
methods may also be external or public (available through the class interface to members of other classes) or internal or private (i.e., *not* available through the interface).
In C++, they may also be protected by which means they are public to the subclass
and private otherwise. The total number of methods of a class (NOM) may thus be
divided into the number of external methods (NEM) and the number of internal (hidden) methods (NHM) or, alternatively, into the number of instance methods (NIM)
and the number of class methods (NCM) (Lorenz and Kidd, 1994). Thus,

$$\text{NOM} = \text{NHM} + \text{NEM} = \text{NIM} + \text{NCM} \tag{6.3}$$

Thus, the NOM metric of Li and Henry (1993) is actually NEM (a measure of the
interface)—confirmed by Li (1994, personal communication).

Furthermore, the number of methods could probably be related partly to function points, or a more recent modification thereof (e.g., task points), and again is relatively easily counted. However, unlike simple datalike attributes, methods are not
coherent in the distribution of their size and structural complexity. As well as a total
count of the number of methods per class (perhaps divided between public, private,
and in C++, protected methods), the size of each could be assessed in LOC or statements and the mean and standard deviation (and possibly even the class distribution)
could be found. As a complement, the structural complexity, using $V(G)$ (see Section 5.3.2), could be calculated for each method (public, private, and/or total). Again
means, standard deviations, and the distribution could be calculated. This permits a
class-level calculation to be made for the $i$th class of

$$s_i = \sum_{j=1}^{m} V_{ij}(G) \tag{6.4}$$

for a class with $m$ methods each of cyclomatic complexity $V_{ij}(G)$ (Li and Henry,
1993), although it should be noted that this ignores any attributes. Equation (6.4) is
essentially the weighted methods per class (WMC) metric of Chidamber and Kemerer (1991) given by

$$\text{WMC} = \sum_{i=1}^{n} c_i \tag{6.5}$$

where $c_i$ is the static complexity of each of the $n$ methods; although in the original
1991 paper the weights all appear to be taken as unity (see similar comments by Sharble and Cohen, 1993). This ambiguity is clarified in Chidamber and Kemerer (1994)
when they note that "complexity is deliberately not defined more specifically here in
order to allow for the most general application of this metric." Thus, if $c_i$ in Equation
(6.5) is given by $V(G)$, then WMC $\equiv s_i$ (of Equation 6.4), whereas if $c_i = 1$, we get

WMC ≡ NOM. WMC does not include NOA and must therefore underestimate class "size." Also simply summing the complexities does not realistically allow for directed acyclic graphs (DAGs) that overlap (see example in Figure 6.16), although this is easily dealt with using the summation rules of Henderson-Sellers and Tegarden (1994b) for callable "subroutines" (see Chapter 5, especially Figures 5.4 and 5.5).

Another minor problem with the WMC metric is that it fails to distinguish attributes (i.e., the get and set access methods) from other methods so that the metric applies well to Smalltalk but not to C++ with its member functions and separate data members. Furthermore, "number of methods" itself is an ambiguous phrase. Does WMC just relate to externally visible methods (i.e., services) or to all methods, public/visible plus private (e.g., Churcher and Shepperd, 1995)? There is no clarification in any of the three Chidamber and Kemerer papers on this point. (For a further discussion and clarification on internal class measures, see Henderson-Sellers, 1995a.)

### 6.3.1.1 Combining Attributes and Methods.

We noted earlier Li and Henry's (1993) SIZE2 metric (= NOA + NEM). This suggests a simple, extended definition of class size, $S_C$, as

$$S_C = \text{NOA} + \text{NOM} \tag{6.6}$$

(unweighted size). Alternatively, some weighting can be applied to the methods to replace their number (NOM) by their total size (TMS) to get a

$$\text{weighted } S_C = \text{NOA} + \text{TMS} \tag{6.7}$$

A slightly different formula from equations (6.4) and (6.7) was proposed by Thomas and Jacobson (1989) and extended later by Henderson-Sellers (1991) in which numbers of attributes and methods, suitably weighted, are summed to give a size value, $s_i$, as

$$s_i = \left(AW_A + MW_M\right)_i \tag{6.8}$$

where $W_A$ and $W_M$ are weights for attributes and methods, respectively, which takes a mean value (probably OOPL dependent) rather than an actual value of method complexity, as in equation (6.4). These weights are likely to be programming language dependent (Thomas, 1989), but of the order of $W_M = 5\text{–}20$, where $W_A = 1$. However, since object-oriented code strongly supports high modularization, both externally and internally, the variance of method lengths is likely to be lower than that for a function point implementation in a procedural programming language. Equation (6.8) is extended by Graham (1995a) to include rulesets[2] such that it becomes

$$WC_{C_i} = \left(AW_A + MW_M L_M + RW_R N_R\right)_i \tag{6.9}$$

where $R$ is the number of rulesets, $N_R$ is the number of rules per ruleset multiplied by the average number of antecedent clauses per rule, and $W_R$ the associated weight-

---

[2]A ruleset is an unordered set of assertions and rules of either IF-THEN or WHEN-THEN form.

ing. The factor $L_M$ is "the proportional excess of SLOCs per method over an agreed language-dependent standard (say, 17 lines)."

This approach then permits the class-level values to be summed across the system. For example, for $N$ object classes, each of size $s_i$ (Henderson-Sellers, 1991),

$$S = \sum_{i=1}^{N} s_i = \sum_{i=1}^{N} \left( AW_A + M W_M \right)_i \tag{6.10}$$

Another view of a class "complexity" is strictly the external, specification, or interface view. Here we see $m$ services being offered to the "world," but there is neither knowledge, nor concern regarding the implementation. The size of the interface is thus $m$ services. These $m$ services may be divided into properties (services that return an object) and operations (services that don't)—an alternative interpretation is that of queries ($q_m$) and commands ($c_M$), respectively. Henderson-Sellers (1995a) suggests extending this to weighted queries and commands such that

$$q'_M = q_M + C_{arglist} \tag{6.11a}$$

$$c'_M = c_M + C_{arglist} \tag{6.11b}$$

where $C_{arglist}$ is 0 for a unary message and 1 for a binary message and is equal to the number of selectors for a selector message.

It should be noted that many of these structural metrics may be grossed up from the class to the system level. So, for instance, we might calculate average method size over the system, average number of methods per class, and average number of instance variables per class (Lorenz and Kidd, 1994). In addition, the number of subsystems and their coupling (Lorenz and Kidd, 1994) and the number of class hierarchies and of class clusters in the system may be of use (Kolewe, 1993)—in some senses cluster here being used as a system level analog of LCOM (Section 6.3.3). Finally, a value for the percentage of non-OO code (for hybrid languages) evaluates the degree to which the object paradigm is being used.

### 6.3.1.2 Incorporating Reuse.

An object-oriented development environment supports design and code reuse, the most straightforward type of reuse being the use of a library class (of code), which perfectly suits the requirements. Perhaps more commonly, a new class will be constructed by using inheritance. In this case a fraction, $I$, of the old code is effectively reused and a fraction $(1 - I)$ written anew. If there are $k$ classes reused "as-is," $l$ classes partially reused and $m$ classes fully coded from scratch (where the total number of classes in the system is $N = k + l + m$), then equation (6.10) is modified as

$$S = \sum_{i=1}^{k} W_{R_i} + \sum_{i=k+1}^{k+l} \left[ \left( AW_A + MW_M \right) \left( 1 - I \right)_i + W_{R_i} \right] \tag{6.12}$$

$$+ \sum_{i=k+l+1}^{k+l+m} \left( AW_A + MW_M \right)_i$$

where $W_{R_i}$ is the (very small) weighting/cost of library reuse, namely, the cost of locating and obtaining a single library class, which is independent of whether all or only part of the code is to be reused. (This approach links with the ROI approach of Chapter 1.)

Yap and Henderson-Sellers (1993) discuss two similarly focused measures similarly designed to evaluate the level of reuse possible within hierarchies, especially those found in or destined to be part of a class library. The reuse ratio, $U$, is given by

$$U = \frac{\text{number of superclasses}}{\text{total number of classes}} \tag{6.13}$$

This ratio indicates the extent to which the implementors of the class library have been able to inherit from their own classes to create new classes. It is clear that $U$ must always be less than 1. A value near to one is characteristic of a linear hierarchy (Figure 6.12(a) where $U = {}^{12}\!/_{13} \rightarrow 1$ as the number of classes gets large) and a value near 0 indicates a shallow depth and a large number of leaf classes (Figure 6.12(b)), where, for $n$ subclasses, $U = {}^1\!/_n \rightarrow 0$ as $n$ increases. Third (Figure 6.12(c)), for high use of multiple inheritance, $U = {}^{(n-1)}\!/_n \rightarrow 1$.

Second, the specialization ratio, $S$, is given as

$$S = \frac{\text{number of subclasses}}{\text{number of superclasses}} \tag{6.14}$$

The specialization ratio measures the extent to which a superclass has captured the abstraction since a large value of $S$ indicates a high degree of reuse by subclassing. Extreme values for single inheritance, as represented in Figure 6.12, run between 1 (part (a)) and $\infty$ (part (b)). For multiple inheritance (part (c)), $S = {}^1\!/_{(n-1)} \rightarrow 0$. Certainly values of $S$ and $U$ near 1 suggest a poor design (insomuch as a linear inheritance tree is generally regarded as poor stylistically). In addition, when multiple inheritance is used (part (c)), values of $S$ can be $\ll 1$, although $U$ must still be less than 1. Table 6.5 summarizes values of $U$ and $S$ for 10 class libraries.

### 6.3.1.3 Inheritance.

All authors note the need to measure inheritance structures: in terms of depths and node density. This can be measured as the depth of each class within its hierarchy (misleadingly called DIT, or depth of inheritance tree) (also called "nesting level" by Lorenz and Kidd, 1994, or class-to-root depth, e.g., Tegarden and Sheetz, 1992), since this is likely to affect the distribution of inherited features. Actual, mean, and maximum values of DIT may be useful. For example, a rough guideline of 6 or 7 is recommended for $\text{DIT}_{max}$. Data for 10 libraries are given in Table 6.6 that support this heuristic.

The average inheritance depth can be calculated by

$$\frac{\sum \text{depth of each class}}{\text{number of classes}} \tag{6.15}$$

In the hierarchical fragment shown in Figure 6.13, the depth for subclass 1 is 1 as it only inherits from one parent, which in turn does not inherit from anything else. The

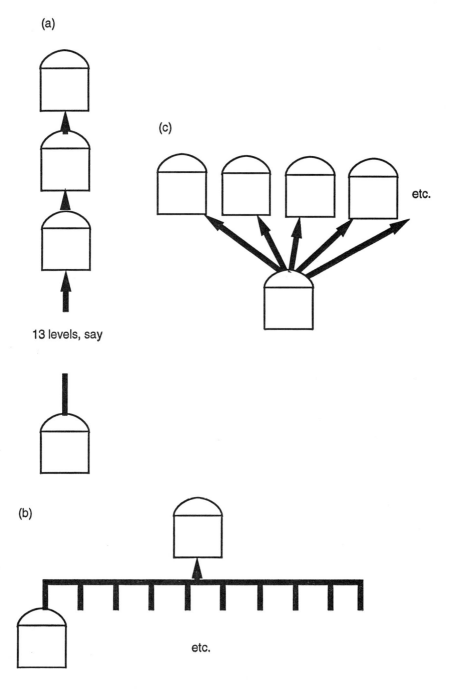

**Figure 6.12**    (a) Linear and deep hierarchy with a value of the reuse ratio, $U$, near to unity; (b) wide, shallow hierarchy with value of $U$ near to zero; and (c) extensive use of multiple inheritance.

| Library | No. of Subclasses | No. of Superclasses | Reuse Ratio | Specialization Ratio |
|---|---|---|---|---|
| Actor 3.0 | 118 | 45 | 0.38 | 2.62 |
| Borland 2.0 | 11 | 27 | 0.37 | 2.45 |
| Borland 3.0 | 67 | 131 | 0.40 | 1.96 |
| Booch components[1] | 4 | 3 | 0.12 | 0.75 |
| C++/Views | 30 | 71 | 0.40 | 2.37 |
| Eiffel/S[2] | 74[3] | 74[4] | 0.99 | 1 |
| NIH C++ | 16 | 63 | 0.24 | 3.94 |
| Smalltalk/V—Windows | 51 | 172 | 0.30 | 3.37 |
| Smalltalk/V for PM | 40 | 138 | 0.29 | 3.45 |
| Zinc interface | 13 | 47 | 0.24 | 3.61 |

[1]Structures and Tools classes only. Note also that Simple_Vector is included in these calculations as classes inherit from it.

[2]The reuse and specialization ratios indicate the direct acyclic nature of the Eiffel/S hierarchy, where everything inherits from ANY and NONE inherits from everything.

[3]All except for NONE.

[4]All except for GENERAL.

depth for subclass 2 is $(2 + 1)/2 = 1.5$ as it inherits from two parents, of which one (superclass 3) inherits from another (superclass 1) and the other (superclass 2) inherits from nothing.

The average depth of inheritance, overall, for this hierarchy is calculated as follows: for the structure in Figure 6.13, the sum of each depth is given as 0 (Superclass 1) + 0 (Superclass 2) + 1 (Superclass 3) + 1 (Subclass 1) + 1.5 (Subclass 2) = 3.5. Thus, the average depth = $3.5/5 = 0.7$. The average depth of inheritance indicates the general level of modeling or abstraction used in the hierarchy (Table 6.4).

However, simply identifying semantic location of classes is only part of the story—it neglects the semantic architecture of the inheritance hierarchy. Yap and Henderson-Sellers (1993) evaluate the structure of a number of class libraries. A single, simple example will suffice. A class that is implemented in most third-party class libraries is STRING (an equivalent class in some libraries as VARIABLE_STRING). This class would probably be used profusely in most applications; yet in 10 class libraries studied, its placement within the hierarchy was very different (Figure 6.14). For example, in Actor 3.0 it inherits from ByteCollection and through four levels to Object; in contrast, it is a second-tier class in Borland C++ and C++/Views. In C++/Views, it is in the same leg of the hierarchy as Container and in Borland C++ in a very different one.

The position of String within the hierarchies seems to be consistent only where the libraries share the same developer—such as Borland C++ versions 2.0 and 3.0 and Smalltalk/V for PM and Smalltalk/V for Windows. String has been classified as an IndexedCollection by Smalltalk/V and Actor (although, in both cases, a different

**TABLE 6.6**   Average depth of inheritance for 10 class libraries: histogram data
(number of occurrences) (after Yap and Henderson-Sellers, 1993)

| Library | 0 | 1 | 1.5 | 1.75 | 2 | 2.5 | 3 | 4 | 4.5 | 4.72[1] | 5 | 5.5 | 6 | 7 | 8 |
|---|---|---|---|---|---|---|---|---|---|---|---|---|---|---|---|
| Actor 3.0 | 1 | 29 | | | 17 | | 27 | 22 | | | 11 | | 7 | 4 | 1 |
| Borland 2.0 | 4 | 8 | | | 7 | | 6 | 3 | | | 1 | | | | |
| Borland 3.0 | 35 | 53 | 1 | | 38 | | 25 | 13 | | | 1 | | | | |
| Booch components[2] | 30 | 3 | | | | | | | | | | | | | |
| C++/Views | 4 | 15 | | | 13 | | 8 | 12 | | | 9 | | 13 | 1 | |
| Eiffel/S | 1 | 1 | | | 1 | | 33 | 21 | 4 | 1 | 7 | 1 | 4 | 1 | |
| NIH C++ | 3 | 16 | | | 26 | | 12 | 8 | | | 1 | | | | |
| Smalltalk/C–Windows | 1 | 39 | | | 57 | | 38 | 21 | | | 14 | | 2 | 1 | |
| Smalltalk/V for PM | 1 | 35 | | | 42 | | 37 | 19 | | | 5 | | | | |
| Zinc interface | 7 | 12 | 1 | 2 | 13 | 4 | 15 | | | | | | | | |

[1]This is the depth calculated for the NONE class. As NONE inherits from everything, its depth is the sum of all other classes' depths (275.5) divided by the number of all other classes (74), plus (1) as it descends from each of those classes (and should be one level deeper), that is, (275.5/74) + 1 = 4.72.

[2]The Simple_Vector class was not described in the Rational (1991, pp. 1–36). It will be assumed that the Simple_Vector class does not inherit from any class, so it has a depth of 0. The total number of classes (for calculating the average depth) will include Simple_Vector.

subclass of IndexedCollection is used as String's direct superclass). Even though Borland C++ versions 2.0 and 3.0, C++/Views, and NIH C++ have Collection objects, String does not inherit from these classes in these libraries, either directly or through the inheritance chain. Instead, String directly inherits from Object in NIH C++. Borland C++ versions 2.0 and 3.0, along with Eiffel/S, classify String as a class that can be ordered or sorted—even through Smalltalk/V and Actor support the concept of ordering through the class Magnitude, String does not inherit from this class in these libraries. For a class that is used so frequently, the inconsistency in String's positions in the various hierarchies is surprising. Users working among libraries cannot automatically apply their knowledge of String's position in inheritance hierarchies from one library to another. Rather, extended periods scouring the hierarchy through a class browser may be required for them to locate the String class.

As well as these system-level assessments of inheritance structures, some class-level considerations are possible. For example, we can count the number of classes inheriting a specific operation (Jacobson *et al.*, 1992; Tegarden and Sheetz, 1992), the number of methods overridden, and the number of methods added (Lorenz and Kidd, 1994). Lorenz and Kidd (1994, p. 72) then use the number of overridden methods (NORM) to calculate the "specialization index" to differentiate between "subclassing by specialization" (high value of index) and "implementation subclassing" (low value of index). This index is then given as $(NORM*DIT)/NOM$ for each class.

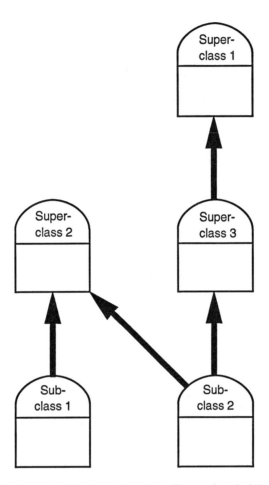

**Figure 6.13**   Fragment of inheritance hierarchy to illustrate the calculation of reuse metrics (after Yap and Henderson-Sellers, 1993).

This possibility of overriding methods inherited from superclasses, compounded with the free access of subclasses to features (operations or methods and attributes) in their superclasses (depending on the inheritance model being used in any chosen OOPL), leads to a paradox in terms of calculating any type of size measure for subclasses. A simple illustration (Figure 6.15) will assist. In this hierarchy

- Classes B and C contain all the features of class A
- Class D contains all the features of classes B and A
- Classes E and F contain all the features of class D

in addition to any new features declared locally to that particular class.

The questions raised by Pant (1993) are (1) what is the system size and (2) what is the size of classes B, D, E, and F? Since class F inherits from class D,

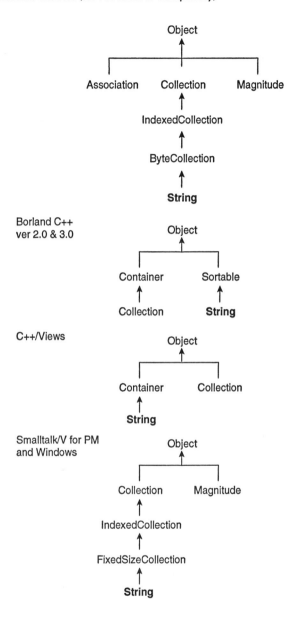

**Figure 6.14**   The positioning of Collection and Container classes in four class libraries (after Yap and Henderson-Sellers, 1993).

should the stated size of class F include (conceptually) the code from class D. Another way of looking at this system is in terms of the functionality of one of the leaf classes, say, E. Using a "flat" tool (such as available in Eiffel) effectively collapses the hierarchy so that, for this example, the contents of class E would be replaced by

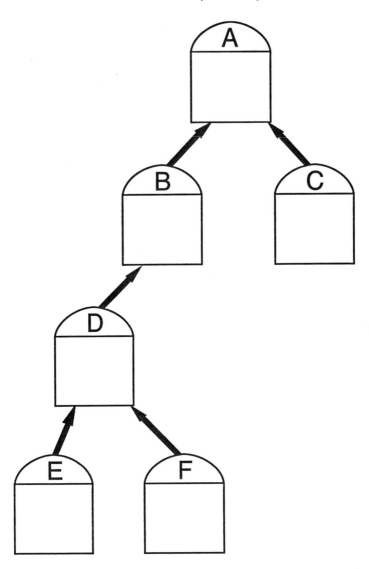

**Figure 6.15**  Inheritance hierarchy in which features are inherited by subclasses so that there are more features available in the classes lower in the hierarchy.

the features of classes A, B, D, and E and in which any overridden features have been automatically updated. Thus, the newly created flat class is behaviorally equivalent to the original class in the hierarchy. However, the "size" of this newly flattened class (call it E') is obviously significantly greater than any straight measure of the "size" of the original class E. Behaviorally the overall system size could be represented by the sum of the flattened sizes of E, F, and C (the lowest leaves). Although this may be attractive for some applications, one of the problem that arises is that the features of class A are included several times (e.g., in classes C, E, and F and the classes B and D appear twice (in E and F). Thus, the system overall appears to be larger than it might otherwise. Furthermore, it is difficult to contemplate, for instance, correlating size with effort since there is an increase of size (by flattening) not commensurate with any additional expenditure of effort. This question about the size of classes within the hierarchy still remains a paradox for metricians.

Chidamber and Kemerer (1991) introduce NOC as the number of children, suggesting classes high in the hierarchy should have more subclasses than those lower down as well as depth of inheritance tree. NOC is a system-level metric (Graham, 1995a). A technique for calculating inheritance-based metrics is given by Sheetz et al. (1991) and Tegarden et al. (1995).

An object-oriented replacement for function points is proposed by Graham (1995a). He suggests as an appropriate measure the "task point." This is the number of atomic tasks in the system and epitomizes the overall complexity, as well as being able to be collected automatically early in the life cycle. Collection of task point data, it is proposed,[3] permits effort estimates to be derived from

$$E = a + pT^k \qquad (6.16)$$

where $E$ is the effort (person-hours), $T$ is the task point count, $p$ is the inverse of productivity in task points per person-hour (an empirical constant), and $a$ and $k$ are constants.

### 6.3.2 Logic Structure Metrics

The application of McCabe's metric to object-oriented systems has not been extensive. Tegarden et al. (1992) include this metric in their evaluation of traditional metrics to four versions of a small accounts system. In Table 6.2 are also given the values of $V(G)$ when polymorphism and inheritance were used. Both improved (decreased) the value of $V(G)$. This is the result of Case statements being replaced by inheritance and/or polymorphism—a traditional advantage of using object technology. Indeed, in many classes, the value of $V(G)$ dropped to its minimum (= 1), suggesting, perhaps, that in a pure object-oriented system, $V(G)$ would typically be small and perhaps a poor discriminator of complexity at the class level.

McCabe's metric (Equation (4.24)) or the Henderson-Sellers and Tegarden metric (Equation (4.23)) can be applied to modularized code in object-oriented systems. This can be evaluated at both module and system level.

A class provides services to the outside world. Each of these services is implemented inside the class as an algorithm, and hence representable as a DAG, which may be self-contained or may reference other algorithms/code chunks within the class. A small schematic illustration is given in Figure 6.16. Here services $S_1$ and $S_2$ are autonomous; services $S_3$ and $S_4$ use the same private method, $S_5$, while ser-

---

[3]As of early 1995, a Metrics Club was being formed internationally to undertake empirical evaluation of this proposal.

vice $S_6$ subcontracts to another class. At this service level (or more usually method level insofar as service is the external nomenclature, method or feature or operation the internal), we can say features 1 and 2 are represented by the DAGs $F_1$ and $F_2$ with cyclomatic complexities of 2 and 3, respectively; features 3 and 4 have complexities of 5 and 6, respectively, for the value of $V(G)$ and 4 and 5 for $V_{LI}(G)$; and feature 6 has a value of $V(G)$ (= $V_{LI}(G)$ here) that requires knowledge of the complexity of the target object for the message send. However, it could reasonably be argued that changing the complexity of the external class should *not* alter the complexity of class MEASURE (Figure 6.16). Consequently, the value of $V(G)$ and $V_{LI}(G)$ for $F_6$ should be reported as 1. Across all the features of a class, one could propose an arithmetic average and standard deviation or variance that could then be used to highlight overly

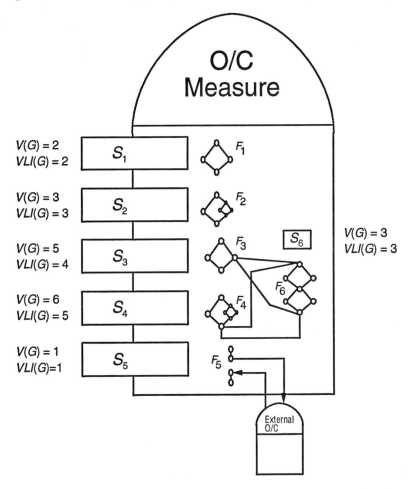

**Figure 6.16**   Object/class MEASURE has five (publicly available) services ($S_1$–$S_5$) and one private service/method ($S_6$). Values for McCabe's (1976) cyclomatic complexity, $V(G)$, and Henderson-Sellers and Tegarden's (1994b) $VLI(G)$ are given.

complex structures: the class method complexity and class method variance. Thus the average cyclomatic complexity would appear to be

$$\overline{V(G)} = \frac{\sum\limits_{i=1}^{6} V(F_i)}{6} = 3.3 \quad \text{and} \quad \overline{V_{LI}(G)} = 3.0$$

$V(G)$ has also been used in a novel application to contracting (Meyer, 1988, 1992b) in which it was shown (Henderson-Sellers and McKim, 1994) that the extra complexity of an error checking contract is linearly proportional to the number of atomic conditions in the precondition.

$V(G)$ is also used as one component in the calculation of "class path coupling" (CPC) by Camapanai and Nesi (1994). This is, in turn, just one component (of five) in the internal class complexity which, when added (with appropriate "tailorable weights"), gives the overall class complexity, CC. This approach is complicated, involves many arbitrary weighting factors and is closely linked to TROL, a "dual object-oriented language."

However, of potentially more interest is the application at the class/class level (a system design metric—Section 6.1). Simply averaging the method complexities and then averaging these over all the classes in the system cannot portray system-level complexity (compare Kolewe, 1993) since that procedure does not describe interclass coupling in any way. Rather than view each class as a module whose internal complexity we need to incorporate (cf. McCabe and Butler, 1989), we could propose making each class a node and each "service call" an edge. Figure 6.17 illustrates this procedure applied to the simple system of Figure 6.2. A similar example is shown by Kolewe (1993) (Figure 6.18, using Booch's notation). He proposes, as an analog to $V(G)$, an association complexity metric, AC, given as

$$AC = A - C + 2P \tag{6.17}$$

where $A$ = number of associations in the class diagram (edges), $C$ = number of classes in the class diagram (nodes), and $P$ is the number of disconnected parts. There is, however, an obvious disadvantage in the application of cyclomatic complexity at this interclass level; that is, the basic assumptions of $V(G)$ require that graphs are connected. In Figure 6.17, the connections do not represent the flow of control in the same way that nodes and edges in a DAG of a method represent a chronological chain. More realistically, system level interclass connections should be measured by fan-in/fan-out *except* for the scenario known as use cases, pioneered by Ivar Jacobson in his Objectory methodology. These really do reflect a control flow across objects, and an extension of McCabe's (1976) metric could be developed for these in the future. Graham (1995a) suggests measuring the "homology" (i.e., Betti number) of the usage structure, although the operationalization remains a research issue.

Indeed, this interaction and complementarity between the fan-in/fan-out metric and cyclomatic complexity can be exploited further in the context of object-oriented systems, since they possess more abstraction/modularization levels than a traditional

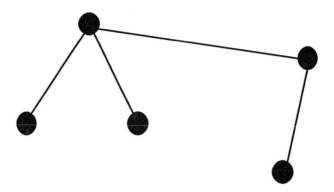

**Figure 6.17**    DAG corresponding to Figure 6.16.

system. If we equate the modularization level of subprogram with class, then at a more detailed level, modularization exists within classes since each feature (operation or attribute) can itself be regarded as a modularized chunk, offering (possibly) an external interface to other classes as well as links to other features in the same class (including private features). Thus we can propose depicting the internal structure of a single class as a set of coupled chunks. At the system level, the related chunks (nodes), as we noted earlier, are classes (Figure 6.2). At the class internal level, the same measures apply, but now the nodes are features (see Figure 6.19). For each feature we can calculate a fan-in and/or a fan-out value and then for the total class, the overall value can be given by equation (4.3). For the class shown in Figure 6.16 this would give a value of the mean intermodule complexity, $\overline{C_I}$ from equation (4.3), as $\overline{C_I} = {}^{18}\!/_5 = 3.6$, which takes into account all the internal features. Such a measure would seem to be appropriate for maintenance. However, in the specification phase, private features should be hidden. Thus, *all* services offered in the interface have an apparent fan-out of unity. Thus, in these early phases, the value of $\overline{C_I}$ must always be 1 ($= \Sigma_{i=1}^{n} 1/n$). At the system level, then, the fan-out values shown in Figure 6.2 would be useful ($A$ has value 3, $B$ a value 1, and the rest are zero). From equation (4.3), the value of $\overline{C_I}$ for this small, five-class system would thus be $2 = (\frac{3^2+1^2}{5})$. Then, if we assume high cohesion ($C_h \simeq C_{hmax}$) and an externally viewed value of $C_M$ of zero, then from equation (4.2), the overall system complexity, $C_S$, is given also as 2. These calculations highlight the need for further evaluation of fan-in/fan-out and cyclomatic complexity to object systems as well as emphasizing the urgent need for different metrics at different life-cycle stages—an area still awaiting detailed exploration.

     In object-oriented systems, abstractions are manifest in the form of encapsulated object classes connected through networks. Indeed, object modeling focuses on the use of various levels or degrees of abstractions as a crucial tool (Henderson-Sellers, 1992a; Selic *et al.*, 1992). As we move to higher levels of abstraction, we tend to concern ourselves with progressively smaller volumes of information and fewer overall items. As we move to lower levels of abstraction, we reveal more

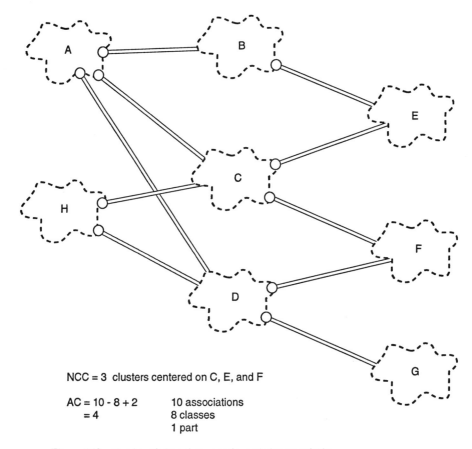

NCC = 3  clusters centered on C, E, and F

AC = 10 - 8 + 2        10 associations
    = 4                8 classes
                       1 part

**Figure 6.18**   Number of class clusters and association complexity.
*Source:* Kolewe, R. 1993. Metrics in object-oriented design and programming, *Software Development,* October 1993, 53–62.

details, typically encountering more individual items, thus increasing the volume of information with which we must deal. Further research on object-oriented structural complexity is clearly warranted, although we note that initial investigation of the usefulness of an unmodified McCabe cyclomatic number (Tegarden *et al.,* 1992) suggests that direct application of $V(G)$ can at least highlight the impact of polymorphism and inheritance, although its use for detecting problems in these areas awaits evaluation since $V(G)$ and $V_{LI}(G)$ are best suited to describing control flow structures not architectural configurations.

In terms of complexity measures for object-oriented systems, Lorenz and Kidd (1994) discuss McCabe's (1976) $V(G)$ but instead suggest that method-level structural (logical flow) complexity is measurable by application programming interface (API) calls, assignments, binary expressions, keyword messages, nested expressions, parameters, primitive calls, temporary variables, and unary expressions, all weighted

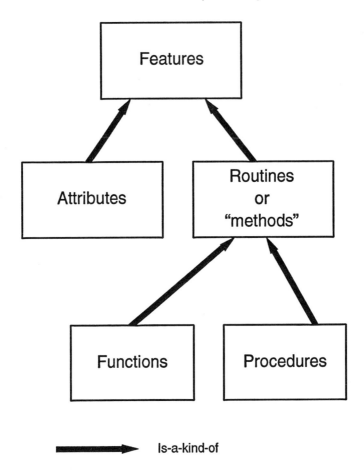

**Figure 6.19**   Classification of the various internal details of a class.

by arbitrary (but predetermined) factors. They note that good object-oriented methods should contain few, if any, Case statements and IF blocks that are the focus of $V(G)$'s control flow complexity.

### 6.3.3 Other Procedural Complexity Measures

In object-oriented systems, module decomposition is no longer focused on functionality. Consequently, the cohesion scale of Figure 5.8 has been extended by Macro and Buxton (1987) by adding a level 7 of "abstract cohesion." In contrast, Fenton (1991) proposes not a separate level, but a separate scale for *data cohesion.*

Chidamber and Kemerer (1991) suggest a metric to evaluate the internal cohesion by considering the number of disjoint sets formed by the intersection of the $n$ sets created by taking all the instance variables used by each of $n$ methods. For a class C with methods $M_1, \ldots, M_n$, consider the set of instance variables used by method $M_i$, labeled $I_i = \{I_{ij}\}$. For $n$ methods, there are $n$ such sets $I_1, \ldots, I_n$ [alternatively written as $\{I_{1j}\}, \ldots, \{I_{nj}\}$]. Then the lack of cohesion of methods metric is given formally by Chidamber and Kemerer (1991, p. 203) as

$$\text{LCOM} = \text{the number of disjoint sets formed} \atop \text{by the intersection of the } n \text{ sets.} \tag{6.18}$$

That this is ill defined is easily seen. The intersection of a number of sets is a single set containing element(s) common to *all* the original sets. Formally, we can state that the intersection $\cap$ of sets $S_i\,(i \in I)$ is given as

$$\cap_{i \in I} S_i = \left\{ x \,|\, x \in S_i \,\forall\, i \in I \right\} \tag{6.19}$$

(Fraleigh, 1967, p. 68). In other words, the result is a *single* set. On the other hand, the notion of disjointedness involves two (or more) sets: two sets $A$ and $B$ are disjoint if $A \cap B = \varnothing$. We must presume, therefore, that Chidamber and Kemerer (1991) meant something different; the most likely rephrasing might be the number of partitions formed by counting the number of subsets of $I\,(= I_1, I_2, \ldots, I_n)$ such that the methods that use members of this subset do not use its complement.

The LCOM measure is derived from Bunge's (1977) definition of "similarity" between two objects as the intersection of the sets of their properties. The degree of similarity $\sigma(\ )$ between two methods is given by

$$\sigma\!\left(M_1, M_2\right) = I_1 \cap I_2 \tag{6.20}$$

Thus, if there are no common properties, similarity = 0.

One problem occurs in the inappropriate extension in Chidamber and Kemerer (1991) of this definition to $m$ sets where

$$\sigma\!\left(M_1, M_2, M_3, \ldots, M_m\right) = I_1 \cap I_2 \cap I_3 \ldots \cap I_m \tag{6.21}$$

(correcting the set notation of Chidamber and Kemerer, 1991). In general, such an intersection is likely to be small or zero.

Perhaps Graham's (1995a) interpretation of LCOM as a measure of "the nonoverlapping of sets of instance variables used by the methods of a class" or Li and Henry's (1993) interpretation that LCOM = number of disjoint sets of local methods is nearer the intended meaning; yet even here maximum similarity would give LCOM = 1, whereas all authors discuss full similarity as occurring when LCOM = 0. For an example, see Figure 6.20. In the first part of this example, $I_i = \{i1, i2\}$ and $I_2 = \{i3\}$. Hence $I_1 \cap I_2 = \varnothing$ and LCOM = 2. In the second case, $I_1 \cap I_2 = \{i1, i2\} \neq \varnothing$ and LCOM = 1, since $I_1 \subset I_2$ there is only one (disjoint) set.

It is intended that a small value of LCOM should imply high similarity, whereas a high value of LCOM can be used to indicate that a class may be more successful if split into two or more classes.

A more useful measure that quantifies these intuitive relationships might be

$$\text{LCOM}' = |I_i \cap I_j = \varnothing, \forall i, j, i \neq j| \tag{6.22}$$

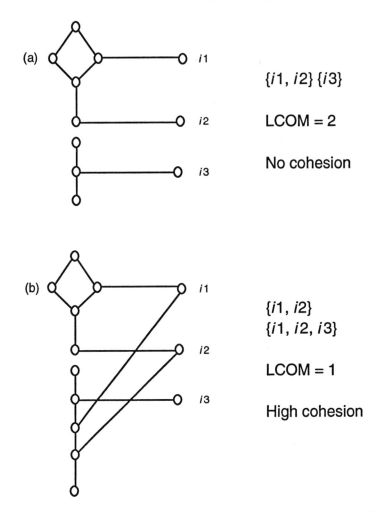

**Figure 6.20** Two classes drawn as DAGs. In (a), a class with two disparate methods is illustrated. This class should probably be divided, and this is reflected in a "high" value of LCOM of 2. A lower value of LCOM is seen in (b), which has a much more cohesive nature.

that is, the number of empty sets formed from taking the intersection of pairs of variable sets $I_i, I_j$ ($i \neq j$). This would give, for the two examples in Figure 6.20, values of LCOM' of 1 and 0, respectively.

However, in Chidamber and Kemerer (1993), the definition of LCOM is altered to read: if $P = \{(I_i, I_j) | I_i \cap I_j = \varnothing\}$ and $Q = \{(I_i, I_j) | I_i \cap I_j \neq \varnothing\}$, then

$$\text{LCOM} = |P| - |Q| \qquad \text{if } |P| > |Q| \tag{6.23}$$

$$= 0, \qquad \text{otherwise}$$

In this case, the revised values of LCOM for the two examples of Figure 6.20 are (a) LCOM = 1 ($|P| = 1$, $|Q| = 0$) and (b) LCOM = 0 ($|P| = 0$, $|Q| = 1$). In words, "LCOM is a count of the number of method pairs whose similarity is 0 (i.e., $\sigma()$ is a null set) minus the count of method pairs whose similarity is not zero." Thus, when there is no cohesion, we expect the cardinality of the set $P$ (the number of pairs that have no similarity) to be high and of set $Q$ (the number of pairs which have some similarity) to be low or zero—and thus LCOM has a large value.

Another concern is that LCOM attempts to measure only structural cohesion, whereas a major focus of OO is its ability to create logically (i.e., semantically) co-hesive modules (classes). LCOM makes no attempt to measure this difficult, yet im-portant, characteristic of an OO system.

Another test of the validity and usefulness of a measure is whether two classes with equal values of LCOM are intuitively of the same cohesion. Consider Fig-ure 6.21(a). The set $\{I_i\}$ has elements given as $I_1 = \{1\}, I_2 = \{2\}, I_3 = \{3\}, I_4 = \{5\},$ $I_5 = \{5, 6\}$. Intuitively, we expect a low cohesion. Our intuitive advice might go so far as to suggest this example would be better as four separate classes. Using equa-tion (6.23), we find that $|P| = 9$ and $|Q| = 1$ (since $I_4 \cap I_5$ is the only nonempty set). In other words, the LCOM value is 8—which does seem to be significantly nonzero (but can we say sufficiently large?) to indicate low cohesion.

In contrast, consider the example in Figure 6.21(b). Henderson-Sellers *et al.* (1995) show that $|P| = 18$ and $|Q| = 10$. Every method accesses at least two data elements, and all data are accessed, most of them by more than one method. The general impression is of a cohesive class, or more realistically it would be difficult to see any easy way to divide the class into a number of smaller ones. Yet the value

(a)

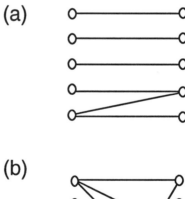

(b)

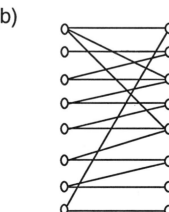

**Figure 6.21**  Two extreme and more elabo-rate (compared with Figure 6.20) examples are illustrated: (a) a highly noncohesive class for which LCOM (1994) = 8 and (b) a highly cohesive class for which LCOM (1994) = 8.

of LCOM (8) is identical to that of Figure 6.21(a)! In that sense, one of the basic axioms of measurement theory, that a measure should be able to distinguish two dissimilar entities, is violated by the 1994 LCOM definition given in equation (6.23).

Furthermore, it is of concern that, while a high value of LCOM implies low similarity and therefore low cohesion, a value of LCOM = 0 does not imply the reverse. If $|P| \leq |Q|$, LCOM = 0, and this can occur even for cases of obvious dissimilarity. For instance, consider extending Chidamber and Kemerer's (1994) example by adding $I_4 = \{x, y, z, d\}$ (Figure 6.22). When all four sets are considered, LCOM $\doteq$ 0, implying a good cohesive structure, yet intuitively, $M_1$ and $M_2$ are a pair of cohesive methods as are $M_3$ and $M_4$, and the designer would suspect that two classes should be formed, not one. Yet LCOM suggests high cohesiveness. In other words, this measure is not very discriminating (i.e., it fails Weyuker's basic first axiom) for low cohesive structures. A second example will reinforce the point. Intuitively, a class with four methods accessing variables according to $I_1 = \{a, b, c\}$; $I_2 = \{c, d, e\}$; $I_3 = \{e, f, g\}$; $I_4 = \{a, g, h\}$ does not seem to be a candidate for good cohesion. Yet LCOM is readily shown to be equal to zero.

One further observation on LCOM is offered. Chidamber and Kemerer (1994) state that if no methods use any instance variables, they have no similarity (agreed) and therefore LCOM = 0. But such a situation should be reflected in a large value of $|P|$ and a zero value for Q (and thus *large* LCOM to indicate the disparate nature of the class—although a class without data is a better sign of a non-OO program). It can therefore be concluded from Chidamber and Kemerer's (1994) discussion, that a zero value of LCOM (1994 definition) could be (1) a highly cohesive class, (2) a not very cohesive class, or (3) a class with no cohesion at all! Clearly, much clarification and research is needed to devise a useful measure of internal cohesion.

It should be noted that in many commentaries and applications of LCOM (e.g., Li and Henry, 1993; Kolewe, 1993) it is the 1991 definition of equation (6.18) that is supposedly used. Lorenz and Kidd (1994) also note this work and use the phrase "patterns of instance variable usage by methods."

---

$$I_1 = \{a, b, c, d, e\}$$
$$I_2 = \{a, b, e\}$$
$$I_3 = \{x, y, z\}$$
$$I_4 = \{x, y, z, d\}$$

Consider a class supporting the first three sets.

$$|P| = 2, |Q| = 1 \Rightarrow \text{LCOM} = 1$$

Consider a class supporting all four sets.

$$|P| = 3, |Q| = 3 \Rightarrow \text{LCOM} = 0$$

**Figure 6.22** Extension of Chidamber and Kemerer's (1994) example for the calculation of LCOM.

**6.3.3.1  A New Measure for LCOM.**    As was noted earlier, there are two serious problems with the 1994 version of LCOM (and of course the 1991 version violates all known axioms of measurement giving all values equally zero!): (1) There are a large number of dissimilar examples, all of which will give a value of LCOM = 0 (which, in fairness, is noted in footnote 28 of Chidamber and Kemerer, 1994); hence, while a large value of LCOM suggests poor cohesion; a zero value does not necessarily indicate good cohesion. And (2) there is no guideline on the interpretation of any particular value. Is a value of 8 an indicator of medium, low, or abysmal cohesion? Indeed, in Figure 6.21, we indicated that such a value might belong to a class requiring splitting (abysmal cohesion—Figure 6.21(a)) or to a fairly cohesive class (Figure 6.21(b)).

This suggests that (1) the requirements for LCOM (and indeed any other measure) *must* include the ability to give values across the full range and not for any specific value (in the foregoing a preferred value of zero) to have a higher probability of attainment than any other, all other things being equal, and (2) the measure must give values that can be uniquely interpreted in terms of cohesion. Henderson-Sellers *et al.* (1995b) suggest that a better LCOM measure should have values on a percentage range; in other words, consider the notion of "perfect cohesion" and then present any particular datum as a fraction/percentage of that perfect value.

In the following, consider a set of $m$ methods accessing a total of $a$ data/attributes. Perfect cohesion is considered to be when all methods access all attributes. For this we expect our new LCOM, call it LCOM*, to have a (fractional) value of 0. At the opposite end of the spectrum, consider that each method only accesses a single variable. In this case, we expect LCOM* = 1 (and, of course, $m = a$).

Consider a set of methods $\{M_i\}$ $(i = 1, \ldots, m)$ accessing a set of attributes $\{A_j\}$ $(j = 1, \ldots, a)$. Let the number of attributes accessed by each method, $M_i$, be written as $\alpha(M_i)$ and the number of methods which access each datum be $\mu(A_j)$. Henderson-Sellers *et al.* (1995b) propose that the simplest metric from a counting viewpoint that satisfies these criteria is

$$\text{LCOM*} = \frac{\left(\frac{1}{a}\sum_{j=1}^{a}\mu(A_j)\right) - m}{1 - m} \tag{6.24}$$

Not only are the values easier to calculate, but this second version assigns a similar value for cases (a) and (b)—the case for splitting—of unity indicating extreme lack of cohesion.

**6.3.3.2  Coherence.**    Another approach to cohesion is proposed by Durnota and Mingins (1993). Basing their approach on the concept that "a class is coherent if the methods work together to carry out a single, identifiable purpose," they identify the set of method calls that is recursively extended to the set of $n$-calls within a specified visibility boundary. As well as the similarity between methods (as defined earlier), they define the co-response of two methods with visibility boundary B as the common set of methods called from the two methods; in other words, similarity between methods is considered from a pairwise viewpoint. This co-response is defined as

$$\sigma_B^+(m, n) = \text{calls}_B^+(m) \cap \text{calls}_B^+(n) \tag{6.25}$$

They suggest that the larger the co-response set compared to the total number of distinct methods called from the two methods, the greater is the degree of cohesion. This gives them the *coherence distance*

$$d_B(m, n) = \frac{\left|\sigma_B^+(m, n)\right|}{\left|\text{calls}_B^+(\{m, n\})\right|} \tag{6.26}$$

where $0 \le d_B(m, n) \le 1$. These coherence distances are then represented in a distance matrix and used to perform cluster analysis, which then permits the authors to draw a dendogram (Figure 6.23). For total dissimilar methods (Figure 6.24(a)), the side branches occur at the top of the dendogram and for totally similar methods (Figure 6.24(b)), they are at the base.

An interval-weighted coherence is then calculated (Figure 6.25) as the sum of the lengths raised to the power of the number of clusters within that interval. The authors comment that one problem with this metric is that it is unevenly distributed across its range (which is the closed interval [0, 1]) and that this results in the need often to calculate a large number of significant digits to discriminate between dendograms. Data from several Eiffel projects were analyzed using this technique by Mingins *et al.* (1993) to identify used versus unused variables as well as features renamed or redefined.

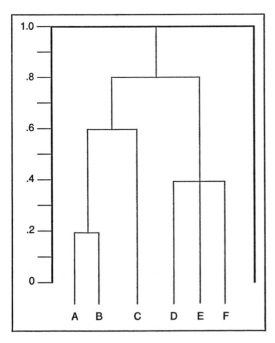

**Figure 6.23** A sample dendrogram (after Durnota and Mingins, 1993).

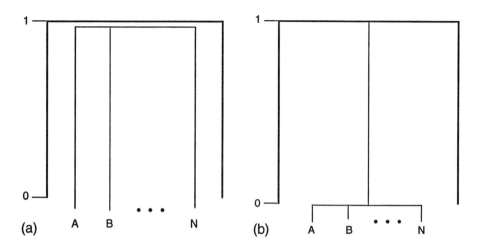

**Figure 6.24**    Dendrogram for (a) totally dissimilar methods and (b) totally similar methods (after Durnota and Mingins, 1993).

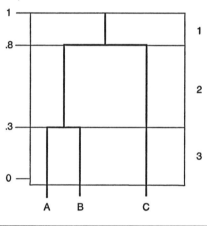

| interval | $l$ | $n$ | weight | | |
|---|---|---|---|---|---|
| [0, 0.3] | 0.3 | 3 | $0.3^3$ | = | 0.027 |
| [0.3, 0.8] | 0.5 | 2 | $0.5^2$ | = | 0.25 |
| [0.8, 1] | 0.2 | 1 | | | |
| | | | sum | = | 0.277 |
| | | | $c_{iw}$ | = | 1 - 0.277 |
| | | | | = | 0.723 |

$l$ = interval length
$n$ = number of branches

**Figure 6.25**    Dendrogram partitioned for defining the interval-weighted coherence (after Durnota and Mingins, 1993)

**TABLE 6.7** Evaluation of the Chidamber and Kemerer (1991) metrics against seven of the Weyuker (1988) axioms (after Chidamber and Kemerer, 1991)

| Metric | 1 | 3 | 4 | 5 | 6 | 7 | 9 |
|--------|---|---|---|---|---|---|---|
| WMC | Y | Y | Y | Y | Y | N | N |
| DIT | Y | Y | Y | N | Y | N | N |
| NOC | Y | Y | Y | Y | Y | N | N |
| RFC | Y | Y | Y | Y | N | N | N |
| LCOM | Y | Y | Y | Y | Y | N | N |
| CBO | Y | Y | Y | Y | Y | N | N |

### 6.3.4 Some Applications of Weyuker's Axioms and Measurement Theory

Chidamber and Kemerer (1991) evaluate their six metrics against seven of Weyuker's axioms (Table 6.7). It is interesting and perhaps not surprising to note that all six metrics fail to satisfy properties 7 (statement order) and 9 (summing complexities)—order within OO is of little import (see property 7) while many metrics (e.g., WMC) build on traditional metrics (e.g., cyclomatic complexity), which themselves do not satisfy property 9 (Table 4.5). Chidamber and Kemerer also note that the other violations (properties 5 and 6) were of those properties questioned by Zuse (1990) and Fenton (1991)—see Section 4.3.2. Chidamber and Kemerer (1993) note that property 7, which deals with permutations, may be totally inappropriate for OO designs since ordering of services within an O/C has no relevance (Cherniavsky and Smith, 1991). While accepting this to be in general true, we would raise the comprehension concern related to "views" (Bielak and McKim, 1993) and "interface contracts" (Low et al., 1995). We would argue that, at the code level, grouping of features/methods along such semantic lines, could, arguably, enhance readability, and hence comprehension, especially in the context of maintenance. Empirical studies are lacking to confirm or reject this hypothesis.

Zuse (1994) applies measurement theory ideas to the six metrics of Chidamber and Kemerer (1994) by defining a concatenation operator that is the intersection of the sets of instance variables and methods. Since the classes being concatenated are likely to possess both subclasses and superclasses, the property of $\mu(A \circ B) = \mu(A) + \mu(B)$ in general does not hold. Zuse notes that this means that such measures are not valid on a ratio scale "because many object-oriented software measures do not assume an extensive structure" (Zuse, 1994). For example, DIT is valid only on an ordinal scale; NOC is not additive since there may be "children." In fact, Zuse suggests that none of these six OO metrics is valid on a ratio scale and thus cannot be used as predictors.

## 6.4 RECOMMENDED METRICS SUITES

Proposals to date for commercially collectible OO metrics have been minimal. These can be briefly summarized as follows:

TABLE 6.8    Items recommended by Lorenz (1993) as useful design metrics

| Metric | Item Being Measured |
|---|---|
| 1. Average method size | Size |
| 2. Average number of methods per class | Size |
| 3. Average number of instance variables per class | Coupling |
| 4. Class hierarchy nesting level (or DIT) | Size |
| 5. Number of subsystem/subsystem relationship | Coupling |
| 6. Number of class/class relationships within each subsystem | Cohesion and coupling |
| 7. Instance variable usage | Semantic complexity |
| 8. Average number of comment lines | Cognitive complexity |
| 9. Number of problem reports per class | Process |
| 10. Number of times class is reused | Process |
| 11. Number of classes and methods thrown away | Process |

- Eleven metrics proposed by Lorenz (1993) as design metrics (Table 6.8). Some of these address measurements for size, others for coupling, others for process, and so on.

- Six metrics proposed by Chidamber and Kemerer (1991); mostly focused on size, coupling, and cohesion (Table 6.9). Chidamber and Kemerer (1991) are careful to ground each of their six proposed metrics in measurement theory and to incorporate the ontological ideas of Bunge (1977). This allows them to present mathematical definitions of some of their measures. However, reliance on Bunge's ontology is questioned by Graham (1995a, p. 410), who notes that this philosophy is atomistic and assumes objects to be defined by their properties, whereas in object technology *all* an object's properties can change without altering the object's inherent identity.

Their first measure, WMC, uses equation (6.10) where all the weightings are unity. As noted earlier, this gives, simply, WMC = number of methods. They argue that O/Cs with a large number of methods "are likely to be more application-specific, limiting the possibility of reuse." It is unclear (e.g., Graham, 1995a) how weightings should be quantified (if nonunity)—presumably some version of control flow complexity.

Deeper inheritance trees lead to lower-level O/Cs using directly ancestral methods. Thus, from a maintenance viewpoint, complexity is likely to be increased. At the same time, Chidamber and Kemerer (1991) propose that it is better to have

TABLE 6.9    Metrics proposed by Chidamber and Kemerer (1991)

| | Metric | Item Being Measured |
|---|---|---|
| 1. WMC | Weighted methods per class | Size and complexity |
| 2. DIT | Depth of inheritance tree | Size |
| 3. NOC | Number of children | Size/coupling/cohesion |
| 4. CBO | Coupling between objects | Coupling |
| 5. RFC | Response for class | Communication and complexity |
| 6. LCOM | Lack of cohesion in methods | Internal cohesion |

depth than breadth in the inheritance hierarchy so that this NOC measure, which counts the number of immediate subclasses, has larger values for poorer designs.

CBO counts class/class connectivity other than by inheritance. It is thus a measure of fan-out, that is, number of "collaborators." Systems in which one class has a high CBO count and all other classes have a value zero indicates a structured not an object-oriented design, with a main "driver" class (Kreindler and Mickel, 1993, personal communication). Many classes with a large CBO value may (but not necessarily) indicate that the designer have been overly enthusiastic (Kolewe, 1993) and the classes are of too fine a granularity.

RFC measures both internal and external communication. It represents the number of message paths but does not discriminate between two messages sent to the same method but from different parts of the class (Figure 6.26).

Chidamber and Kemerer's (1991) final metric in their proposed suite is the lack of cohesion of methods. As discussed, this is intended to be an internal measure of cohesion. A high value for this metric should reflect that the methods in the class are not really related to each other nor, therefore, to a single overall abstraction. A high value therefore should suggest that the class should be split into two or more classes. However, its definition is ambiguous (Graham, 1995a) and differs between the 1991 definition and that in Chidamber and Kemerer (1994). A new revision to the LCOM measure is to be found on page 147. See also Henderson-Sellers *et al.* (1995b).

The relation of these six metrics to elements in the design process is shown in Table 6.10 using Booch's (1991) terminology. Chidamber and Kemerer (1991) also evaluated their measures against Weyuker's (1988) axioms (see Chapter 4, Table 4.5).

These six metrics were used in an empirical study of two companies, the details of which are discussed in detail in Chapter 8.

• Interestingly, this same metrics suite (Chidamber and Kemerer, 1991) was used for a different purpose in the empirical study of Sharble and Cohen (1993). In this study the suite of six metrics was supplemented by three other measures: (1) weighted attributes per class (WAC), (2) number of tramps (NOT) defined as the

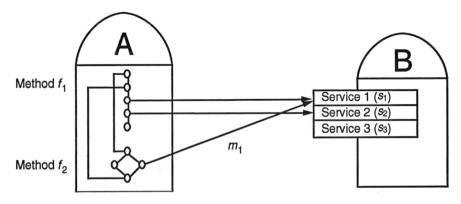

**Figure 6.26**   Two methods in class A ($f_1$ and $f_2$) access the same service class B ($s_1$).

TABLE 6.10    Relation of the six metrics of Chidamber and Kemerer (1991)
to the design process (after Chidamber and Kemerer, 1991)

| Metric | Object Definition | Object Attributes | Object Communication |
|--------|-------------------|-------------------|----------------------|
| WMC    | Y                 | Y                 |                      |
| DIT    | Y                 |                   |                      |
| NOC    | Y                 |                   |                      |
| RFC    |                   | Y                 | Y                    |
| CBO    |                   |                   | Y                    |
| LCOM   |                   | Y                 |                      |

total number of extraneous parameters in the signature of the methods (a metric that should of course always be zero), and (3) and violations of the law of Demeter (VOD). In this comparison of two OO development methods, they evaluated two contrasting designs of a brewery control system (Table 6.11). Based on their attribution of these nine metrics as either relating to class, interaction or inheritance, they portrayed these data in a graphical format (Figure 6.1). The polygonal areas thus formed not only give an easy interpretation to Sharble and Cohen's (1993) research hypothesis testing, but provides, more generically, an easy-to-understand visualization of any coherent set of OO metrics.

• Three coupling complexity metrics and an interface metric proposed by Henry and Li (1992). These are, respectively, coupling through inheritance (= depth of inheritance tree + number of children, i.e., number of subclasses), message-passing coupling, data abstraction coupling, and number of methods per class (Table 6.12).

• Li and Henry (1993) consider three groups of metrics: five of the six proposed by Chidamber and Kemerer (1991), a suite of additional metrics, and some OO size metrics. They assess DIT, NOC, RFC, LCOM, and WMC in the first group, but not CBO. In the second group they introduce (1) message-passing coupling (MPC), which measures the "number of send statements defined in a class"; (2) the coupling through data abstraction coupling (DAC), which is defined as "the number of ADTs defined in a class"; and (3) the number of local methods (NOM), which they use as an interface metric. (These authors use the word "local" to mean those offered locally by the class under consideration (Li, 1994, personal communication) that is, the number of methods often described as public methods). Finally, Li and Henry (1993) propose two size metrics: SIZE1 = number of semicolons in a class (actually the

TABLE 6.11    Comparison of two versions (a data-driven design
and a responsibility-driven design) of the same system
using nine selected metrics (after Sharble and Cohen, 1993)

|                             | WMC | DIT | NOC | CBO | RFC | LCOM | WAC | NOT | VOD |
|-----------------------------|-----|-----|-----|-----|-----|------|-----|-----|-----|
| Data-driven design          | 130 | 21  | 19  | 42  | 293 | 64   | 64  | 0   | 40  |
| Responsibility-driven design| 71  | 19  | 13  | 20  | 127 | 21   | 44  | 0   | 0   |

TABLE 6.12    Current research (adapted from Henry and Li, 1992)

---

**Coupling Complexity**
Coupling through inheritance: DIT (depth of inheritance tree) + NOC (number of children)
Coupling through message passing: MPC = message-passing coupling
Coupling through data abstraction: DAC = data abstraction coupling

**Interface Metric**
NOM = number of methods per class

---

number of noncommented lines of code: Li, 1994, personal communication), and SIZE2 = number of attributes + number of local methods (i.e., the number of services in the interface). They then evaluate these three sets of metrics in relationship to maintenance data that had been collected. They found little usefulness for SIZE1 and SIZE2 and concluded that it was possible to predict maintenance effort in OO systems using a simple additive regression equation with eight independent variables (DIT + NOC + MPC + RFC + LCOM + DAC + WMC + NOM).

- A large number of metrics are proposed by Tegarden and Sheetz (1992) for the variable level, for the object level, for the method level, and for the system level (Table 6.13).

TABLE 6.13    Major proposed metrics of Tegarden and Sheetz (1992)

---

| **Variable Level** | **System Level** |
|---|---|
| Fan-In | Number of classes |
| Fan-Out | Number of abstract classes |
| Fan-Down | Number of concrete classes |
| Polymorphism | Max depth/breadth of inheritance hierarchy |
| **Method Level** | Max depth/breadth of uses hierarchy |
| Fan-In/fan-out/fan-down | Max depth/breadth of message graph |
| Method size (LOC) | Number of inheritance/uses links |
| Message path length | Number of unique messages sent between objects |
| Polymorphism | Number of root objects |
| Arguments passed to the method | Average/max fan-in/fan-out |
| Arguments passed by the method | Average/max fan-up/fan-down |
| **Object Level** | |
| Fan-In/fan-out | |
| Used-by/uses | |
| Arguments passed by object (methods) | |
| Arguments passed to object (methods) | |
| Fan-up/fan-down | |
| Object-to-root depth | |
| Object-to-leaf depth | |
| Number of local variables/methods | |
| Number of inherited variables/methods | |
| Number of subclass variables/methods | |
| Average/max path length | |

---

- Rajaraman and Lyu (1992a or 1992b)[4] focus on coupling. They define a method-coupling metric (MC), as the number of local references per method. These values are then grossed up for each class to give a value for the class-coupling metric, CC and averaged to give the average method coupling, AMC. They also introduce class inheritance-related coupling (CIC) and class noninheritance-related coupling (CNIC), where CC = CIC + CNIC. Thus, their suite of coupling metrics is not orthogonal and does not differentiate clearly between inheritance and client/server effects on structural complexity, which is a different approach to many other metrics suites.

- Based on the foregoing suggestions, Henderson-Sellers and Edwards (1994) recommend a list of nine quantitative measures (Table 6.14) plus the qualitative evaluation of the semantic cohesion of each class.

- Kolewe (1993) endorses Chidamber and Kemerer's (1991) metrics, five of which he describes as being at the class or interclass level and only one (NOC) at the system level (although it could be argued that class coupling and DIT, which require more than one class to exist, would be better described as a system-level metric). At this larger scale, he adds (1) number of class hierarchies, (2) number of class clusters (defined analogously to LCOM at the method level), and (3) association complexity, using equation (6.17). Kolewe describes some observations on moderate-sized C++ programs that "classes with class-coupling values greater than about 7 account for most problems, as do classes with a response for a class values greater than about 50."

- Brito e Abreu (1994) suggests that a suite of six metrics is needed. Some of these are original (i.e., not included in any of the other sets described here): attribute hiding factor, method inheritance factor, attribute inheritance factor, coupling factor, clustering factor, polymorphism factor, and reuse factor. It is suggested that upper and/or lower limits are set for each of these six metrics—determining those values has yet to be accomplished. This set is relatively immature but is likely to make a significant contribution to the literature in the future.

- In SOMA, Graham (1995a) builds on the methodology of object-oriented software engineering systems (MOSES) metrics (Henderson-Sellers and Edwards, 1994)

TABLE 6.14   **Recommendations of Henderson-Sellers and Edwards (1994)**

Collect at least the following:
- Fan-out (coupling)
- Average and standard deviation of the number of methods per class
- Average and standard deviation of the method size
- Average and standard deviation of the cyclomatic complexity of the methods
- Mean and maximum depths of inheritance hierarchies
- Reuse ratio, $U$
- Specialization ratio, $S$
- Time spent in development (effort)
- Time spent on generalization

---

[4]The two papers are in essence identical.

and the work of Chidamber and Kemerer (1991) and introduces some new metrics emphasizing rulesets (equation (6.9)). In addition, Graham (1995a) suggests the collection of data on fan-ins and fan-outs; structure depths (a generalized form of DIT); the numbers of concrete and abstract classes; and the number of interface, domain, and application objects incorporated into the project. A second set of metrics (for tasks) includes the number of external objects in the context model, the weighted complexity of each task, fan-ins and fan-outs, structure depths, and the number of atomic tasks (the leaf nodes of the task tree). Finally, he suggests the possible utility of collecting information on the homology of usage structures, cyclomatic complexity of methods at the coding stage, and the number of interface objects during the logical design stage. He also stresses the lack of empirical work in this whole area.

• In an empirical evaluation of the difficulty of reskilling traditional programmers into OO habits, Miller *et al.* (1995) developed a tool to count average number of methods per class, average number of instance variables per class, average method size per class, average class complexity, average method complexity (measured by $V(G)$ following Graham (1994)), average number of children, maximum DIT per program, together with two overloading metrics not discussed elsewhere: average instances of (1) function overloading and (2) operator overloading per class. Interestingly, they found statistically significant (at the 5% level) differences for all metrics except average method size and average method complexity. Since methods are essentially procedural in nature (in this C/C++ environment), that is perhaps understandable.

• Lorenz and Kidd's (1994) suite of metrics is certainly the most extensive. They list over 30 different product/design metrics (Table 6.15), most of which have been discussed.

**TABLE 6.15    Lorenz and Kidd's (1994) suite of design metrics**

| | |
|---|---|
| *Method Size* | *Method Inheritance* |
| Number of message sends | Number of methods overridden by a subclass |
| Number of statements | Number of methods inherited by a subclass |
| Lines of code | Number of methods added in a subclass |
| Average method size | Specialization index |
| *Method Internals* | *Class Internals* |
| Method complexity | Class cohesion |
| Strings of message sends | Global usage |
| *Class Size* | Average number of parameters per method |
| Number of public instance methods per class | Use of friend functions |
| Number of instance methods per class | Percentage of function-oriented code |
| Average number of instance methods per class | Average number of comment lines per method |
| Number of instance variables per class | Average number of commented methods |
| Average number of instance variables per class | Number of problem reports per class or contract |
| Number of class methods per class | *Class Externals* |
| Number of class variables per class | Class coupling |
| *Class inheritance* | Number of times a class is reused |
| Class hierarchy nesting level | Number of classes/methods thrown away |
| Number of abstract classes | |
| Use of multiple inheritance | |

## 6.5 CONCLUSIONS AND RECOMMENDATIONS

Building on the MDF (Section 3.4) and the discussions in this chapter, here we go systematically through the various perspectives: inside a class, external at the class level (i.e., the specification or interface), system-level (but ignoring relationships), system-level relationships (excluding inheritance), and inheritance coupling (Henderson-Sellers, 1995a).

### 6.5.1 Inside a Class

A coded class can be considered to contain $n$ public methods (those that appear as services in the interface) and, in some languages, $m$ public attributes. There are also $r$ private methods and $s$ private attributes. Each method is a piece of procedural code that may or may not send messages to other objects (see Section 6.5.4). For each of these $n + r$ methods, we can calculate a control flow complexity. This can be accomplished by local application of the cyclomatic complexity, $V(G)$ or $V_{LI}(G)$. Since there is a $V(G)$ for each method, there must be $n + r$ such values. (Note: These metrics are only collectible once the design has been implemented, i.e., the code exists.)

*For each class,* we can therefore count or calculate

- A distribution of $V(G)$ ($n + r$ values)
- A median value for $V(G)$
- A mean value for $V(G)$ (if it can be shown that $V(G)$ is on an interval or ratio scale—see Zuse, 1990)
- A standard deviation for $V(G)$ (if it can be shown that $V(G)$ is on an interval or ratio scale—see Zuse, 1990)
- A class total $V(G)$—this is one interpretation of WMC of Chidamber and Kemerer (1991)

As well as cyclomatic complexity, we could characterize each method by its size (assuming that a consistent definition for size is used). This gives $n + r$ values in the class for method size.

*For each class,* we can therefore count or calculate

- A distribution of method size ($n + r$ values)
- A median value for method size
- A mean value for method size
- A standard deviation for method size
- A class total method size—this is labeled TMS

*For each class,* we can also do a straightforward count of

- A class total number of methods (public, private, and, in C++, protected)
- A class total number of attributes = NOA

These values give one way of representing overall *class size, $S_C$,* as

* A weighted calculation of method and attribute sizes = NOA + TMS
* An unweighted calculation of method and attribute sizes = NOA + NOM

We can also count the number of preconditions and postconditions. For reliable software contracting (Meyer, 1992), each method should have both a pre- and a postcondition. Thus the ratios of (number of preconditions/number of methods) and (number of postconditions/number of methods) should both tend to unity. Small values imply less reliability and low robustness.

The final structural "complexity" measure internal to a class is the LCOM metric of Chidamber and Kemerer (1991)—as corrected by Henderson-Sellers *et al.* (1995). Again this is a value that can be calculated *for each class.*

One other metric is needed purely for C++ classes, that is, the number of declared "friend" classes, which adds structural (and probably psychological) complexity to the interaction. We class this as internal rather than external for obvious reasons, although it is arguably better categorized as a component of inter-O/C coupling (Section 6.5.4).

### 6.5.2 External at the Class Level

External to the class, we see only the interface or the specification. We can characterize this as a total number of services, some of which are queries and some of which are commands (Figure 6.27). We see, from the outside, no indication of (internal) size or complexity. We can thus count

* Number of commands for $i$th class, $c_i$
* Number of queries for $i$th class, $q_i$

We might alternatively prefer to weight these with the number of arguments by adding one for each argument to the unweighted count; that is,

* Number of weighted commands, $c_i' = (c + \sum_{j=1}^{c} C_{arglist_j})_i$
* Number of weighted queries, $q_i' = (q + \sum_{k=1}^{q} C_{arglist_k})_i$

where $C_{arglist_j}$ is the cardinality of the argument list for the $j$th service

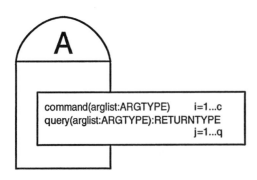

command(arglist:ARGTYPE)        i=1...c
query(arglist:ARGTYPE):RETURNTYPE
                                j=1...q

**Figure 6.27**    A class offers a number of services in its interface. These may be queries (which return an object) and commands (which don't).

### 6.5.3 System Level but Ignoring Relationships

At this level, we simply gross up some of the measures we have already identified. A first, simple measure is

- Total number of classes in system, $C_S$. This is an extremely rough measure, but one can say that a system with 1000 classes in it is likely to be bigger (in all sense of the word) than one with only 20 classes.

We can then look at systemwide averages, assuming we have the appropriate interval or ratio scale, derived from the lower-level measures:

- A mean value for the number of commands per class across the system, given simply as $\frac{1}{C_s} \sum_{i=1}^{C_s} c_i$
- A standard deviation for $c_i$
- A mean value for the number of queries per class across the system, given simply as $\frac{1}{C_s} \sum_{i=1}^{C_s} q_i$
- A standard deviation for $q_i$
- A mean value for the number of weighted commands per class across the system, given simply as $\frac{1}{C_s} \sum_{i=1}^{C_s} c_i'$
- A standard deviation for $c_i'$
- A mean value for the number of weighted queries per class across the system, given simply as $\frac{1}{C_s} \sum_{i=1}^{C_s} q_i'$
- A standard deviation for $q_i'$
- Average class size $= \frac{1}{C_s} \sum_{i=1}^{C_s} S_{c_i}$
- Standard deviation for $S_{C_i}$
- Distribution of class size, $S_{C_i}$
- Average number of methods per class $= \frac{1}{C_s} \sum_{i=1}^{C_s} NOM_i$
- Standard deviation for $NOM_i$
- Distribution of class size, $NOM_i$

### 6.5.4 System-Level Relationships but Excluding Inheritance

Coupling is epitomized at both a design level where only a single client/server relationship between any pair of classes is considered. This is the CBO metric of Chidamber and Kemerer (1991) and the more detailed message passing metrics, discussed earlier, of Li and Henry (1993). Collaborators that require such connections are related to the declarations of ADTs within the class body and are thus also equivalent to Li and Henry's DAC metric. This measure, CBO or "design fan-out," is easily calculable from a design diagram. Since multiple objects from the same class will probably not add significantly (a hypothesis that has yet to be tested) to the psychological complexity of the class being measured, this design level metric can be done at the class level. Another way of thinking about this metric is simply as the "number of other classes referenced."

A useful insight into the "object-orientedness" of the design can be gained from the systemwide distribution of the class fan-out values. For example, we have already noted that for a system in which a single class has a very high fan-out and all the other classes have low or zero fan-outs, we really have a structured, not an OO, system (Kreindler and Mickel, 1993, personal communication). This also agrees with the guidelines of Wirfs-Brock *et al.* (1990) about ensuring that the total behavior is distributed fairly evenly across the system.

At the detailed design level, however, CBO is inadequate. The establishment of a connection between two O/Cs permits several services of the server O/C to be used. The sum of the services used across all the server O/Cs (i.e., the collobora-tors) gives a value for the metric NRM (number of remote methods). Of course, $NRM \geq CBO$. This leads to two further metrics: RFC and MPC. RFC is the sum of the number of local methods and the number of remote methods; that is,

- RFC = NLM + NRM (and is one of Chidamber and Kemerer's, 1991, six metrics)

However, RFC simply addresses the notion of "how many methods do I have access to from within the class in question." It does not make any statement regard-ing the frequency of use, from different parts of the class, of those methods. This can be addressed, for the external methods by MPC (the message-passing coupling of Li and Henry, 1993) and for the internal methods, to some degree, by $V(G)$.

As noted, friend classes should probably be counted separately, but the RFC count of a friend class will also reflect this "friendship."

### 6.5.5 Inheritance Coupling

Inheritance can be addressed initially by those metrics already proposed; al-though it should be noted that no one has yet seriously addressed, theoretically, the "complexity" introduced by the use of polymorphism. Thus, we have

- DIT = depth of each class in the hierarchy
- Max depth of inheritance tree
- Mean depth of inheritance tree
- $NOC_i$ = number of children for each class

which leads to

- Average NOC for the whole inheritance tree
- Standard distribution of NOC for the whole inheritance tree
- Distribution of NOC for the whole inheritance tree

(see the example in Figure 6.28).

Kolewe (1993) also suggests that the number of distinct inheritance hierarchies might reflect the number of broad domain foci within the system, although there seems little reason to start averaging the NOC values listed earlier (per hierarchy)

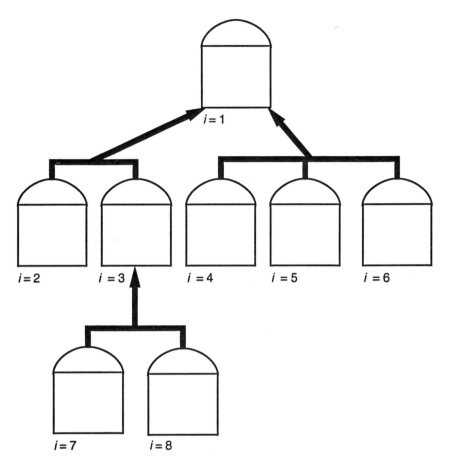

NOC(1) = 5
NOC(2) = 0 = NOC(4) = NOC(5) = NOC(6) = NOC(7) = NOC(8)
NOC(3) = 2

Average NOC = 7/8
  or 7/2 excluding leaf classes

**Figure 6.28**    Example values of NOC for an inheritance hierarchy.

across the whole system. Dvorak (1994) introduces the notion of conceptual entropy, which suggests that deeper hierarchies are less likely to be true specializations.

It is clear that further work on inheritance metrics is urgently required; for instance, to address the issues of renaming and redefinition, polymorphism in design as well as code, and genericity (which is grouped here under the general heading of inheritance although not strictly correctly so).

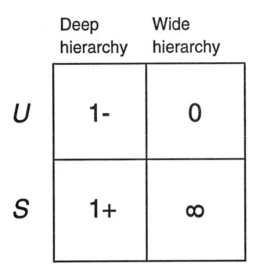

**Figure 6.29**   Extreme values of the reuse and specialization ratios ($U$ and $S$, respectively) for single inheritance structures.

Finally, the reuse metrics $U$ and $S$ are available:

- Reuse ratio, $U$, which gives an indication of developers inheriting from existing classes, is always less than 1. A value nearer 0 indicates a shallow, broad hierarchy (Figure 6.29).
- Specialization ratio, $S$, which also gives an indication of width (large values of $S$) additionally gives an indication (Figure 6.29) of the extent to which multiple inheritance is used since
- For a leafy (broad, shallow) structure, $S \gg 1$
- For lots of multiple inheritance, $S \ll 1$

Finally, some of these calculations are summarized in an example in Figure 6.30. Of the 13 classes, 10 are superclasses and 11 subclasses. Thus $U = {}^{10}\!/_{13} = 0.76$ and $S = {}^{11}\!/_{10} = 1.1$. There is thus significant reuse (review Figure 6.28), but it is still fairly linear, implying low use of specialization. The values of $NOC_i$ is ${}^{16}\!/_{13} = 1.25$ or ${}^{16}\!/_{10} = 1.6$ if the leaf nodes are excluded.

## 6.6 CHAPTER SUMMARY

In this chapter we have discussed the potential application of traditional metrics to object-oriented systems as well as the necessary object-oriented extensions. The format mirrors that of the traditional approaches discussed in Chapter 5: intermodule metrics versus module metrics. Module metrics are then discussed under the headings of semantic complexity and procedural complexity and procedural complexity is itself subdivided into size, logic structure, and "others." We also include a section on the application of the ideas of Chapter 4 to these OO metrics. Based on

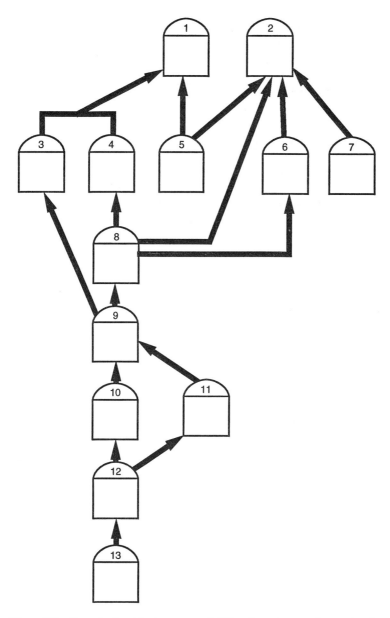

**Figure 6.30**  Example of an inheritance network. Values for various metrics are given in the text.

these discussions, we then summarize the technical features of the metrics in terms of suites that have been recommended in the literature.

While the focus is currently at the code level, being the simplest and most concrete to measure, it is vital that life cycle concerns are incorporated. This is especially true for object technology as a result of the incremental delivery style of the life-cycle model, a topic that is not addressed by any traditional metrics set. The subject of OO complexity metrics is in its infancy. We hope this chapter both offers guidelines to the technical aspects of setting up a metrics program as well as stimulating researchers to investigate this challenging area of OT. Managerial aspects of metrics programs are discussed in Chapter 8.

## 6.7 BIBLIOGRAPHIC DETAILS

Much of the work reported here comes from our own work, published in part in Henderson-Sellers and Edwards (1994) and Henderson-Sellers (1995a). Initial work was also presented at a number of international OO conferences in collaboration with David Monarchi of the University of Colorado and David Tegarden, currently at Virginia Tech.

# 7

# COGNITIVE
# COMPLEXITY MODEL[1]

## 7.1 INTRODUCTION

As we have seen, there is no accepted definition of software complexity. The *Macquarie Dictionary* defines the common meaning of complexity as "the state or quality of being complex," that is, "composed of interconnected parts" or "characterized by an involved combination of parts . . . an **obsessing notion**." This definition is intuitively appealing. It recognizes that complexity is a feature of an object being studied, but that the level of perceived complexity is dependent upon the person studying it. For example, a person unfamiliar with an object may find it far more difficult to understand than someone who has studied the object many times before. However, the definition has two deficiencies as a technical definition upon which to base research. The first is that it ignores the dependency of complexity on the task being performed. As Ross Ashby (quoted in Klir, 1985 p. 326) noted,

> . . . although all would agree that the brain is complex and a bicycle simple, one has also to remember that to a butcher the brain of a sheep is simple while a bicycle, if studied exhaustively . . . may present a very great quantity of significant detail.

The second problem with the definition is that it does not allow complexity to be operationalized as a measurable variable. The factors described as determining complexity are very general and therefore lack the specificity required for measurement.

---

[1]This chapter was contributed by S. N. Cant, D. R. Jeffery, and B. Henderson-Sellers.

It was probably with these problems in mind that Basili (1980) formulated his definition of "software complexity" as

> a measure of resources expended by a system [human or other] while interacting with a piece of software to perform a given task.

Although this definition addresses the two deficiencies in the dictionary definition, it may be too broad. As the dictionary definition indicates, complexity is usually regarded as arising out of some characteristic of the code, on which the task or function is being performed and therefore does not include characteristics of the programmer that affect resource use independently of the code. A suitable compromise may be the definition proposed by Curtis (1979, p. 102) and used throughout this book as an operational definition. He claimed that software complexity is

> a characteristic of the software interface which influences the resources another system will expend while interacting with the software.

This definition is broad enough to include characteristics of the software that interact with characteristics of the system carrying out the task, in such a way as to increase the level of resource use. However, it is not so broad as to include arbitrary characteristics of the programmer that affect his or her ability generally. This distinction is illustrated in Figure 7.1. The left and center areas cover those characteristics relevant to software complexity as defined in this paper.

The other advantage of Curtis's definition, which it shares with Basili's definition, is that complexity is measurable. If one includes the qualification that complexity is dependent on the task being performed, then the definition covers all the suggested ingredients of complexity. Therefore, the following definition will be adopted.

> The cognitive complexity of software refers to those characteristics of software that affect the level of resources used by a person performing a given task on it.

This chapter examines the complexity of software only in respect of tasks performed by programmers that involve analyzing code. The tasks for which this is appropriate are manifold, including maintaining, extending, and understanding code.

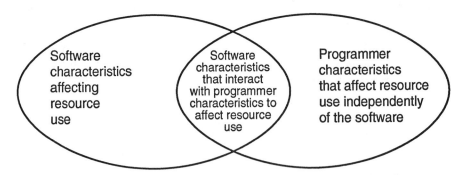

**Figure 7.1**   Characteristics relevant to cognitive complexity (after Cant *et al.*, 1995).

The cognition processes common to these tasks are essentially reading code (chunking) and searching through code (tracing) as discussed in the paragraphs that follow.

## 7.2 THEORETICAL APPROACHES TO COMPLEXITY

Cant *et al.* (1995) argued that the most appropriate approach for a model of *cognitive* complexity is to develop a framework based on research into the cognitive processes used by programmers in performing the relevant tasks. Such an approach has been endorsed by Curtis (1979), Davis (1984), and Kearney *et al.* (1986) among others.

Existing theoretical approaches to formulate such "complexity" metrics include the use of information theory from signal processing (e.g., Halstead, 1977; Mohanty, 1979; Davis and LeBlanc, 1988), approaches based on analogs with graph theory (e.g., McCabe, 1976), or on lattice theory (e.g., Harrison and Magel, 1981). Munson and Khoshgoftaar (1989) adopt a more inductive approach, using factor analysis. These, and other, approaches are summarized in Table 7.1.

TABLE 7.1    **Taxonomy of theoretical approaches taken in existing metrics**

| Theoretical Approach | Metric or related research |
|---|---|
| Information theoretic | Chen's (1978) MIN (nesting) |
| | Harrison's (1992) AICC |
| | Halstead's (1977) effort |
| | Ramamurthy and Melton's (1988) weighted pair |
| | Hansen's (1978) complexity pair—control flow and operators |
| | Davis and LeBlanc's (1988) entropy |
| | Woodfield *et al.*'s (1981b) logical module complexity |
| | Gannon *et al.*'s (1986) number of generic packages |
| Graph theoretic | McCabe's (1976) cyclomatic number, $V(G)$ |
| | Gill and Kemerer's (1991) complexity density |
| | Woodward *et al.*'s (1979) knots |
| | Myers' (1977) complexity interval |
| | Damerla and Shatz (1992) |
| | Gilb's (1977) logical complexity |
| | Harrison and Magel's (1981) scope ratio (nesting) |
| | Gaffney's (1979) jumps |
| | Adamov and Richter (1990) structural complexity |
| | Oviedo's (1980) branches |
| | Chen's (1978) MIN (nesting) |
| | Lakshmanan *et al.* (1991) |
| | Ramamurthy and Melton's (1988) weighted pair |
| | Hansen's (1978) complexity pair—control flow and operators |
| | McCabe and Butler's (1989) subtree complexity |
| | Tsai *et al.*'s (1986) data structure complexity |
| | Emerson's (1984) cohesion metric |
| | Nejmeh's (1988) NPATH complexity |
| | Fenton and Whitty's (1986) structural measures |
| | Prather's (1984) complexity metrics based on sequence, decisions and loops |
| | Henderson-Sellers and Tegarden's (1994a) $V_{LI}(G)$ cyclomatic metric |

*(continued)*

**TABLE 7.1    (Continued)**

| Theoretical Approach | Metric or related research |
|---|---|
| Graph theoretic (cont) | Piwowarski's (1982) nesting measure |
| | Henderson-Sellers et al.'s (1993a) product complexity |
| | Sagri's (1989) rated and operational complexity |
| Lattice theoretic | Harrison and Magel's (1981) scope number |
| Communication theory | Henry and Kafura's (1981) information flows |
| | Shepperd's (1990) information flows |
| | Bieman and Debnath's (1985) data dependency graph |
| Empirical | Tanik (1980) |
| | Troy and Zweben (1981) |
| Other | Harrison et al.'s (1982) span |
| | Munson and Khoshgoftaar's (1993) data structure complexity |
| | Basili and Turner's (1975) segment global usage pair |
| | Oviedo's (1980) reachability |
| | Munson and Khoshgoftaar's (1990) relative complexity |
| | Oviedo's (1980) weighted complexity |
| | Yau and Collofello's (1980) stability measure |
| | Tian and Zelkowitz (1992) |
| | McClure's (1978) program complexity analysis method |
| | Iyengar et al.'s (1982) logical complexity |
| Cognitive science | Atwood and Ramsey's (1978) propositional analysis |
| | Davis and LeBlanc's (1988) review measure |
| | Soloway et al.'s (1983) plan analysis |
| | Bastani's (1983) complexity model |

One feature common to all these approaches is that they begin with certain characteristics of the software and attempt to determine what affect they might have on the difficulty of the various programmer tasks. A more useful approach would be first to analyze the processes involved in programmer tasks, as well as the parameters that govern the effort involved in those processes. From this point one can then deduce, or at least make informed guesses, about which code characteristics will affect these parameters. In other words, it is necessary to start with the symptoms of complexity, which are all manifested in the mind, and then attempt to understand the processes that produce those symptoms. By doing so, we are more likely to discover the cause of complexity than if we simply examine the full range of possible causes, blindly searching for a determining factor.

## 7.3  COGNITIVE COMPLEXITY

To understand the cognitive complexity of software fully, the comprehension process and the limits on the capacity of the human mind must first be understood, and research from cognitive science will consequently be utilized significantly in this chapter. Evaluation of such cognitive processes enabled Cant *et al.* (1994, 1995) to formulate a new approach to software complexity metrics.

### 7.3.1 Architecture of the Mind

The mind is usually modeled by dividing it into activated (short-term) and long-term memory. The characteristics of short-term memory are that distraction causes forgetting of recently learned material after about 20–30 seconds (Tracz, 1979, p. 29; Sutcliffe, 1989, p. 26). Other simultaneous inputs or similar inputs impair recall; while recall is improved by presenting both a word and a picture together (Sutcliffe, 1989, p. 26). The limits on the language-based subcomponent of short-term memory are a relatively fast access time, a rapid loss of information unless refreshed (Sutcliffe, 1989, p. 27), and a capacity of $7 \pm 2$ chunks (Miller, 1956), although this capacity is reduced while performing difficult tasks (Kintsch, 1977). The rate of memory decay can be slowed down by mental rehearsal of the information, as we all know personally. Furthermore, the effective capacity of short-term memory is expanded by chunking, which involves abstracting recognized qualities from the information and storing the abstraction (in terms of a single symbol) instead of the complete information.

Long-term memory has "virtually unlimited" capacity, and memory loss appears to be largely a problem of retrieval (Tracz, 1979, p. 26). However, the factors that determine recall ability appear to be similar to those for short-term memory. Thus, pictures presented together with associated text tend to be remembered better than text alone. Furthermore, memory recall is retarded by extraneous "noise" but is enhanced by structure, particularly when the structure or its components already exist in long-term memory (Tracz, 1979; Sutcliffe 1989, pp. 28–33). The structure of knowledge in long-term memory and the process of chunking involved in comprehension (a subtask of debugging and extending) are intimately related.

### 7.3.2 The Cognitive Processes in Comprehension

Debate continues about the exact mental processes involved in debugging, extending, or simply understanding a section of code. The generally held view is that programmers *chunk* (Miller, 1956; Shneiderman and Mayer, 1979; Badre, 1982; Davis, 1984; Ehrlich and Soloway, 1984, p. 114), which involves recognizing sections of code and recording the presence of that section in short-term memory by means of a single reference or memory symbol. Chunking involves recognizing groups of statements (not necessarily sequential) and extracting from them information that is remembered as a single mental abstraction. These chunks are then further chunked together into larger chunks and so on, forming a multileveled, aggregated structure over several layers of abstraction (somewhat akin to a layered object model). However, there is also evidence that programmers perform a type of *tracing*. This involves scanning quickly through a program, either forward or backward, in order to identify relevant chunks. (For example, Weiser, 1981, and, later, Bieman and Ott, 1994, examined "slicing," which includes tracing backward to ascertain the determinants of a set of variables at a point in a program.) Tracing may be required to allow knowledge to be acquired about certain variables or functions that are scattered throughout a program. These two processes, of chunking and tracing, both have implications for software complexity. Furthermore, both processes are involved in the three programmer tasks of understanding, modifying, and debugging.

Shneiderman and Mayer (1979) suggest that the chunking process involves utilizing two types of knowledge: semantic and syntactic. Semantic knowledge includes generic programming concepts from structures as basic as loops to more complex concepts such as sorting algorithms. This semantic knowledge is stored in a way which is relatively independent of specific programming languages. Furthermore, the information is systematically organized in a multileveled structure so that related concepts are aggregated into a single concept at a higher level of abstraction. Syntactic knowledge is specific to particular languages and allows semantic structures, implemented in those languages, to be recognized. By chunking, syntactic knowledge is used to convert the code into semantic knowledge, which is then stored as a multileveled representation of the program in memory. In a critique of this model, Gilmore and Green (1984, p. 463) suggest that recognition of semantic constructs may, to some extent, be dependent upon syntactic aspects of its presentation.

Ehrlich and Soloway (1984) propose a more comprehensive model of chunking based on "control flow plans" and "variable plans"—a model adopted in this chapter. Control plans describe control flow structures, while variable plans rely on a range of features common to variables with particular roles. Examples of such roles include countervariables and variables in which user input is stored.

### 7.3.3 Contingency Model of Programmer Tasks

In the range of tasks performed by a programmer, it is often necessary to locate the required chunk before comprehension can begin. A number of models of the various problem-solving tasks performed by programmers on programs have incorporated this process of tracing. Tracing, like chunking, has a large impact on complexity.

A broad model of programmer problem solving suggested by Green et al. (1981, pp. 223–224) takes into account a wider variety of tasks performed by programmers. To answer "sequential questions" (concerning the order of events), a programmer must work forward, possibly chunking, from the given point. However, "circumstantial questions" (concerning the conditions required for a particular action to take place) are resolved by finding a "signpost" (i.e., some point in the program that directly causes an action under certain conditions) and working backward from that point. Although usually related to debugging, tracing backward may also be required for both understanding and modifying. In particular, attempting to resolve a variable dependency while reading code, a programmer may have to trace backward finding references to the variable until the "variable plan" is understood and/or the determinants of its value ascertained. Most procedural languages tend to be "asymmetrical" so that it is simple to trace forward, but difficult to trace backward (Green et al., 1981, pp. 223–224).

In the rest of this chapter, the term "tracing" will be used to refer to the process of searching through code to identify (but not comprehend) relevant chunks. Note that the term "chunking" will be used to refer to the process of comprehending those chunks.

## 7.4 A NEW GENERAL MODEL

In this section a comprehensive model of programmer problem solving is proposed (Cant *et al.*, 1995), which involves a strong intertwining of the chunking and tracing processes. When a programmer is primarily chunking, there are control and variable dependencies that, to be resolved, require that the programmer perform a certain amount of tracing forward or backward to find the relevant sections of code. Having found that code, programmers will once again chunk to comprehend it. Conversely, when programmers are primarily tracing, they will need to chunk to understand the effect of the identified code fragments. For example, they may need to analyze an assignment statement to determine its effect, or they may need to analyze a control structure to understand how it interacts with the assignment statements contained in it, to create certain effects.

Keeping the interaction of these processes in mind, we can define an incremental model to describe the three programmer tasks of understanding, modifying and debugging based on chunking and tracing. This model appears in Table 7.2. The effects of chunking and tracing difficulty on complexity can be graphically demonstrated by modeling the various programmer tasks as "landscapes" (Figure 7.2). The markers, at a single level, delineate each chunk. For example in Figure 7.2, at the top level, there is a single chunk visible, delineated by the two markers ($A$ and $B$); at the second level, there are two chunks delineated by the two pairs of markers ($C$, $D$ and $D$, $E$); and at the lowest level, there is a single chunk: $F$, $G$. Note that although the chunk $CD$ is interrupted by a lower-level chunk, its integrity remains as a result of its semantic integrity. The complexity of the top-level chunk is thus represented by the sum of the two line segments $Ax_1$ and $x_4B$; the overall system complexity being visualized by the total distance between the end points of the chunk: $A$ and $B$.

While reading an upper-level chunk, a dependency requires that the programmer suspend reading of the original code segment because of the need to undertake tracing to understand fully the chunk currently being analyzed. The "vertical drop" (e.g., $x_1C$) represents visually the work required in *tracing* the relevant code section. The length of time and amount of work required to resolve the dependency is a function of the aggregate depth of the dependency "valley" and the aggregate breadth

TABLE 7.2    The incremental model of programming tasks

---

**Understanding**
   Chunking forward for comprehension.
   Tracing to find related chunks to comprehend control and variable plans used in the immediate chunk.
**Modifying**
   Understanding to permit modification plus tracing forward to identify ripple effects.
   Chunking to understand variable references and associated control structures that contribute to change propagation.
**Debugging**
   Tracing backward to diagnose faults.
   Chunking to understand variable definitions and related control structures that determine the values of variables related to the faults. Modifying to correct fault.

---

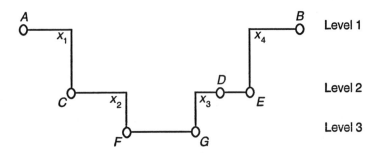

**Figure 7.2** Landscape model of program comprehension.
*Source:* Cant, S. N., Henderson-Sellers, B., and Jeffery, D. R., 1994. Application of cognitive complexity metrics to object-oriented programs, *J. Object-Oriented Programming,* 7(4), 52–63.

of the dependency "valley." The total *depth* of the "nested valleys" depends on the length of the chain of dependencies that must be traced to satisfy the programmer's inquiry and the difficulty of performing the tracing involved in each link of the chain. In addition, the number of "steps" involved indicates the number of chunks that need to be considered. The total *breadth* of the "nested valleys" is determined by the effort required to understand each chunk in the dependency chain.

For example, Figure 7.3(a) illustrates the type of landscape that might represent the tracing of a chain of variable dependencies, either backward or forward. In contrast, Figure 7.3(b) illustrates the type of landscape that might represent reading a series of nested chunks. Note that the first subchunk in Figure 7.3(b) involves significant tracing. This could represent a called module, for example. The lowest subchunk involves almost no tracing (the minimal drop shown is to indicate that it is a nested chunk rather than a sequential chunk). This chunk is embedded within its immediate superchunk. For example, it could represent a loop nested within a module.

In mathematical terms, the difficulty of solving a programming inquiry focused on the $i$th chunk is given by the complexity, $C_i$. This is the sum of the difficulty of understanding the immediate ($i$th) chunk, $R_i$, and the difficulty in moving from the original top level (the whole program) down to the current ($i$th) chunk. That difficulty occurs from both chunking and tracing, summed over all the levels between the top level and the current chunk (as seen in Figure 7.2). For example, in Figure 7.2, to understand chunk $FG$ ($R_i$), we need to understand chunk $CD$ ($C_{CD}$) and to trace from $CD$ to $FG$ ($T_{CD}$ represented by "depth" $x_2F$ or $x_3G$). Recursively, then, to understand $CD$ we need to also understand $AB$ ($C_{AB}$) and trace from $AB$ to $CD$, namely, $x_1C$ ($T_{AB}$). Thus, total complexity related to understanding $FG$ is represented by

$$C_i = R_i + C_{CD} + T_{CD} + C_{AB} + T_{AB} \qquad (7.1)$$

Generalizing this over the full set of chunks, denoted by $N$, on which the $i$th chunk is directly dependent for a given task

(a) Tracing a variable dependency

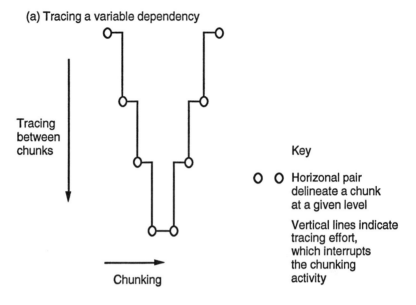

Tracing
between
chunks

Key

O  O  Horizonal pair
delineate a chunk
at a given level

Vertical lines indicate
tracing effort,
which interrupts
the chunking
activity

Chunking

(b) Tracing a series of nested chunks

Tracing
between
chunks

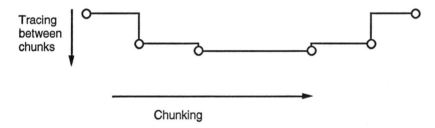

Chunking

**Figure 7.3**   Landscape for a variable dependency compared with that for a series of nested chunks (after Cant *et al.*, 1995).

$$C_i = R_i + \sum_{j \in N} C_j + \sum_{j \in N} T_j \qquad (7.2)$$

where $T_j$ is the difficulty of tracing a particular dependency.

Clearly equation (7.2) is a recursive definition, so that for most levels of nesting, $C_i$ will be partly determined by $C_j$. At the lowest level of nesting $C_i$ will be equal to $R_i$, since there will be no more nested chunks. For a program with only one chunk, $C_1 = R_1$ as expected. Factors determining $R_i$, $N$, and $T_i$ will be discussed shortly.

This "landscape" visualization illustrates the basic approach of the cognitive complexity model (CCM) of Cant *et al.* (1992, 1995), and the following examples will demonstrate briefly how the landscape model can be used to depict different levels of complexity associated with different program design structures. Application to object-oriented designs and code will then be studied in detail.

The program skeletons contained in Figure 7.4 represent programs containing several layers of nesting. In program A the nested chunks are embedded within the

```
program A;                          program B;
begin                               begin
    .                                   .
    .                                   .
    while still_true do                 outer_loop;
    begin                               .
        .                           end.
        .
        while inner_loop_true do    procedure outer_loop;
        begin                           begin
            .                               while still_true do
            if inner_conditional then       begin
                .                               .
                .                               inner_loop;
        end;                                    .
        .                                   end
    end;                                end;
    .
    .                               procedure inner_loop;
    end;                                begin
    .                                       while inner_loop_true do
end.                                        begin
                                                .
                                                .
                                                inner_conditional;
                                                .
                                            end
                                        end;

                                    procedure inner_conditional;
                                        begin
                                            if inner_conditional_true then
                                                .
                                                .
                                            end
                                        end;
```

**Figure 7.4**  Skeleton programs with nested chunks: program A (embedded) and program B (modularized).
*Source:* Cant, S. N., Henderson-Sellers, B., and Jeffery, D. R., 1994. Application of cognitive complexity metrics to object-oriented programs, *J. Object-Oriented Programming,* 7(4), 52–63.

superchunks. In program B the nested chunks are remote dependencies. In other words they are chunks located in other parts of the program, which are invoked by subprocedure calls from the superchunk.

In program A reading the relevant chunks, especially those at a higher level, is difficult because they are dispersed over a greater expanse of code by the nesting of the chunks. Furthermore, if the nested chunks are read sequentially by the programmer, they will disrupt the process of comprehending the superchunks, which will lead to even greater complexity. Therefore, the landscape (Figure 7.5) for program A is wider, representing more effort required in chunking. In program B, reading of the relevant chunks is easy because the information is concentrated within a small area. Furthermore, module calls give some cues as to the operations performed by nested chunks, because of the reference to the module identifier. Therefore, the landscape for program B is less wide, representing less effort required for understanding by chunking.

To read program A, a programmer needs simply to read the program from top to bottom, performing minimal tracing. To read program B, a programmer must find the modules referred to (i.e., trace) and then chunk those modules before returning to the original chunk. The relatively large amount of tracing required causes a disrup-

(a)  Program A

(b)  Program B

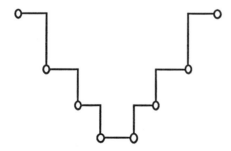

**Figure 7.5**   Landscapes for programmer seeking detailed understanding of programs A and B given in Figure 7.4.
*Source:* Cant, S. N., Henderson-Sellers, B., and Jeffery, D. R., 1994. Application of cognitive complexity metrics to object-oriented programs, *J. Object-Oriented Programming,* 7(4), 52–63.

tion in the reading of the superchunks making them more complex. Although program B requires tracing, the difficulty of tracing a single procedure may well not outweigh the difficulty resulting from the dispersion of code associated with program A.

It can be seen that the effect of modularization on complexity is highly task dependent. This is illustrated visually by the landscape diagrams. For a detailed understanding, programs that are highly modularized may require significant tracing. This is of especial relevance to object-oriented systems where a high degree of modularization leads to a significant number of module interconnections, potentially adding to the effort of tracing. For a cursory understanding, programs that are not modularized may make it difficult to identify and read the relevant chunks.

This brief example in terms of visualization (Figure 7.5) and mathematical representation (equation (7.2)) provides a solid base from which to explore the application of this CCM approach to object-oriented software complexity metrics.

## 7.5 OPERATIONALIZING THE COGNITIVE COMPLEXITY MODEL

To operationalize the cognitive complexity model, as defined by equation (7.2), we need to understand what characteristics of the code and the programmer are relevant to quantifying these processes of chunking and tracing. Analysis of each of these processes, in turn, leads to the identification of independent variables that can be measured. Each of these must be shown to be valid in terms of both measurement theory and practicality. In the sections that follow, we make no attempt to categorically identify these necessary components of the CCM; rather, we identify the conceptual concerns necessary for identification of these component measures and, when available, draw *one illustrative example* from the literature. The aim here is more to focus on a research agenda likely to provide useful results than to support any particular "brand" of component metric.

### 7.5.1 The Definition of a Chunk

It is difficult to determine exactly what constitutes a chunk since it is a product of a programmer's semantic knowledge, as developed through experience. However, generalizations can be made in order to operationalize the construct encapsulated in equation (7.2). For example, Mayer (1979) classified chunks as "mandatory" or "nonmandatory." Mandatory chunks are those in which one statement must always be followed by a second statement. For example, in certain languages, a FOR must always be followed by a NEXT, and an IF must always be followed by a THEN and an ENDIF. Nonmandatory chunks are those that a programmer uses for convenience, such as search loops. Here, for purposes that involve only normal chunking forward, the corresponding delimiters of each control construct (e.g., loop, conditional) will be used to distinguish each chunk. One special case that will be defined is where a routine contains a single loop or decision structure at the next level of nesting. In this case, the code surrounding the decision or loop structure is often simply associated with initialization, and therefore the whole structure should be considered as one chunk.

This definition of a chunk is inadequate when describing processes that primarily involve tracing. Where a programmer is tracing a variable forward or backward, each chunk would often be a single statement containing a variable definition. Therefore, when considering tracing, the instruction line containing the definition should be regarded as a chunk. Again, the exception to this is where the variable definition is contained within a conditional control structure or a series of nested conditional control structures. Under such circumstances, all the conditional control structures containing the variable definition should be regarded as relevant and divided into chunks in the normal way.

Chunks may be classified as elementary or compound. Elementary chunks consist only of sequentially self-contained statements. Compound chunks are those that contain other chunks within them. Routines containing a number of procedure calls should be considered compound chunks rather than elementary chunks, since the identifier of each procedure is usually a cue to some abstract programming unit, which is itself a chunk. At the same time, routines containing no routine calls may also be compound chunks. If a routine contains more than one recognizable subunit, it is equivalent to a module containing many routine calls in the sense that both contain within them multiple subchunks. This conforms with the notion that a loop or decision structure can be considered a nested dependency in much the same way as can a procedure call.

### 7.5.2 Factors Affecting *R*: The Complexity of the Immediate Chunk

Both elementary and compound chunks are influenced by a range of factors determining the complexity of the immediate chunk, some of which were shown explicitly in Figure 3.12 in Chapter 3. Cant *et al.* (1994, 1995) suggest that these should likely include (1) the size ($R_S$), (2) the difficulty of comprehending the control structure within which the chunk is contained ($R_C$), (3) the difficulty of comprehending Boolean expressions contained in the chunk ($R_E$), (4) the recognizability ($R_R$), (5) the visual structure/layout of the program ($R_V$), (6) the disruptions caused by dependencies of those chunks ($R_D$), and (7) the familiarity ($R_F$) that influences speed of recall; that is,

$$R = R\big(R_S, R_C, R_E, R_R, R_V, R_D, R_F\big) \qquad (7.3)$$

Each of these will be reviewed in the following seven subsections in which some tentative proposals for possible submodels will be made, while recognizing that there remain a significant number of good alternatives. Selection of these alternatives may indeed be task dependent (e.g., maintainability; compared with comprehensibility: Basili and Rombach, 1988; Fenton, 1994) and require extensive evaluation and validation.

### 7.5.2.1 Chunk Size ($R_S$).

There are two issues to the size question. The first is the complexity of the actual chunk, as read by the programmer, resulting from its size, as exemplified by lines of code. The second is the psychological complexity of identifying a chunk where a long contiguous section of nonbranching code must be divided up to be understood by the programmer.

A possible equation describing the effect of the size of any chunk was proposed by Cant *et al.* (1992) as

$$R_s = \begin{cases} aS_i, & \text{if } S_i \leq L_{max} \\ aS_i + b\left(\dfrac{S_i - L_{max}}{L_{max}}\right), & \text{if } S_i > L_{max} \end{cases} \tag{7.4}$$

where $R_S$ is the complexity resulting from chunk size $S_i$ is the size of the chunk $L_{max}$ is some limit on the size of a chunk that may be estimated empirically and $a$ and $b$ are empirically determined coefficients. One difficulty may be that the limit, $L_{max}$, would probably vary from programmer to programmer.

### 7.5.2.2 The Type of Control Structure in Which It Is Enclosed ($R_C$).
Intuitively, a conditional control structure is more complex to understand than a normal sequential section of code. However, it is also highly likely that different levels of complexity are associated with different types of control structures. To understand a decision structure, a programmer must first understand the Boolean expression and then analyze the distinction between the alternative code. To understand a loop, a programmer must "inductively" develop an understanding of the effect of the loop. If the function of the loop is not immediately recognized, then a programmer must symbolically iterate the function of the code contained in the loop to follow how the values of variables contained in the loop change. This distinction between loops and decision structures is supported by Bastani (1983), Iyengar *et al.* (1982), Evangelist (1984), and Nejmeh (1988). This distinction is not included in McCabe's cyclomatic complexity, $V(G)$. Although this has led to a number of criticisms (e.g., Evangelist, 1984; Nejmeh, 1988), McCabe's (1976) original intention was to provide a measure of decisions for use in the development of testing procedures.

For example, equations for $R_C$ are given by Iyengar *et al.* (1982) and Bastani (1983), the latter emphasizing the iterative nature of comprehension of loop structures, suggesting that

$$R_C = \sum_{j=1}^{\infty} C_i^{(j)} p^{2^{j-1}-1} \tag{7.5}$$

where $C_i^{(j)}$ is the complexity of the $i$th chunk after the $j$th iteration and $p$ is the probability of failure after the first iteration.

Empirical evidence for the usefulness of these, and other, metrics for $R_C$ remains indecisive (e.g., Gaffney, 1979).

### 7.5.2.3 The Difficulty of Understanding Complex Boolean and Other Expressions ($R_E$).    Boolean expressions are an important issue associated with control flow structures. There is very little understanding of the impact of control structures on complexity. McCabe (1976) assumes that each conditional within

a Boolean expression adds the same level of difficulty as an entire control structure. A similar assertion is made by Nejmeh (1988). Such a treatment of conditionals effectively ignores the debate about whether long Boolean expressions are more or less complex than extended sequences of nested conditional structures.

Myers (1977) argues that a series of conditionals contained in a Boolean expression is considerably simpler than the equivalent array of nested control structures. Green *et al.* (1981, p. 225) suggested that complex Boolean expressions would significantly increase the mental workload required to understand a chunk, thereby increasing the likelihood of mistakes. Evangelist (1984, pp. 390–391) points out that logical expressions are no more difficult to explicate than normal arithmetic operations. He claims that the complexity of Boolean expressions needs to be determined empirically. However, the exact effect of Boolean expressions on psychological complexity is not well understood. A simple summation provides the simplest acceptable model that, based on the principle of scientific parsimony, can be proposed as

$$R_E = b_1 \sum_{\substack{\text{all Boolean} \\ \text{expressions}}} B_i \qquad (7.6)$$

where $B_i$ is the number of predicates in the $i$th Boolean and $b_1$ an empirical constant. A formula such as equation (7.6) is purely tentative at this stage and provides an indicator of a useful area for further research.

Despite the obvious importance of this issue, it is by no means settled. The most useful approach is probably to highlight both excessively complicated sequences of nesting, and also overly complicated Boolean expressions. To ensure that the cognitive complexity model is consonant with this approach, long Boolean expressions should be taken into account. The effect of deep sequences of nested conditionals is already accounted for by the level of disruption (see Section 7.5.2.6) to the comprehension of superchunks (outer conditional structures). Empirical evaluation of $R_E$ thus remains an open question.

### 7.5.2.4 The Recognizability of a Chunk ($R_R$).    Soloway and Ehrlich (1984) have argued that complexity is largely dependent on qualitative factors, including programming experience, which determine how easily a chunk is recognized. They conducted experiments that demonstrated that "programming plans" are not recognized by experienced programmers when the "rules of discourse" are not followed. For example, programmers will find it significantly harder to recognize a routine to find the minimum value from an input stream if the variable containing the result is called MAX. Furthermore, programmers will not recognize structures requiring a conditional, if a "while" statement is used where a simple "if" would suffice. This theory is supported by Gilmore and Green's (1984, p. 463) experiment, which showed that the mental abstraction of a program was highly dependent on the syntactic form of the program.

Cohesion may also have an important impact on the recognizability of a chunk. The importance of cohesion was identified by Yourdon and Constantine (1979). Cohesion refers to the "degree to which the tasks performed by a single program module are functionally related" (IEEE, 1983). This concept may be applied to a chunk, as defined here, to determine to what extent functions performed by a chunk are related. Where a chunk contains two or more functions, related only by the same control structure, it is likely that the chunk will be significantly harder to recognize.

These two factors (conformance with rules and cohesion) may be quantified separately

$$R_R = r_R + r_C \tag{7.7}$$

where $r_R$ and $r_C$ represent the complexity of these two factors, respectively. The value of the factor $r_R$ may be described by Moher's (1985) metric, which gives

$$r_R = -\log_2\left[\prod_{k=1}^{N} P(t_k)\right] \tag{7.8}$$

where $P(t_k)$ is the probability of the $k$th token being drawn from a vocabulary of $n$ tokens specified within the "rules of discourse." However, it should be noted that a significant difficulty in deriving values for $r_R$ using equation (7.8) is the enormous task of compiling the large number of rules of discourse against which to judge the expectedness of any particular token.

The second factor, cohesion, as originally proposed by Yourdon and Constantine (1979), has seven different levels, although only three groups are used by Emerson (1984) who gives[2]

$$r_C = \frac{|M_i| \dim M_i}{|VF - \{T\}| \dim VF} \tag{7.9}$$

where the set of nodes, $VF$, in a directed graph, $F$, contains a subset $\{M_i\}$ and $T$ is the terminal vertex. The dimension of $A$ is equal to $1 + V(G)(A)$. The metric $r_C$ then gives the cohesion of this module to the average cohesion of the reference sets using equation (7.9) or an acceptable alternative.

### 7.5.2.5 The Effects of Visual Structure ($R_V$).

A related issue is the visual structure provided by a program. Green et al. (1981, pp. 225, 227–228) note that chunks that are visible and tractable (i.e., separable from the rest of the program) considerably reduce the difficulty of comprehending a chunk. Note, however, that natural chunks may be larger for experienced programmers, particularly where they have experience with the program and/or language under consideration.

There are essentially three levels of chunk identification difficulty, common to most programs:

1. Chunks delineated by routine boundaries are the easiest to identify, especially if well named.
2. Chunks delineated by control structure boundaries only are less easily identified since there are fewer cues provided concerning their function and the chunk is not as obviously separated from the surrounding code.

[2]Upon correcting typographical errors in the source.

3. Chunks not delineated by any boundaries are the most difficult to identify. One of the reasons that a chunk may be in this category is because a chunk in one of the higher categories becomes so large that it can no longer be understood as a single unit. The point at which this occurs will differ widely from programmer to programmer and from chunk to chunk, making it difficult to quantify the process.

Hence it is reasonable to model these effects, at their simplest, as

$$R_V = a_1 V \tag{7.10}$$

where $V \in \{1, 2, 3\}$ represents the three levels of identification difficulty just outlined and $a_1$ is an empirical constant that still requires evaluation experimentally.

### 7.5.2.6 Disruptions in Chunking Caused by Dependencies ($R_D$).

In the process of understanding a chunk, dependencies often arise such that knowledge of some other "variable plan" and/or "control flow plan" is needed to understand that chunk fully. Often the programmer may recall the necessary program plans from memory. However, at other times, the dependencies must be resolved by reviewing the relevant sections of code. This often involves tracing the relevant sections and then chunking them to acquire understanding. Resolving dependencies, in this manner, disrupts the comprehension of the original chunk. Since short-term memory has only limited capacity, and a rapid decay rate that is worsened by distraction (Sutcliffe, 1989, p. 26), disruptions to the chunking process may cause knowledge of the original chunk to be lost.

This disruption effect is not simply a result of the effort involved in tracing, but also a result of the effort in understanding the nested chunks. Therefore, the effect of disruption is applicable not only to remote dependencies (a point emphasised in the empirical study of Cant *et al.*, 1994) requiring tracing, but also to embedded dependencies, such as nested loops or decision structures, which must be understood before the chunk within which it is nested may be understood.

A possible equation for the disruption effect, $R_D$, of set of chunks $N$, and their descendants, on the $i$th chunk is

$$R_D = d \sum_{j \in N} C_j + e \sum_{j \in N} T_j \tag{7.11}$$

where $R_D$ is that part of the complexity of a chunk resulting from disruptions by nested chunk, for example, subroutine calls; $N$ is the set of chunks on which the $i$th chunk is directly dependent for a given programmer task; $T$ is the difficulty of tracing a particular dependency; and $d$ and $e$ are empirically determined constants.

### 7.5.2.7 Speed of Review or Recall ($R_F$).

The ability of a programmer to understand a chunk is often affected by the number of times that the programmer has read that particular chunk on previous occasions. This may be referred to as chunk familiarity. Chunk familiarity may be looked at from two aspects. The first is by considering the number of times that a programmer has had to review a chunk to understand the section of code that is being worked on in a particular session. The second is by considering the experience that the programmer has had generally with the relevant chunk or with the program in general or indeed with that "pattern" (Gamma *et al.*, 1995).

Woodfield (1980; see also discussion of Davis, 1984) found that repeated reviews of the same chunk reduced the amount of time required to understand that chunk. A good approximation of this effect involves assuming that each review takes two-thirds of the time of the previous review. Woodfield (1980) then derives an equation for program complexity in which the chunk complexity is expressed as

$$C_i = \sum_{m=0}^{(\text{fan-in})_i} R_i f^m \qquad (7.12)$$

where $R_i$ is the complexity of the $i$th chunk, equated in Woodfield's analysis simply to the number of lines of code in the $i$th chunk. The factor $f$ is a review constant $\sim 2/3$. The summation over $m$ represents the number of chunks affected by a particular chunk. Thus, we can revise this for the cognitive complexity model as a multiplicative recall factor, $R_F$, for the $i$th chunk ($R_{Fi}$) given as

$$R_{Fi} = \sum_{j \in N} f^j \qquad (7.13)$$

for use in equation (7.3)—and hence in equation (7.2).

**7.5.2.8 Operationalizing R.** The terms in equation (7.3), based on the preceding discussion, would appear to be likely to be generally additive (with the exception of $R_F$, which is clearly multiplicative). Empirical research is still required to validate this hypothesis and is the next stage in the research program.

### 7.5.3 Operationalizing the Dependency Construct

"Dependency" in a chunk may refer to any part of a program that must be understood to determine the effect of (part of) a chunk. Therefore, dependencies may be functional dependencies or variable dependencies. Functional dependencies refer to procedures or functions called from within a chunk that must, as a result, be read to understand that chunk. Variable dependencies may refer not only to definitions that may affect the variable reference under consideration, but also to variable references which may be affected by a variable definition currently under consideration. These will be distinguished by calling the former "determinants" and the latter "effects."

Dependencies may also be embedded, local, or remote. Remote dependencies are those that extend across modular boundaries. Local dependencies are contained within these modular boundaries (but for our purposes, not within the chunk concerned). Embedded dependencies are physically contained within the chunk itself.

### 7.5.3.1 Factors Affecting the Number of Dependencies Traced, N.
The number of actual dependencies may be determined by identifying all the dependencies of each of the various types. However, the relevant dependencies depend

on the programmer task being considered. In understanding a chunk, variable "determinants" and functional dependencies will be relevant, whereas in tracing ripple effects, variable "effects" will be relevant and in isolating errors, variable "determinants" will be relevant. Remote variable "determinants" may be parameters passed to the module containing the chunk, values returned by called procedures, or global variables referenced in the chunk. Similarly, remote variable "effects" may arise from definitions of global variables, parameters passed to called procedures or from values returned to the calling module.

Local variable "determinants" and "effects" may occur before or after the chunk because of loops within which the chunk may be embedded. Note also that variable dependencies may be indirect, in the sense that the value of a variable may depend on a control structure (decision or loop) and therefore upon the variables that control the execution of that control structure.

For embedded functional dependencies such as nested loops or nested decision statements, it can generally be assumed that they are always read. The corollary of this is that variable dependencies contained within the same chunk will usually not require tracing, because they have been read recently, or will be read shortly after reading the program statement concerned. Although these assumptions are not necessarily always valid, they are found to be generally applicable and allow simplifications to be made which may be useful for developing a metric.

When simply reading for understanding, dependencies are only traced to the extent necessary to give a general idea about the "control plan" or "variable plan" of the particular module or variable referenced. Therefore, one factor that bears on whether a particular dependency will be traced depends on the depth already traced and the depth of understanding required.

Another factor that affects whether a dependency will be traced is the level of cues in the program text that helps recall of the relevant control flow or variable "plans" (see Section 7.5.2.7). This is supported by Woodfield *et al.* (1981a) who found that the use of comments within the code significantly increased the level of programmer comprehension. The only difficulty with comments and other cues is that they are difficult to analyze automatically. Therefore, measures of the level of cues provided will either need to be subjectively based or based on heuristics.

When reading a program to trace the ripple effects of a change, "effects" must be traced until the programmer is satisfied that the change will not be propagated beyond that point. Similarly, when reading a program to isolate a bug, "determinants" must be traced until the bug is found.

### 7.5.4 Factors Affecting *T,* the Difficulty of Tracing

The difficulty of tracing is a function of many factors including the localization of the dependencies ($T_L$), the ambiguity of the dependency ($T_A$), the spatial dependency of the dependency ($T_S$), the level of cuing of the dependency ($T_C$), and the familiarity of the dependency ($T_F$).

$$T = T\left(T_L, T_A, T_S, T_C, T_F\right) \tag{7.14}$$

**7.5.4.1 Localization ($T_L$).** This is the degree to which a dependency may be resolved locally. The various levels are embedded, local, and remote. The simplest equation might be

$$T_L = a_2 L \tag{7.15}$$

where $L \in \{1, 2, 3\}$ represents the three levels of embedded, local, and remote and $a_2$ is an empirical coefficient requiring empirical evaluation.

**7.5.4.2 Ambiguity ($T_A$).** Where there are several alternative chunks on which a section of code may be dependent or may be affected by a section of code, the ambiguity increases the complexity of tracing the alternative chunks. Since there is no specific limit to the number of alternatives, then for any particular alternative there is no indication that it actually exists. For example, one may be uncertain about how many references there are to a global variable. Because of this ambiguity one must continue searching even when all the references may have been found (Dunsmore and Gannon, 1980). The same is true of tracing global variables definitions and tracing calls to a procedure. An equation might be

$$T_A = a_3 A \tag{7.16}$$

where $A \in \{0, 1\}$. Here a value of 1 represents ambiguity and 0 no ambiguity.

**7.5.4.3 Spatial Distance ($T_S$).** This is factor representing the distance, $\Delta S$, possibly in lines of code, between two chunks for which there is a dependency. It can be expressed simply as

$$T_S = b_2 \Delta S \tag{7.17}$$

where $b_2$ is an empirical constant. It is conceivable that this would affect the difficulty of tracing.

**7.5.4.4 Level of Cuing ($T_C$).** When searching for a procedure, its name is usually found at the beginning. When searching for procedure calls, they are often obscured by being embedded within the text. Other cuing difficulties may be identified for specific programming languages.

$$T_C = a_4 B \tag{7.18}$$

where $B \in \{0, 1\}$. Here $B = 1$ represents the existence of obscure references.

**7.5.4.5 Dependency Familiarity ($T_F$).** Dependency familiarity is similar to chunk familiarity and would be incorporated into equation (7.14) as a multiplicative factor.

$$T_{Fi} = \sum_{j \in N} f^j \tag{7.19}$$

**7.5.4.6 Operationalizing the Tracing Difficulty.**   Empirical research on the functional form of the tracing difficulty, $T$, as given by equation (7.14), still remains to be undertaken. If the simple binary representation for $T_A$ and $T_C$ are appropriate, then once the weightings have been determined, the simplest likely representation for $T$ would be

$$T = \left(T_L + T_A + T_S + T_C\right)T_F \qquad (7.20)$$

## 7.6 APPLICATION TO OBJECT-ORIENTED SYSTEMS

### 7.6.1 Adapting the Model

A crucial way in which object-oriented programs reduce complexity is through data encapsulation, which reduces the complexity of tracing backward to resolve variable dependencies ("determinants") or tracing forward to follow ripple "effects" (Cant *et al.*, 1992, 1995). However, other facilities that are part of the object-oriented paradigm, in particular inheritance, may have varying effects on complexity for different tasks.

A system developed using object-oriented design is organized entirely differently from one developed using structured design. Whereas in structured design, the system is decomposed according to the functions it will perform, in the object-oriented paradigm, systems are decomposed based on the objects that will be manipulated. This involves characterizing the system as a collection of abstract data types.

**7.6.1.1 Acquiring Variable Plans.**   Even from this general level, it is possible to see how complexity may be lessened. As indicated in the model of comprehension complexity (Cant *et al.*, 1992, 1995), one of the most difficult tasks in functionally designed systems is the acquiring of "variable plans" that rely on a range of features common to variables with particular roles, such as counter variables and variables in which user input is stored. This involves understanding the role of the variable or data structure in the program. However, the abstract data type upon which an object-oriented class is based itself contains all the most important features necessary to understand a "variable plan" in its interface. An abstract data type describes a data structure in terms of the services that can be performed on it, and the properties of those services (Meyer, 1988, pp. 53–54). It is these services that best characterize the responsibilities of each object at the system level. Therefore, it is reasonable to argue that the information required to develop a system-level "variable plan" may be best evinced from an abstract data type, implemented, in most object-oriented systems, as a class. The essential element of an abstract data type is not its underlying data structure, since implementation can often use one of a variety of data structures. For example, a stack could be implemented using an array, a linked list or any of a variety of other structures. The most important characteristics of an abstract data type, and of a "variable plan," are the services that may be performed on the data and not how those data are structured. These services reflect the external responsibilities as made available to external "clients" of this "supplier" class.

In a class, the implementation details should be effectively hidden from the user, so that the user cannot modify the data directly, but can request only that some service be performed (Wirfs-Brock and Wilkerson, 1989). Therefore, only those details that best describe a "variable plan" need be understood by a programmer wishing to use a particular class. In other words the interface of a class visible to its user is the set of services that a programmer can perform on the objects described by the class. This is also the information by which a "variable plan" can be best understood. Therefore, acquiring a system-level variable plan involves understanding the abstract data type or the role of a particular variable. It is only when complexity of individual classes is considered that implementation details and local, class-level variable plans are relevant.

In terms of the general model of comprehension (Cant *et al.*, 1995), an object-oriented program should result in a shallower landscape (as illustrated in Figure 7.6) than would result from a program developed using structured design, since significantly less tracing is required to acquire "variable plans" (which describe the use of variables in particular roles, e.g., as counter variables or storage variables) as a result of the high degree of localization and encapsulation supported by the object-oriented paradigm.

Acquiring a general variable plan for a class is often not sufficient. Sometimes, particularly in debugging or modifying, a programmer will need to trace the exact determinants of a variable or data structure, referred to in an assignment, or alternatively trace the impact of an assignment on the rest of the program. This involves tracing through the execution flow of a program to discover which modules (classes) in the system influence the values of the relevant data structure.

**7.6.1.2 Parameters.**   Determining which other modules in the program may pass parameters to the module under consideration is a problem common to

(a) Acquiring variable plans in object-oriented programs

(b) Acquiring variable plans in functional programs

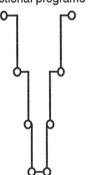

**Figure 7.6**   Landscapes for acquiring variable plans in object-oriented programs as compared with programs developed using structured design.
*Source:* Cant, S. N., Henderson-Sellers, B., and Jeffery, D. R., 1994. Application of cognitive complexity metrics to object-oriented programs, *J. Object-Oriented Programming, 7*(4), 52–63.

both object-oriented and procedural languages. It may be a more difficult task in an object-oriented language because in procedural languages the flow of control is usually explicitly understood in terms of the hierarchical model of execution, which matches the model of decomposition. In object-oriented languages, however, the system is decomposed as a set of interacting objects and the exact flow of control is not explicitly modelled as it is in structured design (Meyer, 1988, p. 71).

In many object-oriented languages, this problem is attacked by reducing the need to identify the passers of parameters, for example, by use of assertions (Meyer, 1988, pp. 111–163; Masotti, 1991). The strict adherence to these "contractual obligations" means that errors are manifested in the routines that cause them. Good exception handling mechanisms thus significantly reduce the need to trace calls between classes to trace errors. The theory of programming with contractual obligations also reduces the need to trace forward, following modifications. When postconditions are specified correctly, you can be sure that a class will have few and possibly no ripple effects, because it must meet those conditions. Similarly, one can be sure that if the routine still meets all the pre-conditions of the classes that it calls, then there should be no ripple effects propagated through such called routines. Therefore, correct and strict specification of all post- and preconditions ensures that errors can be isolated in the routine in which they are caused.

In terms of the general model of comprehension (Cant *et al.,* 1995), there are two opposing effects. First, parameters are more difficult to trace in an object-oriented system than in a traditional, structured system since there is usually no explicit model of the flow of execution, and routines are often called by several different client classes. This is manifested as deeper drops to the relevant levels in the landscape model of an object-oriented system. The second effect results from assertions, which reduce the depth to which a dependency must be traversed before a ripple effect or an error is understood. In the model, this is manifested as a reduced number of levels in the relevant section of the landscape (Figure 7.7). Two aspects of tracing effort can thus be visualized: the number of levels indicating the number of "subchunks" investigated and the depth indicating the effort of finding the location of those "subchunks."

(a) Tracing ripple effects
through routine arguments
in object-oriented programs

(b) Tracing ripple effects
through routine arguments
in functional programs

**Figure 7.7**    Visualization of tracing variable values through routine arguments in object-oriented and traditional programs.
*Source:* Cant, S. N., Henderson-Sellers, B., and Jeffery, D. R., 1994. Application of cognitive complexity metrics to object-oriented programs, *J. Object-Oriented Programming,* 7(4), 52–63.

### 7.6.1.3 Common Variables.

A second method through which values are often communicated is through variables or data structures that are common to a number of routines. In programs developed using structured design, there is relatively little regard given to the communication paths between modules through global variables and data structures (this should be contrasted with Henry and Kafura, 1981, who concentrate on fan-in and fan-out resulting from argument lists not from globally accessible variables). As a result, such communication paths are not made explicit. This makes such dependencies very difficult to resolve. In object-oriented design, common variables, and their associated routines, may be encapsulated within the same class or inherited from one or more superclass. Therefore, all communication through those variables and data structures is localized within the one class or in a well-defined inheritance hierarchy, making tracing significantly easier. In the general model of comprehension (CCM), this is reflected in a reduction in the drop between levels where the drop corresponds to tracing a dependency through a common variable (Figure 7.7).

### 7.6.1.4 Resolving Functional Dependencies.

An important facility in the object-oriented paradigm, inheritance, introduces a number of difficulties in terms of functional dependencies. Not only are the routines implementing the services offered by some classes in fact contained in the code of other classes, but some routine calls may be syntactically ambiguous as a result of "polymorphism" making them very difficult to trace by inspection of the code. However, the semantic consistency implicit in polymorphic calls counterbalances this tracing difficulty to some degree (Monarchi, personal communication, 1992).

For a simple nonpolymorphic routine call, strongly typed object-oriented programs may allow easier tracing to the relevant routine. This is because the message structure is a combination of the target object name and the desired routine. Given that a programmer knows the class of this object, or can at least determine its class easily from the attribute declarations of the current class, then the tracing process is more effectively directed. In a similar way to that in which houses are identified by a number, a street name, and a suburb, a routine is identified by its name (including signature) and its class. Therefore, resolving basic routine calls may be a simpler process in an object-oriented system than in a traditional system, reflected in the general model of comprehension as a shorter drop between levels of the relevant chunks.

### 7.6.1.5 Routines for Services Located in Other Classes.

The facility of inheritance can cause new difficulties in two respects. First, in simply trying to understand a class, many of the routines available within the class are in fact located in the parent class; in other hierarchies, routines declared in a deferred parent class may not be implemented until a descendant class. To understand the entire class, a programmer must therefore consider all the classes from which a class inherits routines or methods. Furthermore, in some object-oriented languages (notably, C++) routines may include a reference to the equivalent routine in a superclass, possibly redefining this routine. This means that a routine cannot be fully understood, unless the equivalent routine in the "parent class" is understood. In the general model of comprehension, this would mean that a chunk that might have been contained on a single level may be split on to different levels (Figure 7.8). However, at least one tool is available to collapse inheritance hierarchies and thus obviate the need to trace up and down the inheritance tree. In the Eiffel environment, the use of the FLAT tool permits analysis of code to be undertaken more simply, thus reducing the inherent complexity during the maintenance phase.

### 7.6.1.6 Ambiguity Arising out of Polymorphism.

The second aspect of inheritance that can cause problems is polymorphism. When a polymorphic request for service is issued, you can determine which routine provides the service only if you know the type of the object referred to by the entity (pointer in C++) specified in the request. Often the type of that object can be known only at runtime. In this case, the call may be (syntactically) ambiguous when the static code is read, although when the signature and side effects remain constant, only the method's interface has to be understood (no additional complexity) (Moser, personal communication, 1995). For a programmer to understand the possible outcomes of such a call, all the possible routines must be read and understood. Although this would seem to add a large degree of complexity, it could be argued that to achieve the same level of flexibility in

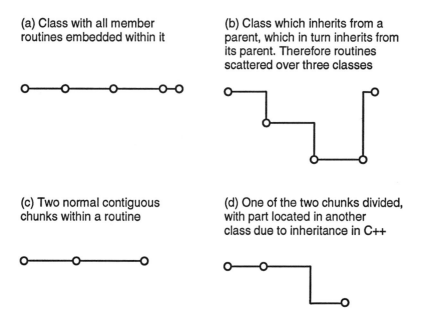

(a) Class with all member routines embedded within it

(b) Class which inherits from a parent, which in turn inherits from its parent. Therefore routines scattered over three classes

(c) Two normal contiguous chunks within a routine

(d) One of the two chunks divided, with part located in another class due to inheritance in C++

**Figure 7.8**  Splitting of classes and chunks caused by inheritance.
*Source:* Cant, S. N., Henderson-Sellers, B., and Jeffery, D. R., 1994. Application of cognitive complexity metrics to object-oriented programs, *J. Object-Oriented Programming,* 7(4), 52–63.

a normal functional program, a programmer would need to continually embed decision statements to determine which routine should be called.

Clearly both methods have advantages and disadvantages. Where a programmer needs to read a called routine to understand it, the complexity is reduced by having a decision structure in which the identifiers of all candidate routines are specified. However, where the identifier provides a sufficient indication of the function it performs, it is preferable to have a single call. Since in polymorphic requests for service, the nature of the service is usually semantically the same, a single call is conceptually neater. Furthermore, all the candidate routines that might be called would probably be best recognized under the same name. Polymorphism allows this (as also does "operator overloading"; see Stroustrup, 1986, Chapter 6), while the procedural programsming alternative does not. The exact effect of polymorphic requests on complexity is contingent upon the programmer's familiarity with the program (and with the called routines in particular), upon the degree of meaning incorporated within the labeling and also upon the nature of the task being performed by the programmer. If the task requires tracing of the exact flow of control, polymorphism is likely to increase cognitive complexity although it has been suggested that the use of polymorphism decreases the structural complexity (Tegarden *et al.*, 1992). In terms of the landscape model of comprehension, this will be manifested as a greater number of vertical drops resulting from a single function call (Figure 7.9). However, where a programmer is reading for understanding and does not need to resolve the dependencies, the conceptual simplicity of a polymorphic routine call will be reflected in the general model of comprehension as a shorter chunk at the relevant level. This indicates less effort required to comprehend the immediate chunk.

**7.6.1.7 Class Chunks.**    One important type of compound chunk (i.e., a chunk that contains other "subchunks") is a class. Often a whole class will not need to be understood, in which case the most abstract chunk that need be considered is a routine. However, sometimes a whole class will need to be understood as a single conceptual unit. In this case understanding the class will effectively involve understanding the abstract data type that it embodies; in other words, its external interface and the constraints determining its range of responsibilities.

(a) Ambiguity resulting
from polymorphism

(b) All function calls in
functional languages are
unambiguous

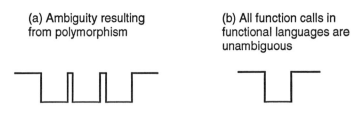

**Figure 7.9**    Landscapes illustrating the ambiguity resulting from polymorphism. *Source:* Cant, S. N., Henderson-Sellers, B., and Jeffery, D. R., 1994. Application of cognitive complexity metrics to object-oriented programs, *J. Object-Oriented Programming,* 7(4), 52–63.

Elementary chunk complexity can be measured best using token or line metrics (e.g., Henry and Kafura, 1981; Davis and LeBlanc, 1988; and compare equation (7.2)). Compound chunk complexity would be measured best by counting control structures, such as intramodule branch counts, internal routine counts, or external dependency counts. Note that when analyzing the size of a compound chunk by counting its constituent chunks, you should only consider the chunks at the next level of nesting. This is based on the assumption that chunks at even deeper levels of nesting are already aggregated into the abstractions of chunks immediately below the chunk under consideration.

The last kind of local dependency is the class-local dependency, which is only relevant to the object-oriented paradigm. These may be functional or variable dependencies. Functional dependencies arise when one routine calls another routine within the same class. Variable dependencies occur when a class attribute defined by one routine is referenced by another routine. These dependencies may be more difficult to resolve than routine-local dependencies. However, they are significantly easier to resolve than remote dependencies since all the relevant information may be found locally.

One situation where this may not be true is tracing a polymorphic routine call in an object-oriented program. In this case there is no clear indication of how many routines may be invoked by the call. Furthermore, only the class (and therefore its type) to which the message is sent can be identified in the "calling" object. The object receiving the message may subcontract (e.g., Meyer, 1992a) to an object of another class (type), thus involving a class that cannot be identified from the code of the original calling object. Therefore, tracing remote functional dependencies may be harder in object-oriented programs for polymorphic routine calls.

**7.6.1.8 Global Variables Versus Class Attributes.**    In object-oriented programming the problem of positioning and scope of variables is alleviated by removing the need for most global variables. Since classes encapsulate both variables and the routines that operate on them, interaction through these variables can be understood through local information. Class attributes (which usually replace global variables found in procedural programs) may generally be considered local dependencies, since routines operating on them are encapsulated within the one class.

This assertion is confirmed by Woodfield *et al.* (1981a) who found programs organized as abstract data types significantly easier to understand and by Rombach (1987) who found that "object-oriented" programs, written in the language LADY, required less effort to isolate errors than equivalent procedural programs.

**7.6.1.9 Reuse.**    Finally, there may be a long-term effect on object-oriented design resulting from reuse. One of the central aims of object-oriented design is to foster the reuse of program components. In the long term, regular use of the same classes should mean that programmers become very familiar with them, making them easier to understand and also improving a programmer's confidence in the correctness of the class.

In terms of the landscape model of comprehension, confidence in the correctness of classes will reduce the number of levels in the landscape of a programmer attempting to isolate an error or tracing a ripple effect. Increased familiarity will reduce the width of all the chunks contained in reused modules, indicating a reduction in the effort to required to comprehend them.

### 7.6.2 Case Study

A case study was performed (Cant *et al.,* 1994) to test some of the proposals of Cant *et al.* (1992) as applied here to object-oriented systems. It also serves as an illustration of the nature of the analysis required to fully validate their complexity model and explores the problems that may be encountered. The study focused on remote dependencies because it was believed that these usually have the greatest impact on complexity out of all the factors considered in the CCM (Cant *et al.,* 1992, 1995). This is supported by the empirical research carried out on the metrics of Henry and Kafura (1981) and Shepperd (1990).

Three research questions, all relating to remote dependencies, were analyzed in this initial case study. They were

1. Does the complexity of understanding a chunk increase with the number of functional and backward variable dependencies (determinants)?
2. Does the complexity of modifying a chunk increase with the number of remote forward variable dependencies (effects)?
3. Does the complexity of isolating an error manifested in a chunk increase with the number of determinants?

#### 7.6.2.1 Rules for Counting of Remote Dependencies.    For the purposes of functional or variable dependencies (see the example in Figure 7.10), functions are regarded as remote if (1) they are contained in a distinct class, (2) they are contained in a parent class, and (3) they are a calling function where the present function is a public or protected function.

1. Functional dependencies occur whenever a remote function is called.
2. Backward dependencies occur wherever there is a reference to an entity which may have been modified by a remote function. Therefore,
   a. A reference to a parameter passed by the calling function is regarded as a backward dependency on the calling function.
   b. A reference to a pointer to an object where a pointer to that pointer was passed as a parameter to a function called earlier in the present function is counted as a backward dependency on that called function
   c. A reference to a simple type entity where a pointer to that simple type entity was passed as a parameter to a function called earlier in the present function is counted as a backward dependency on that called function
   d. Where a function returns a value, the assignment of that value is counted as a backward dependency on that called function.
3. Forward dependencies occur wherever an entity's value is passed to a remote function. Therefore,

```
class EXAMPLE : public PARENT {
public:
    int     FUNCTION(OTHER_CLASS**, OTHER_CLASS*)
    void    CLASS_LOCAL_FUNCTION( )
private:
    OTHER_CLASS* class_private_pointer_to_object
}

PUBLIC int EXAMPLE::FUNCTION (OTHER_CLASS** pointer_to_pointer_to_object,
OTHER_CLASS* pointer_to_object)
{
    int     function_private_int
    CLASS_LOCAL_FUNCTION() // not counted because it is local
    class_private_pointer_to_object = pointer_to_object
                        // counted as a remote backward dependency on the
                        // calling function because of the reference to a parameter
                        // passed by the calling function
    function_private_int = PARENT_FUNCTION (pointer_to_object,
        pointer_to_pointer_to_object)
                        // calling the parent function is counted as a
                        // functional dependency.
                        // again the two references to parameters passed by
                        // the calling function are counted as additional
                        // backward dependencies on the calling routine
                        // The assignment of the return value from the called
                        // function is counted as a backward dependency
                        // on the called function
                        // The passed parameters are counted as two
                        // forward dependencies on the called function
    if( *pointer_to_pointer_to_object == class_private_pointer_to_object)
                        // reference to the pointer to an object which may have
                        // modified by the function called in the previous line
                        // is counted as a backward variable dependency on
                        // that function
    {
        ......
    }
    return (function_private_int)
}
```

**Figure 7.10**    Example to illustrate rules for counting remote dependencies.
*Source:* Cant, S. N., Henderson-Sellers, B., and Jeffery, D. R., 1994. Application of cognitive complexity metrics to object-oriented programs, *J. Object-Oriented Programming,* 7(4), 52–63.

a. A parameter passed to a called function is a forward dependency on that function.

b. A value returned to a calling function is a forward dependency on that function.

The study, carried out within the Australian research arm of a large multinational computer firm, analyzed a C++ project undertaken by a team of 12 (7 of whom were active at any one time). Five classes were examined in this case study. These were chosen from a selection provided by the project manager as representative of different levels of complexity. The five classes chosen all contained a similar number of routines and a similar number of lines. The only exception was one class (referred to later as class D) that contained approximately 60% more routines than the others. However, since it was substantially larger, any finding of low complexity would verify that the complexity measure was measuring something other than length. Thus, it introduces no bias towards false positives.

A comparison of the perceived complexity of *understanding* against the predicted complexity value based on comprehension is shown in Figure 7.11. Figure 7.11(a) illustrates the relative ratings of the five classes by two programmers who had substantial experience with them. Figure 7.11(b) illustrates the average number of dependencies in a routine for each class. Figure 7.11(c) illustrates the maximum number of dependencies of any routine in a class. Overall, the figures demonstrate a high correspondence between perceived and predicted complexities. The only striking exception is class D, which, although being the median in terms of its perceived complexity rating, had a very low predicted complexity. This may due to a distortion in perceived complexity resulting from the fact that D had a much larger number of routines than any of the other classes. This might have made it appear more complex than the other classes even though each routine was simpler. An alternative explanation for the high perceived complexity was suggested by one of the team members who noted that "the maintenance of internal pointers in some of the methods" and the intricacy of some of the algorithms were the main sources of complexity. These would not be exposed by counts of remote dependencies.

A comparison of the perceived complexity of *tracing modifications* with the complexity predicted using remote dependencies appears in Figure 7.12. Once again, the overall impression is that predicted complexity is consistent with perceived complexity. The main discrepancy is once again class D. Predicted complexity is substantially lower than perceived complexity for this class. As discussed in the previous section, it is likely that this is due either to the large number of routines or the internal complexity of the routines neither of which are measured by a metric based on the number of forward connections.

A comparison of the predicted complexity of *isolating errors* manifested in the classes against the perceived complexity appears in Figure 7.13. Overall, there is consistency across all the figures. One exception is the greater average number of dependencies in class A relative to class B. However, Figure 7.13(c) reveals that this is largely due to a single routine in class A that contains a large number of determinants.

A second exception is the greater number of dependencies in E relative to D. However, distortion created by D has already been highlighted. This is probably again a manifestation of the high perceived complexity resulting from internal features of the class.

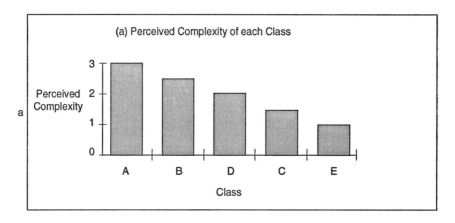

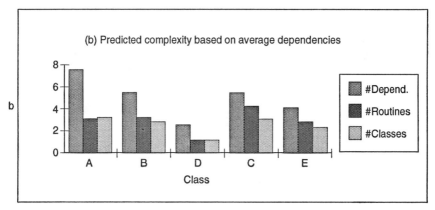

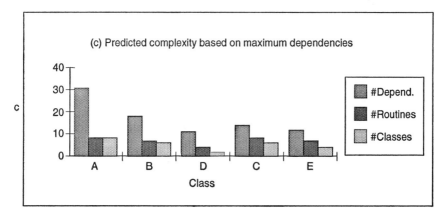

**Figure 7.11**    Perceived and predicted understanding.
*Source:* Cant, S. N., Henderson-Sellers, B., and Jeffery, D. R., 1994. Application of cognitive complexity metrics to object-oriented programs, *J. Object-Oriented Programming*, 7(4), 52–63.

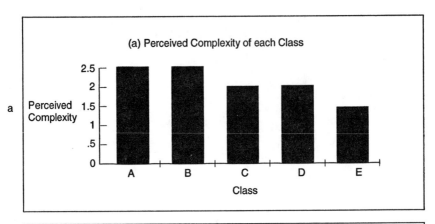

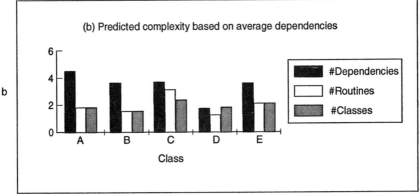

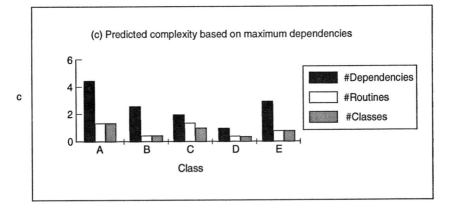

**Figure 7.12**   Perceived and predicted effort for tracing modifications.
*Source:* Cant, S. N., Henderson-Sellers, B., and Jeffery, D. R., 1994. Application of cognitive complexity metrics to object-oriented programs, *J. Object-Oriented Programming,* 7(4), 52–63.

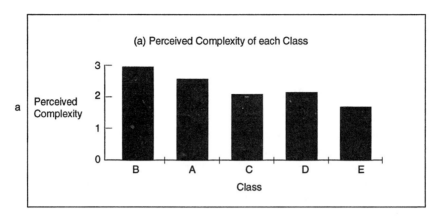

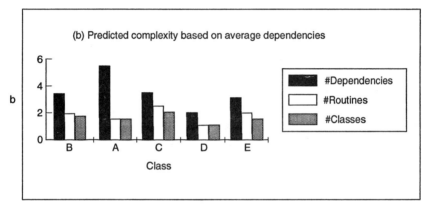

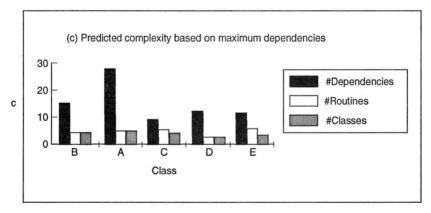

**Figure 7.13**   Perceived and predicted effort to isolate errors.
*Source:* Cant, S. N., Henderson-Sellers, B., and Jeffery, D. R., 1994. Application of cognitive complexity metrics to object-oriented programs, *J. Object-Oriented Programming,* 7(4), 52–63.

The applicability of the cognitive complexity model to object systems still awaits final empirical validation. It potentially offers a new type of tool for project management, including as it does cognitive behavioral characteristics.

## 7.7 CHAPTER SUMMARY

A conceptual model of cognitive complexity based on an analysis of the programming process, rather than the program product, has been described (Cant *et al.*, 1992, 1994, 1995). This model takes two forms: a graphical representation via the landscape diagram and a mathematical representation.

The landscape diagram is approximate and useful for human judgment processes concerned with a rough appreciation of the cognitive complexity of code for a defined programming purpose. The mathematical expression of cognitive complexity given is, as yet, also a conceptual model requiring considerable work before a fully operational version can be provided. Only tentative formulas for describing the constituent parts of chunking and tracing have been discussed, purely as material illustrative of the underlying concepts. The complexity model is designed to be useful in all programming paradigms, and current research is aimed at exploring its operational applicability to the object-oriented paradigm, initially in terms of the significant effect of remote dependencies. For example, Cant *et al.* (1994) have showed that for object-oriented programs written in C++, an evaluation of dependencies did suggest agreement between perceived and predicted values in three contexts: understanding, tracing modifications, and effort to isolate errors.

The model proposed defines the meaning of cognitive complexity and, based on this, provides metrics of this complexity that can be used for benchmarking, prediction, and control once the necessary empirical work has been carried out to establish the efficacy of the model. Some preliminary case study-based empirical work in Cant (1991) and for C++ programs in Cant *et al.* (1994) shows initial support for the model proposed.

## 7.8 BIBLIOGRAPHIC DETAILS

The cognitive complexity model was originally developed as part of a student's honours thesis (Cant, 1991). Further refinement led to an internal report (Cant *et al.*, 1992). The work was then extended into a theory paper (Cant *et al.*, 1995) and an OO applications paper (Cant *et al.*, 1994).

# 8

# INDUSTRIAL APPLICATION
# OF A METRICS PROGRAM

Much of OO metrics is only just emerging from the theoretical discussions into the empirical evaluation stage. The suite of six metrics of (Chidamber and Kemerer 1993, 1994) have had some very small amount of industrial validation. Other groups (e.g., those at Clemson University/Software Architects and at University of Technology, Sydney) are beginning on large-scale evaluation programs in collaboration with local industry and the international Metrics Club was recently initiated. The (sparse) data to date that have been published are presented in Section 8.1. In Section 8.2 we look briefly at some of the issues in implementing a metrics program within an object-oriented software development environment.

## 8.1 INDUSTRIAL DATA

### 8.1.1 MIT Studies

The six metrics of Chidamber and Kemerer were used in an empirical study of two companies, one using Smalltalk, one using C++ (Chidamber and Kemerer, 1994). Site A, a software vendor using C++, provided data on 634 classes from two C++ libraries. Site B, a semiconductor manufacturer using Smalltalk, provided data on 1459 classes. The summary statistics are given in Table 8.1. Values of weighted methods per class (WMC) were similar for the two sites. Most classes tend to have less than 10 methods, although one had as many as 106 (site A). Depth of inheritance tree (DIT) values supported the intuition of hierarchy depths less than about 7, although the preponderance with DIT values near zero leads the authors to comment that "the designers may not be taking advantage of reuse of methods through inheritance" (which seems a fairly limited view of both reuse and inheritance).

TABLE 8.1  Summary statistics for site A and
site B for the six MIT metrics (compiled from
Chidamber and Kemerer, 1993).

|  | Site A C++ | | Site B Smalltalk | |
|---|---|---|---|---|
|  | Median | Range | Median | Range |
| WMC | 5 | 0–106 | 10 | 0–346 |
| DIT | 1 | 0–8 | 3 | 0–10 |
| NOC | 0 | 0–42 | 0 | 0–50 |
| CBO | 0 | 0–84 | 9 | 0–234 |
| RFC | 6 | 0–120 | 29 | 3–422 |
| LCOM | 0 | 0–200 | 2 | 0–17 |

In the case of number of children (NOC) for the two sites, the high majority of classes (73% for site A and 68% for site B) had zero "children"—which of course ties in with the dominant value of DIT of 1. Coupling between objects (CBO) describes reuse by collaboration, and the values highlight the differences between Smalltalk and C++, the former having a higher emphasis on pure OO message passing. The median values are 0 and 9, respectively, and the maximum values 84 and 234, respectively. Response for a class (RFC) values again showed interlanguage differences. Here the median values were 6 and 29, respectively, with maximum values of 120 and 422 (Table 8.1). The higher median values for Smalltalk are again attributed to the adherence to object-oriented principles in that language.[1] Finally, the lack of cohesion of methods (LCOM, 1994 definition) has a very different distribution at the two sites (Figure 8.1). Although both sites show low median values, the ranges are very different. Smalltalk classes appear to be designed much more cohesively than equivalent classes in C++.

### 8.1.2  Li and Henry's Studies

Li and Henry's (1993) metrics were evaluated on two commercial systems written in Classic-Ada. Data collection took three years and measured maintenance effort in terms of the number of lines changed per class. Their extended statistical analyses of the data led to the conclusion that their metrics could be useful in predicting maintenance effort by combining eight measures using a linear regression approach.

### 8.1.3  Lorenz and Kidd's Studies

Lorenz and Kidd (1994) apply their extensive suite of metrics to five commercial systems, again in Smalltalk or C++ or a mixture of the two language environments.

---

[1]It is difficult to avoid using an OO style in Smalltalk, yet extremely easy in C++. Indeed, many programs supposedly written in C++ are in effect C programs with little influence of OO style. No metrics have yet been validated that will discriminate clearly between an OO C++ program and a non-OO C++ program.

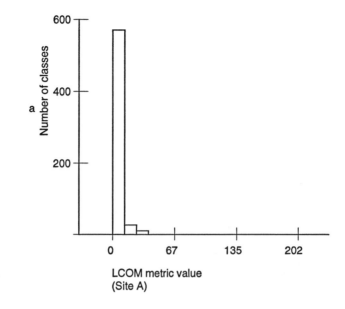

(a)

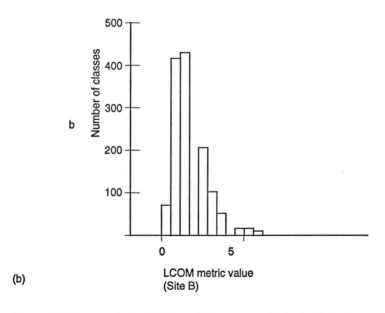

(b)

**Figure 8.1**   Histogram for the LCOM metric for two sites: (a) site A, (b) site B.
*Source:* Chidamber, S. and Kemerer, C., 1994. A metrics suite for object-oriented design, *IEEE Trans. Software Eng.,* 20(6), 476–493. © 1994 IEEE.

Four of the projects are relatively small (projects 1, 2, 4, 5 have less than about 100 classes) whereas the third system, that of Smalltalk/V™ OS2 itself, has over 700 classes. Despite the disparity in class numbers comprising each of these five systems, the number of message sends is more uniform (two clusters of projects 1, 2, 3 and projects 4, 5, Figure 8.2). Metric data were collected with a tool written by Lorenz and Kidd (OOMetric™), which formed the data source of project 4.

DIT values differed across projects. While all projects showed relatively low maximum values, the distribution shapes are contrasting. In the first project, the mode is 4, and the distribution is roughly symmetrical; in the second, third, and fourth project, the mode is 2 and the distribution skewed; while in the final project the distribution is bimodal (1 and 4). Lorenz and Kidd (1994) comment that for the projects with a low-range mode (they suggest all classes at levels below four), there is a need to look for more abstractions and for projects with many deep hierarchies, there may be poor or excessive subclassing.

The authors note the perturbing influences of browser classes and low-level functionality such as data and file classes, as well as framework classes that embody a different philosophy—that of providing an abstract framework that *must* use inheritance to reify it. Indeed, most of the authors' comments are useful and pragmatic and have the flavor of "alarm levels" (Section 2.5).

### 8.1.4 UTS Studies

An extensive set of metrics, as described in Henderson-Sellers (1995a), has been collected by researchers at the University of Technology, Sydney (UTS), on four systems using OOMTool (Sevel, 1994). The systems used were (1) Smalltalk-80, (2) a

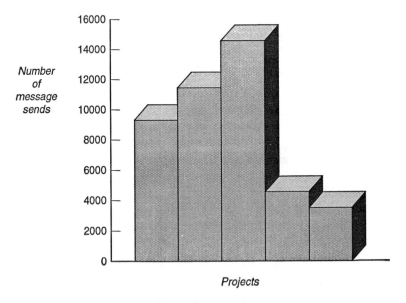

**Figure 8.2**   Number of message sends for five projects (after Lorenz and Kidd, 1994).

set of 25 C++ classes of Pant (1993), (3) the generalized versions of these, and (4) the prototype of the CASE tool Aaron (Henderson-Sellers *et al.,* 1994). In addition to values on statements, lines of code (LOC), $V(G)$ and message-passing coupling (MPC) (which, at least for ST80, agree with previous published metrics values), results are also given for $C^3$. For ST80, there is a predominant modal value of 12 (with a count of about 8000) with all other counts being less than 1000. For the C++ classes of Pant, ranges tend again (for C++) to be larger. For instance, mean method size is 17 LOC as against the ST80 value of 6. As noted, since Smalltalk is a pure OO language, it operates only by message passing. Hence its $V(G)$ counts are always zero. For the C++ classes, this is not so, and the value of $V(G)$ has a maximum for this data set of 26 with a mean of 3. Once these classes had been generalized (Pant *et al.,* 1995b), lines of code (both maximum and mean) were significantly smaller, as was the value of $V(G)$ (maximum of 13, mean of 2.7). It should be noted that this generalization effort created classes that were cleaner abstract data types (ADTs) but did not address the second part of the generalization process which is the creation of inheritance hierachies. This research experiment was highly useful in accomplishing this discrimination.

The application of OOMTool to Aaron (Lebrun and Guigne, 1994) showed a message-passing distribution skewed, with a maximum value of 119 and a mean of 7.1. $C^3$ values were low (around 12) with a very low tail, although the maximum (outlier) was 632. Again, we can use such data as triggers to undertake an investigation of those outliers. In this system (written in ST80), the DIT values showed a maximum depth of 11 with a mode of 4—somewhat more use being made of inheritance than in some of the systems reported by Lorenz and Kidd (1994) in the same language. An interesting conjecture here is that the development team for Aaron were well versed in the OO paradigm and had not originally learned structured programming techniques prior to Smalltalk.

Data from a commercial project, written in C++, are given for the cognitive complexity model (Cant *et al.,* 1994) in Chapter 7. Other data can be extracted from the same source. Table 8.2 gives the number of methods and attributes (both public and private) along with DIT, NOC, and LCOM. No real quantitative analysis is possible, yet some interesting comments can be made. In general, these eight classes show a good object-oriented approach since they have no public attributes, a reasonable balance between public and private methods and relatively low values of DIT. However, the values of LCOM are interesting—classes 3 and 7 have extremely high values of LCOM. For at least class 7, there are no attributes suggesting that this class is more of a "functional object."

## 8.1.5 Sharble and Cohen's Studies

The study of Sharble and Cohen (1993) was aimed at elucidating differences between a data-driven methodology and a responsibility-driven methodology. It used a suite of metrics to do this, which included the six of Chidamber and Kemerer (1991). The industrial system studied was a brewery control system that consisted of an inventory system, a production system, and a recipe library. Their results, summarized

TABLE 8.2   Summary data for eight classes from the analysis of a commercial system

|  | Number of Methods | | Number of Attributes | | | | |
| --- | --- | --- | --- | --- | --- | --- | --- |
| Class Label | Public | Private | Public | Private | DIT | NOC | LCOM |
| Class 1 | 40 | 29 | 0 | 8 | 2 | 2 | 0 |
| Class 2 | 9 | 1 | 0 | 7 | 1 | 0 | 0 |
| Class 3 | 10 | 3 | 0 | 3 | 3 | 0 | 48 |
| Class 4 | 33 | 11 | 0 | 10 | 2 | 0 | 0 |
| Class 5 | 18 | 1 | 0 | 1 | 3 | 0 | 0 |
| Class 6 | 24 | 1 | 0 | 3 | 2 | 3 | 4 |
| Class 7 | 7 | 4 | 0 | 0 | 4 | 0 | 45 |
| Class 8 | 7 | 2 | 0 | 1 | 3 | 0 | 0 |

in Table 8.3, showed that while both systems had a number of tramps (NOT) value of zero, the value of violations of the law of Demeter (VOD) was 40 for the data-driven approach. RFC values for the data-driven approach are more than twice the values for the responsibility-driven approach. These striking differences illustrate the more complex design that resulted from the data-driven approach.

## 8.2 INTRODUCING A MEASUREMENT PROGRAM

Management of any production process is simplified if some measures of progress toward a quality product are collected and analyzed. In manufacturing, tolerance limits are prescribed and individual components assessed against these "standards." Excessive product rejections suggest that the process producing them is at fault. Costs are tracked during the process and compared with estimates made initially ("variances").

As noted earlier in the book, software development shares with manufacturing industry the need to measure costs, productivity, and quality. The main difference lies in the "one-off" nature of software. Nevertheless, quality can be evaluated against prespecified criteria, progress toward the goal evaluated on a temporal basis and final costs compared with estimated costs. Specific goals could include the ability (1) to do cost estimation from the requirements analysis; (2) to estimate maintenance costs

TABLE 8.3   Summary data from the brewery control
system of Sharble and Cohen (1993)

| Metric | Data Driven | Responsibility Driven |
| --- | --- | --- |
| WMC | 130 | 71 |
| DIT | 21 | 19 |
| NOC | 19 | 13 |
| CBO | 42 | 20 |
| RFC | 293 | 127 |
| LCOM | 64 | 21 |
| WAC | 64 | 44 |
| NOT | 0 | 0 |
| VOD | 40 | 0 |

from the code; (3) to evaluate the reusability of designs, frameworks, and code; and (4) to allocate resources most wisely. Such aims require collection of data on the process, effort expended (often measured in time resources × people resources), and objective measures of the code itself.

In introducing a measurement program, an initial question is often: "What is to be measured?" A more appropriate question is: "What is the goal which we want to attain?" For example, is the goal to increase programmer productivity, to decrease the number of defects reported per unit of time, to improve the efficiency of the overall development process, or to attain ISO 9000 accreditation? Until that goal is defined, recommendations on the optimum measurement program cannot be made. A widely used framework here is the goal/question/metric (GQM) paradigm (Figure 8.3) of Basili and Rombach (1988). As its name suggests, the first step of

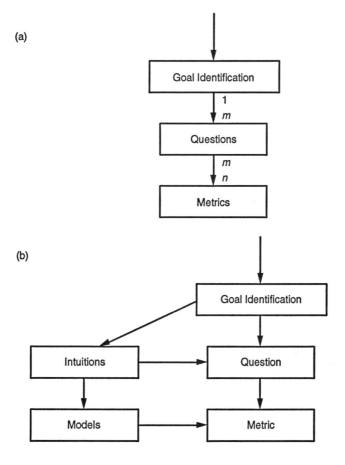

**Figure 8.3**    (a) The basic goal/question/metric paradigm of Basili and Rombach (1988) and (b) its adaptation and extension by Sheppherd (1990).
*Source:* Shepperd, M., 1990, Early life-cycle metrics and software quality modules, *Information and Software Technology,* 32(4), 311–316.

selecting metrics is to identify the goal, G (as has been illustrated). This leads to questions, Q, such as how to increase code quality and decrease enhancement schedules. In turn, these questions help to elucidate the appropriate metrics, M, that need to be be collected. Shepperd (1990) argues that an additional, vital component is the interrelationship with theories and modeling (Figure 8.3(b))—a viewpoint with which we concur. Models permit explicit description of relationships between components and properties of interest within the realm of the stated goal.

GQM evaluates the goals and questions, thus leading to choice of an appropriate metric. The problem with the application of this approach to OO metrics is that the set of metrics available may be empty. Thus, a complementary activity is the one described here, predominantly in Chapters 5 and 6, of identifying simply the M component of GQM *independently* of specific goals and questions (Henderson-Sellers, 1995a). Our major first step is thus identification of a large number of "potentially useful" metrics (Figure 8.4). Then (part b), when a characteristic requiring

### (a) Identify "potentially useful" metrics.

### (b) Identify characteristic requiring evaluation.

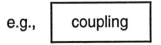

e.g.,   coupling

Note: Characteristic needs to have empirical relation.

### (c) Use GQM to select metric$_n$ from (newly created) set. Also take into consideration needed scale type.

**Figure 8.4**   (a) The "pool" of potentially useful OO metrics that need (b) to identify some characteristic requiring evaluation and (c) only then, can we use the GQM framework to select the most appropriate metric.

quantification that has an empirical relational system (Chapter 4) is identified, the GQM approach can be used (part c) to select the most appropriate metric(s), taking the needed scale type into consideration, as identified in part (a).

A second important context for a measurement program is the identification of the organization's level in the capability maturity model (CMM) scale of the Software Engineering Institute (SEI) (Humphrey, 1989). Table 8.4 illustrates the five identified levels that reflect not only the organization's level of process maturity but also strongly reflects the type and extent to which a metrics program might be implementable, sustainable, and useful. Indeed, the existence of different degrees of sophistication within the metrics program is a factor in determining the current status of an organization on this CMM scale. Consequently, introducing or improving a metrics program can be a significant factor in climbing this "process sophistication ladder."

Calculating the organizational level in the CMM is done by answering a 100+ question questionnaire. The baseline is that of "no order," that is, random, chaotic, or ad hoc management of the software development process. Typically, few, if any, metrics will be used. At level 2, the process is considered repeatable. Experience is held within the heads of developers, and they have learned, often individualistically, what works and what doesn't. Some project-level metrics may be collected, but there is no interchange of that information to other parts of the organization. At level 3, the process is well-defined and institutionalized. The focus is on the product being produced, that is, at the departmental rather than individual level. Once the process is well defined (in other words, some well-delineated OO methodology is being used), it is possible to begin to manage that process and to collect metrics that are not purely descriptive (as in lower levels) but are used as feedback to begin to allow the process to be controlled on a quantitative basis. The top level (level 5) of CMM is known as optimizing: here feedback is allowed to actually change the process, often in the middle of a project so that optimization is possible. This progression may also be likened as one moving from ignorance (level 1), to understanding (level 2), to control (level 3) and hence to improvement (level 4) and to optimization (level 5). A case study at Motorola of how to achieve higher CMM levels is given in Daskalantonakis (1994).

TABLE 8.4    SEI's capability maturity model

| Level | Characteristics | Metrics to Use |
|---|---|---|
| 5. Optimizing | Improvement fed back to process | Process + feedback for changing process |
| 4. Managed | Measured process (quantitative) | Process + feedback for control |
| 3. Defined | Process defined, institutionalized | Product |
| 2. Repeatable | Process dependent on individuals | Product |
| 1. Initial | Ad hoc | Baseline |

*Source:* Pfleeger, S. L., 1991. *Software Engineering. The Production of Quality Software* (2nd ed.), Macmillan Publishing Company, New York.

Most organizations find themselves at level 3 or below. A U.S. survey undertaken by SEI in 1990 found 85% at level 1, 14% at level 2, and only 1% at level 3. A later survey in Singapore showed some significant improvements: 72% at level 1, 10% at level 2, 10% at level 3, 1% at level 4, and 7% at level 5 (Tan and Yap, 1995).

A second capability maturity model, known as the PC–CMM (people management capability maturity model, Curtis *et al.*, 1994) uses the same framework, but applied to the people involved rather than the process (Table 8.5). Again, each level is seen as a springboard for moving to the next level of human resources development. Level 1 is again ad hoc, level 2 focuses on performance management, level 3 concerns team building, level 4 is on quantitative people management, and level 5 focuses on improvement and optimization of human resources.

In another framework approach, Rowe and Whitty (1993) describe the application of metrics to industry (AMI) program which focuses on an interlinking of the actions of assess, analyze, metricate, and improve (Figure 8.5). Here the framework encompasses a 12-step method (AMI Consortium, 1992) that embodies both the GQM paradigm and the five-level capability maturity model. The four activities are themselves distinct but interlinked. The AMI method proposes that you

- *Assess* the project environment to define the goals (for GQM).
- *Analyze* these goals in terms of achievable subgoals.
- *Metricate* in terms of a measurement plan.
- *Improve* by using the measured data to feed back to the process (Debou *et al.*, 1995).

Ince (1990) also notes that metrics can be used as a mechanism for evaluating staff performance. Such a use is fraught with problems since it can be counterproductive. Staff resistance can be high because of the appraisal element, or staff may work to optimize one specific metric (e.g., size) if that metric is, unwisely, being used as the sole adjudicator of their productivity/"worth." In a discussion on the etiquette

TABLE 8.5    Curtis *et al.*'s (1994) people management capability maturity model

| Level | Characteristics | To Raise Level of People Management Capabilities |
|---|---|---|
| 5. Optimizing | People management innovation; people management improvement | |
| 4. Managed | Organizational performance alignment; quantitative people management | Continuously improve methods |
| 3. Defined | Team building; competency development; knowledge and skills analysis; people management planning | Quantitatively manage organizational growth |
| 2. Repeatable | Participatory culture; compensation and reward; performance management | Identify primary competencies and align people management with activities |
| 1. Initial/herded | Ad hoc | Instill basic discipline |

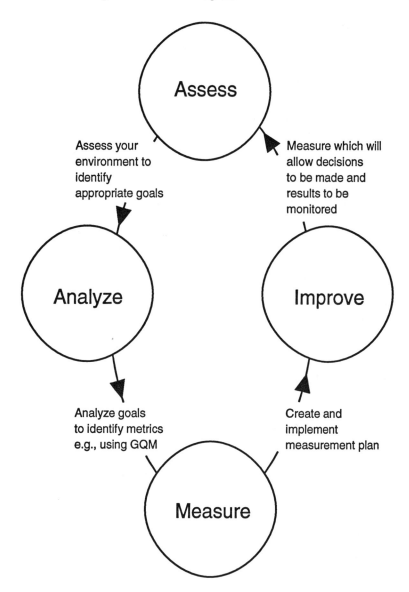

**Figure 8.5**   The AMI framework illustrating the interlinking of assess, analyze, metricate, and improve.
*Source:* A. Rowe and R. Whitty, December 1993,  *Software Quality Journal Vol. 2 No. 4*
Chapman and Hall, London.

of applying software metrics programs, Grady (1993) divides his set of rules (Table 8.6) into three areas: functional management, project management, and the project team. At each level it must be made clear that metrics are to be used to mutual improvement, not to chastise individuals.

TABLE 8.6   Rules of etiquette for applying software metrics (after Grady, 1993)

| | |
|---|---|
| Functional management | 1. Don't allow anyone in your organization to use metrics to measure individuals. |
| | 2. Set clear goals and get your staff to help define metrics for success. |
| | 3. Understand the data that your people take pride in reporting; don't ever use it against them; don't ever even hint that you might. |
| | 4. Don't emphasize one metric to the exclusion of others. |
| | 5. Support your people when their reports are backed by data useful to the organization. |
| Project management | 6. Don't try to measure individuals. |
| | 7. Gain agreement with your team on the metrics that you will track and define them in a project plan. |
| | 8. Provide regular feedback to the team about the data it helped collect. |
| | 9. Know the strategic focus of your organization and emphasize metrics that support the strategy in your reports. |
| Project team | 10. Do your best to report accurate, timely data. |
| | 11. Help your managers to focus project data on improving your processes. |
| | 12. Don't use metrics to brag about how good you are or you will encourage others to use other data to show the opposite. |

*Source:* Grady, R. B., 1993, Software metrics etiquette, Cutter Information Corp., publishers of American Programmer, 6(2), 6–15.

Another use that is often overlooked is the objective assessment of various competing methodologies, techniques, organizational structures, or work patterns,[2] although, as Ince (1990) notes, there is little practical experience with this mode of application of metrics, and Fenton *et al.* (1994) underline the difficulties and realities of research in these areas.

In a study at Contel, Pfleeger (1993) describes the introduction of a metrics program to that organization. She links the appropriateness of the metrics to the SEI maturity level (Table 8.4). She identifies several common themes that contributed to the project's success in Contel and that should be equally important in an object-oriented environment:

- Begin by focusing on the process.
- Keep the metrics close to the developers.
- Focus initially on those who need help—they will then "spread the good word."
- Automate data collection as far as possible.
- Keep things simple to understand.
- Capture whatever information is possible but without burdening developers.
- Don't force the developers to implement a metrics program against their will.
- Some metrics is better than using no metrics.
- Tailor the metrics used to the individuals responsible.
- Criticize the process and the product, but *not* the people.

[2]Or indeed whether the object paradigm is being used at all!

The success of any metrics program requires total commitment and understanding of what can and cannot be achieved and in what time frame. Fenton (1991, quoting Rubin) suggests that success is considered to have been achieved when

- Measurement program results are actively used in decision making.
- They are communicated and accepted outside of information technology (IT) department.
- The program lasts longer than two years.

On the other hand, failure is more likely if

- Management did not clearly define purpose and later saw measures as irrelevant.
- Systems professionals resisted the introduction of a metrics program, perceiving it as a negative commentary on their performance.
- Already burdened project staff were taxed by extensive data collection requirements and cumbersome procedures.
- Program reports failed to generate management action.
- Management withdrew support for the program perceiving it mired in problems and "no-win" situations.

Burgess (1995) suggests that three potential causes for low satisfaction are that measurement is often regarded as an immature (and hence untrustworthy) discipline, that measurement programs are often incorrectly implemented, and that the data collected are often used for other (ignoble) purposes, as highlighted earlier. Lynch (1995), in a study of the Sydney Area Health Service, stresses the necessary objective nature of the data to be collected and the need to negotiate the details of the program before its instigation. He also urges that metrics be linked to business needs and must be useful (i.e., both timely and sensitive) as well as economical to gather.

## 8.3 CHAPTER SUMMARY

Industrial data are beginning to show the real benefits of the use of object-oriented metrics. However, data are really case studies and do not as yet provide global or external validity (Section 2.6.1). Introducing an OO metrics program faces the same problems as introducing a traditional program: the threat feared by individuals, the potential cost of data collection, and the incomprehension of "what this sea of figures means." A more structured approach, such as the goal/question/metric paradigm, is appropriate. The level of likely attainment of the success of the program can be closely linked with the CMM level.

The simplest exhortation is to (1) establish a baseline for the organization; (2) instigate a metrics program *now,* but keeping it simple and minimizing the effort of data collection (say, less than 1 hour a week or, if possible, automatically); (3) analyze data frequently and accurately (avoid the shotgun approach described by Courtney and Gustafson, 1993) and give immediate feedback (beautifully analyzed data 12 months old are virtually useless); and (4) develop an organizational-specific set of key measures, keeping business objectives in mind. A successful metrics program requires commitment from all those involved (project level and senior management level), it is more beneficial if a methodical process exists (i.e., above SEI CMM level 1) and is enhanced if someone on the staff has a reasonable understanding of descriptive statistics—similar requirements for introducing total quality management (TQM) into an organization. Measurements imply facts that lead to decisions that in turn lead to actions. Those actions are to improve the quality of the process and the final (software) product.

## 8.4 BIBLIOGRAPHIC DETAILS

The evaluation of the MIT metrics is best documented in Chidamber and Kemerer (1994). The study by Sharble and Cohen (1993) is also highly illuminating. The data presented by Lorenz and Kidd (1994) are interesting if inconclusive. Some of the best insights for introducing a measurement program come from the very detailed case study at Contel (Pfleeger, 1993).

## 8.5 FINAL SUMMARY

Project management of an object-oriented systems development requires both a new managerial outlook and perception as well as new tools to assist in decision support. Object-oriented metrics are still in their infancy, and the proposals here have yet, in general, to be validated in the global sense. Consideration needs also to be given to the life-cycle phase to which any chosen metric is applicable. Metrics are needed for the static dimensions of (1) analysis, (2) design, (3) code, and (4) maintenance as well as for effort calculations across the life-cycle phases, remembering that the effort peak using object technology is shifted to earlier in the life cycle. Metrics should be theoretically well grounded as well as be subject to extensive empirical evaluation.

Metrics may be collected for a number of reasons: for cost estimation, for project management, for quality assessment, for productivity calculations, for program comprehensibility, for defect detection, and for program maintenance, for instance. While it is possible to guess which of the metrics discussed here are likely to be more useful, empirical work is lacking.

Metrics (and organizational rewards) must reflect the varying roles (Section 1.2), especially between the O/C users and the O/C producers.

In addition, it will be necessary to develop such metrics to permit evaluation of maintenance cost savings that are likely to be realized in an object-oriented software development environment. Planning time scales also have to be reconsidered since the full benefits of adopting the object-oriented philosophy will be realized in the longer, not the shorter, term.

Figure 5.1 detailed the variety of structural complexity metrics. At present, collection of data for each of these categories is needed so that (1) managers can build up a database to support their own, local metrics programs and (2) a database can be built up to assist researchers in developing a theoretically sound and more widely applicable metrics set.

Currently, a metrics program should probably include in its data collection at least the following:

- Fan-out (coupling)
- Average[3] (and standard deviation) of number of methods per class
- Average (and standard deviation) of method size
- Average (and standard deviation) of complexity of methods (e.g., using cyclomatic complexity)
- Mean and maximum depth of inheritance hierarchies
- Reuse ratio, $U$
- Specialization ratio, $S$
- Time spent in development (effort)
- Time spent on generalization

as well as a qualitative evaluation of the semantic cohesion of each class.

All these metrics will need to be evaluated empirically using case studies before final recommendations can be made. In the interim, however, we trust that the reflection of the state of the art in this book provides information useful for project managers until such well-validated metrics and their supporting tools become commercially available.

---

[3]Or, if on an ordinal scale, modes, and medians, which may, of course, also be useful for measures on a ratio or absolute scale.

# REFERENCES

ADAMOV, R. and RICHTER, L., 1990, A proposal for measuring the structural complexity of programs, *Journal of Systems and Software,* **12,** 55–70.

ADAMS, S. and BURBECK, S., 1992, Software assets by design, *Object Magazine,* **2(4),** A–C.

ALBRECHT, A. J., 1979, Measuring application development productivity, *Proc. Joint SHARE/GUIDE/IBM Application Development Symposium,* October, 34–43.

ALBRECHT, A. and GAFFNEY, J., 1983, Software function, source lines of code, and development effort prediction: a software science validation, *IEEE Trans. Software Eng.,* **9(6),** 639–648.

AMBLER, S. W., 1994, In search of a generic SDLC for object systems, *Object Magazine,* **4(6),** 76–78.

AMI CONSORTIUM, 1992, *The AMI Handbook,* South Bank University, London, ISBN 0 9522262 0 0.

ARMSTRONG, J. M. and MITCHELL, R. J., 1994, Uses and abuses of inheritance, *Software Eng. J.,* January 1994, 19–26.

ARTHUR, L. J., 1985, *Measuring Programmer Productivity and Software Quality,* John Wiley, New York, 292 pp.

ATWOOD, M. E. and RAMSEY, H. R., 1978, Cognitive structures in the comprehension and memory of computer programs: an investigation of computer program debugging, Tech. Rep. TR–78–A21, U.S. Army Res. Ins. for the Behavioral and Social Sciences, Alexandria, VA.

BADRE, A., 1982, Designing chunks for sequentially displayed information, in *Directions in Human/Computer Interaction,* eds. A. Badre and B. Shneiderman, Ablex, Norwood, NJ, 179–193.

BAKER, A. L. and ZWEBEN, S. H., 1980, A comparison of measures of control flow complexity, *IEEE Trans. Software Eng.,* **SE–6(6),** 506–512.

BAKER, A. L., BIEMAN, J. M., FENTON, N., GUSTAFSON, D. A., MELTON, A., and WHITTY, R., 1990, A philosophy for software measurement, *J. Systems Software,* **12,** 277–281.

BALDA, D. M. and GUSTAFSON, D. A., 1990, Cost estimation models for the reuse and prototype software development life-cycles, *ACM SIGSOFT Software Engineering Notes,* **15**(3), 42–50.

BASILI, V. R., 1980, Qualitative software complexity models: a summary, in *Tutorial on Models and Methods for Software Management and Engineering,* IEEE Computer Society Press, Los Alamitos, CA.

BASILI, V. R., 1981, Evaluating software development characteristics: assessment of software measures in the Software Engineering Laboratory, *Procs. Sixth Annual Software Engineering Workshop,* SEL–81–013, December, NASA/Goddard Space Flight Center, Greenbelt, MD.

BASILI, V. R. and ROMBACH, H. D., 1988, The TAME project: towards improvement-orientated software environments, *IEEE Trans. Soft. Eng.,* **14**(6), 758–773.

BASILI, V. R. and TURNER, A. J., 1975, Iterative enhancement: a practical technique for software development, *IEEE Trans. Software Eng.,* **1**(4), 390–396.

BASTANI, F. B., 1983, An approach to measuring program complexity, *COMPSAC '83,* IEEE Computer Society Press, Silver Spring, MD, 1–8.

BERARD, E. V., 1992, *Essays on Object-Oriented Software Engineering,* Prentice Hall, Englewood Cliffs, NJ, 392 pp.

BERGE, C., 1985, *Graphs,* 2nd ed., North-Holland, Amsterdam.

BERNS, G. M., 1984: Assessing software maintainability, *Comm. ACM.,* **27**(1), 14–23.

BIELAK, R. and McKIM, J. C., Jr., 1993, The many faces of a class, *J. Obj.-Oriented Pro gramming,* **6**(5), 81–85, 95.

BIEMAN, J. M. and DEBNATH, N. C., 1985, An analysis of software structure using a generalized program graph, *Procs. COMPSAC 85,* Chicago, 9–11 Oct 1985 IEEE, Computer Society Press, Washington DC, 254–259.

BLUM, M., 1967, On the size of machines, *Inform. Contr.,* **11**, 257–265.

BOEHM, B. W., 1981, *Software Engineering Economics,* Prentice Hall, Englewood Cliffs, NJ.

BOEHM, B. W., 1984, Software engineering economics, *IEEE Trans. Soft. Eng.,* **SE–10**, 4–21.

BOEHM, B. W., 1986, A spiral model of software development and enhancement, *ACM Software Engineering Notes,* **11**(4), 14–24.

BOEHM, B. W., BROWN, J. R., KASPAR, H., LIPOW, M., MACLEOD, G. J., and MERRITT, M. J., 1978, *Characteristics of Software Quality,* North-Holland, Amsterdam.

BOLLINGER, T. B. and PFLEEGER, S. L., 1990, Economics of reuse: issues and alternatives, *Inf. Software Technol.,* **32**, 643–652.

BOLLOBÁS, B., 1979, *Graph Theory. An Introductory Course,* Springer-Verlag, New York, 180 pp.

BOOCH, G., 1991, *Object Oriented Design with Applications,* Benjamin/Cummings, Menlo Park, CA, 580 pp.

BOOCH, G., 1994, *Object Oriented Analysis and Design with Applications* (2nd ed.), Benjamin/Cummings, Menlo Park, CA, 589 pp.

BOOCH, G., 1996, *Object Solutions: Managing the Object-Oriented Project,* Benjamin/ Cummings, Menlo Park, CA.

BORGIDA, A., MYLOPOULOS, J., and WONG, H. K. T., 1984, Generalization/specialization as a basis for software specification, in *On Conceptual Modelling: Perspectives from Artificial*

*Intelligence, Databases, and Programming Languages,* eds. M. L. Brodie, J. Mylopoulos, and J. W. Schmidt, Springer-Verlag, New York, 87–114.

BOURQUE, P. and CÔTÉ, V., 1991, An experiment in software sizing with structured analysis metrics, *J. Syst. Software,* 15(2), 159–172.

BOWEN, T. P., WIRGLE, G. B., and TSAI, J., 1984, *Specification of Software Quality Attributes,* Vols. I, II, and III (RADC–TR–85–37), prepared for Boeing RADC, Griffis Air Force Base, NY; reproduced by NTIS, Springfield, VA.

BRITO E ABREU, F., 1994, MOOD—Metrics for object-oriented design, paper presented at OOPSLA '94 Workshop on Pragmatic and Theoretical Directions in Object-Oriented Software Metrics, Portland, OR, October 1994 (unpublished).

BROOKS, F. P., JR., 1975, *The Mythical Man-Month,* Addison-Wesley, Reading, MA.

BUNGE, M., 1977, *Treatise on Basic Philosophy: Ontology I: The Furniture of the World,* Reidel, Boston.

BURGESS, A., 1995, Mad about or mad at measurement? *IEEE Software,* January, 115–116.

BUSH, M. E. and FENTON, N. E., 1990, Software measurement: a conceptual framework, *J. Systems and Software,* 12, 223–231.

CAMPANAI, M. and NESI, P., 1994, Supporting an object-oriented design with metrics, in *TOOLS13,* ed. B. Magnusson, B. Meyer, J.-M. Nerson, and J.-F. Perrot, Prentice Hall, Hemel Hempstead, UK, 227–241.

CANT, S. N., 1991, The cognitive complexity of programs developed using the object-oriented paradigm, Honours Thesis, School of Information Systems, University of New South Wales, Sydney, Australia.

CANT, S., JEFFERY, D. R., and HENDERSON-SELLERS, B., 1992, A conceptual model of cognitive complexity of elements of the programming process, Centre for Information Technology Research Report No. 57, University of New South Wales, Sydney, Australia.

CANT, S. N., HENDERSON-SELLERS, B., and JEFFERY, D. R., 1994, Application of cognitive complexity metrics to object-oriented programs, *J. Obj.-Oriented Programming,* 7(4), 52–63.

CANT, S., JEFFERY, D. R., and HENDERSON-SELLERS, B., 1995, A conceptual model of cognitive complexity of elements of the programming process, *Inf. Software Technol.* 37(7), 351–362.

CARD, D. N., 1991, What makes a software measure successful? *Amer. Programmer,* 4(9), 2–8.

CARD, D. N. and AGRESTI, W. W., 1987, Resolving the Software Science anomaly, *J. Syst. Software,* 7(1), 29–35.

CARD, D. N. and GLASS, R. L., 1990, *Measuring Software Design Quality,* Prentice Hall, Englewood Cliffs, NJ.

CHAN, M. L. and HENDERSON-SELLERS, B., 1990, Corporate object-oriented development environment (CODE), *ACM SIGSOFT. Software Engineering Notes,* 15(1), 42–43.

CHEN, E. T., 1978, Program complexity and programmer productivity, *IEEE Trans. Software Eng.,* SE–4(3), 187–194.

CHEN, J.-Y. and LU, J.-F., 1993, A new metric for object-oriented design, *Inf. Software Technol.,* 35(4), 232–240.

CHERNIAVSKY, J. C. and SMITH, C. H., 1991, On Weyuker's axioms for software complexity measures, *IEEE Trans. Software Eng.,* 17(6), 636–638.

CHIDAMBER, S. and KEMERER, C., 1991, Towards a metric suite for object-oriented design, in *Proc. OOPSLA'91, Sigplan Notices,* 26(11), 197–211.

CHIDAMBER, S. and KEMERER, C., 1993, A metrics suite for object oriented design, Working Paper #249, MIT Center for Information Systems, Cambridge, MA, 40 pp.

CHIDAMBER, S. and KEMERER, C., 1994, A metrics suite for object oriented design, *IEEE Trans. Software Eng.,* **20(6),** 476–493.

CHURCHER, N. I. and SHEPPERD, M. J., 1995, Comments on "A metrics suite for object oriented design," *IEEE Trans. Soft. Eng.,* **21(3),** 263–265.

COAD, P., 1991, OOA & OOD: A continuum representation, *J. Obj.-Oriented Programming,* **3(6),** 55–56.

COAD, P. and YOURDON, E., 1991, *Object-Oriented Design,* Prentice-Hall/Yourdon Press, Englewood Cliffs, NJ.

COLEMAN, D., HAYES, F., and BEAR, S., 1992, Introducing objectcharts or how to use statecharts in object-oriented design, *IEEE Trans. Software Engineering,* **18(1),** 9–18.

CONTE, S. D., DUNSMORE, H. E., and SHEN, V. Y., 1986, *Software Engineering Metrics and Models,* Benjamin/Cummings, Menlo Park, CA.

CÔTÉ, V. and ST-DENIS, R., 1992, Bridging the gap between CASE tools and project management through a decision support system based on metrics, *IEEE Compsac,* 300–309.

CÔTÉ, V., BOURQUE, P., OLIGNY, S., and RIVARD, N., 1988, Software metrics: an overview of recent results, *J. Syst. Software,* **8(2),** 121–131.

COULTER, N. S., 1983, Software science and cognitive psychology, *IEEE Trans. Software Eng.,* **9(2),** 166–171.

COURTNEY, R. E. and GUSTAFSON, D. A., 1993, Shotgun correlations in software measures, *Software Eng. J.,* January 1993, 5–13.

COX, B. J., 1990, Planning the software industrial revolution, *IEEE Software,* **7(11),** 25–33.

COX, B. J., 1992, What if there is a silver bullet? *J. Obj.-Oriented Programming,* **5(3),** 8–9, 76.

CURTIS, B., 1979, In search of software complexity, in *Workshop on Quantitative Software Models,* IEEE, New York, 95–106.

CURTIS, B., 1981, Substantiating programmer variability, *Procs. IEEE,* **69(7),** 846.

CURTIS, B. and CARLETON, A., 1994, Seven ± two software measurement condundrums, in *Procs. Second Int. Software Metrics Symposium,* London, October 24–26, 1994, IEEE Computer Society Press, Los Alamitos, CA, 96–105.

CURTIS, B., HEFLEY, W. E., MILLER, S., KONRAD, M., and BOND, S., 1994, Increasing software talent, *American Programmer,* **7(12),** 13–20.

DAMERLA, S. and SHATZ, S. M., 1992, Software complexity and Ada rendezvous: metrics based on nondeterminism, *Journal of Systems and Software,* **17,** 119–127.

DASKALANTONAKIS, M. K., 1994, Achieving higher SEI levels, *IEEE Software,* **11(4),** 17–24.

DAVIS J. S., 1984: Chunks: a basis for complexity measurement, *Information Processing and Management,* **20(1),** 119–127.

DAVIS, J. S. and LEBLANC, R. J., 1988, A study of the applicability of complexity measures, *IEEE Trans. Software Eng.,* **14(9),** 1366–1371.

DEBOU, C., KUNTZMANN-COMBELLES, A., and ROWE, A., 1994, A quantitative approach to software process management, in *Procs. Second Int. Software Metrics Symposium,* London, October 24–26, 1994, IEEE Computer Society Press, Los Alamitos, CA, 26–34.

DREGER, J. B., 1989, *Function Point Analysis,* Prentice Hall, Englewood Cliffs, NJ.

Dué, R. and Henderson-Sellers, B., 1995, The changing paradigm for object project management, *Object Magazine,* **5(4),** 33–38.

Dunsmore, H. E., 1984, Software metrics: an overview of an evolving methodology, *Information Processing and Management,* **20(1–2),** 183–192.

Dunsmore, H. E. and Gannon, J. D., 1980, Analysis of the effects of programming factors on programming effort, *Journal of Systems and Software,* February **1(2),** 141–153.

Durnota, B. and Mingins, C., 1993, Tree-based coherence metrics in object-oriented design, in *TOOLS12&9,* eds. C. Mingins, B. Haebich, J. Potter, and B. Meyer, Prentice Hall, Sydney, Australia, 489–504.

Dvorak, J., 1994, Conceptual entropy and its effect on class hierarchies, *IEEE Computer,* June 1994, 59–63.

Ehrlich, K. and Soloway, E., 1984, An empirical investigation of the tacit plan knowledge in programming, in *Human Factors in Computer Systems,* eds. J. C. Thomas and M. L. Schneider, Ablex, Norwood, NJ, 113–133.

Ejiogu, L. O., 1987, The critical issues of software metrics, *SIGPLAN Notices,* **22(3),** 59–64.

Ejiogu, L. O., 1991, *Software Engineering with Formal Metrics,* QED Technical Publishing Group, Boston.

Ejiogu, L. O., 1993, Five principles for the formal validation of models of software metrics, *ACM SIGPLAN Notices,* **28(8),** 67–76.

Elshoff, J. L., 1978, An investigation into the effects of the counting method used on software science measurement, *ACM SIGPLAN Notices,* **13(2),** 30–45.

Emerson, T. J., 1984, A discriminant metric for module cohesion, *Int. Conf. Software Eng.,* IEEE Computer Society Press, Washington DC, 294–303.

Emory, C. W. and Cooper, D. R., 1991, *Business Research Methods,* 4th ed., Richard D. Irwin, Homewood, IL.

Evangelist, W., 1983, Software complexity metric sensitivity to program structuring rules, *Journal of Systems and Software,* **3(3),** 231–243.

Evangelist, M., 1984, An analysis of control flow complexity, *COMPSAC '84,* Chicago, Nov 7–9, 1984, IEEE Computer Society Press, Silver Spring, MD, 388–396.

Evangelisti, W. M., 1983, Software complexity metric sensitivity to program structured rules, *J. Systems Software,* **3,** 231–243.

Feghali, I. and Watson, A. H., 1994, Clarification concerning modularization and McCabe's cyclomatic complexity, *Comm. ACM,* **37(4),** 91–92.

Fenton, N. E., 1989, The mathematics of complexity in computing and software engineering, Centre for Software Reliability, City University, Northampton Square, London, May 1989.

Fenton, N. E., 1990, Software metrics: theory, tools, and validation, *IEE Software Engineering Journal,* January, 65–84.

Fenton, N. E., 1991, *Software Metrics: A Rigorous Approach,* Chapman and Hall, London, 337 pp.

Fenton, N. E., 1992, When a software measure is not a measure, *Software Eng. J.,* September, 357–362.

Fenton, N. E., 1994, Software measurement: a necessary scientific basis, *IEEE Transactions on Software Engineering,* **20,** 199–206.

FENTON, N. and KAPOSI, A., 1987, Metrics and software structure, *Information and Software Technology,* **29(6),** 301–320.

FENTON, N. E. and MELTON, A., 1990, Deriving structurally based software measures, *J. Systems and Software,* **12,** 177–187.

FENTON, N. E. and WHITTY, R. W., 1986, Axiomatic approach to software metrication through program decomposition, *Computer J.,* **29(4),** 330–339.

FENTON, N., PFLEEGER, S. L., and GLASS, R. L., 1994, Science and substance: a challenge to software engineers, *IEEE Software,* **11(4),** 86–95.

FIRESMITH, D. G., 1994, Clusters of classes: a bigger building block, *Report on Object Analysis and Design,* **1(4),** 18–21, 25.

FRALEIGH, J. B., 1967, *A First Course in Abstract Algebra,* Addison-Wesley, Reading, MA, 447 pp.

GAFFNEY, J. E., 1979, Program control complexity and productivity, *IEEE Trans. Software Eng.,* **10(4),** 459–464.

GAMMA, E., HELM, R., JOHNSON, R., and VLISSIDES, J., 1995, *Design Patterns: Elements of Reusable Object-Oriented Design,* Addison-Wesley, Reading, MA, 395 pp.

GANNON, J. D., KATZ, E. E., and BASILI, V. R., 1986, Metrics for Ada packages: an initial study, *Comms. ACM,* **29,** 616–623.

GIBBS, S., TSICHRITZIS, D., CASAIS, E., NIERSTRASZ, O., and PINTADO, X., 1990, Class management for software communities, *Comm. ACM,* **33(9),** 90–103.

GILB, T., 1977, *Software Metrics,* Winthrop, Cambridge, MA.

GILL, G. K., and KEMERER, C. F., 1991, Cyclomatic complexity density and software maintenance productivity, *IEEE Trans. Software Eng.,* **17(12),** 1284–1288.

GILMORE, D. J., and GREEN, T. R. G., 1985, The comprehensibility of programming notations, in *Human-Computer Interaction—INTERACT '84,* ed. B. Shackel, IFIP North-Holland, Amsterdam, 461–464.

GOLDBERG, A., 1993, Wishful thinking, *Object Magazine,* **3(1),** 88, 87.

GOLDBERG, A. and RUBIN, K., 1990, Talking to project managers: organizing for reuse, *Hotline on Obj.-Oriented Technol.,* **1(10),** 7–11.

GRADY, R. B., 1992, *Practical Software Metrics for Project Management and Process Improvement,* Prentice-Hall, Englewood Cliffs, NJ.

GRADY, R. B., 1993, Software metrics etiquette, *Amer. Programmer,* **6(2),** 6–15.

GRADY, R. B. and CASWELL, D. L., 1987, *Software Metrics: Establishing a Company-Wide Program,* Prentice-Hall, Englewood Cliffs, NJ.

GRAHAM, I., 1991, *Object-Oriented Methods,* Addison-Wesley, Wokingham, UK, 410 pp.

GRAHAM, I., 1994, *Object-Oriented Methods,* 2nd ed., Addison-Wesley, Wokingham, UK, 473 pp.

GRAHAM, I. M., 1995a, *Migrating to Object Technology,* Addison-Wesley, Wokingham, UK.

GRAHAM, I. M., 1995b, A non-procedural process model for object-oriented software development, *Report on Object Analysis and Design,* **1(5),** 10–11.

GREEN, T. R. G., SIME, M. E., and FITTER, M. J., 1981, The art of notation, in *Computing Skills and the User Interface,* ed. M. J. Coombs and J. L. Alty, Academic Press, London, 221–251.

GRISS, M. L., 1991, Software reuse at Hewlett-Packard, HPL-91-38, Palo Alto, CA, 8 pp.

GRISS, M. L., ADAM, S. S., BAETJER, H., JR., COX, B. J., and GOLDBERG, A., 1991, The economics of software reuse, *Procs. OOPSLA '91,* ACM, New York, NY, 264–270.

GROVER, P. S. and GILL, N. S., 1995, Composite complexity measure (CCM), Chapter 43 in *Software Quality and Productivity. Theory, Practice, Education and Training* eds. M. Lee, B-Z. Barta and P. Juliff, Chapman & Hall, London, 279–283.

HALSTEAD, M. H., 1977, *Elements of Software Science,* Elsevier/North-Holland, New York.

HAMER, P. G. and FREWIN, G. D., 1982, M. H. Halstead's software science—a critical examination, *Procs. IEEE Sixth Int. Conf. on Software Engineering,* Los Alamitos, CA, 197–206.

HANSEN, W. J., 1978, Measurement of program complexity by the pair (cyclomatic number, operator count), *ACM SIGPLAN Notices,* April, ACM, New York, 29–33.

HARARY, F., 1969, *Graph Theory,* Addison-Wesley, Reading, MA, 274 pp.

HARRISON, W., 1992, An entropy-based measure of software complexity, *IEEE Trans. Software Eng.,* **18(11),** 1025–1029.

HARRISON, W. and MAGEL, K., 1981, A topological analysis of computer programs with less than three binary branches, *ACM SIGPLAN Notices,* April, New York, NY, 51–63.

HARRISON, W., MAGEL, K., KLUCZNY, R., and DeKOCK, A., 1982, Applying software complexity metrics to program maintenance, *IEEE Computer,* **15(9),** 65–79.

HAYNES, P. and MENZIES, T., 1994, The effect of class coupling on class size in Smalltalk systems, in *TOOLS15,* eds. C. Mingins and B. Meyer, Prentice Hall, Sydney.

HENDERSON-SELLERS, A., HENDERSON-SELLERS, B., POLLARD, D., VERNER, J., and PITMAN, A. J., Applying software engineering metrics to landsurface parameterization schemes, 1995a, *J. Climate,* **8(5),** 1043–1059.

HENDERSON-SELLERS, B., 1991, Some metrics for object-oriented software engineering, *Technology of Object-Oriented Languages and Systems: TOOLS6,* eds. B. Meyer, J. Potter and M. Tokoro, Prentice Hall, Sydney, Australia, 131–139.

HENDERSON-SELLERS, B., 1992a, Object-oriented information systems: an introductory tutorial, *Australian Computer J.,* **24(1),** 12–24.

HENDERSON-SELLERS, B., 1992b, Modularization and McCabe's cyclomatic complexity, *Comm. ACM,* **35(12),** 17–19.

HENDERSON-SELLERS, B., 1993, The economics of reusing library classes, *J. Obj.-Oriented Programming,* **6(4),** 43–50.

HENDERSON-SELLERS, B., 1995a, Identifying internal and external characteristics of classes likely to be useful as structural complexity metrics, *OOIS'94 Proceedings,* eds. D. Patel, Y. Sun, and S. Patel, Springer-Verlag, New York, 227–230.

HENDERSON-SELLERS, B., 1995b, *A BOOK of Object-Oriented Knowledge,* 2nd ed., Prentice Hall, Sydney, Australia.

HENDERSON-SELLERS, B., 1995c, Towards a process metamodel architecture: II Analysis and design issues, *Report on Object Analysis and Design,* **2(4),** 48–51.

HENDERSON-SELLERS, B. and EDWARDS, J. M., 1990, The object-oriented systems life cycle, *Comm. ACM* **33(9),** 142–159.

HENDERSON-SELLERS, B. and EDWARDS, J. M., 1993, The fountain model for object-oriented system development, *Object Mag.,* **3(2),** 71–79.

HENDERSON-SELLERS, B. and EDWARDS, J. M., 1994, *BOOKTWO of Object-Oriented Knowledge: The Working Object,* Prentice Hall, Sydney, Australia.

HENDERSON-SELLERS, B. and McKIM, J. C., Jr., 1994, Contracting: what's in it for the supplier?, in *TOOLS14,* eds. R. Ege, M. Singh, and B. Meyer, Prentice Hall, Englewood Cliffs, NJ, 179–186.

HENDERSON-SELLERS, B. and PANT, Y. R., 1993, When should we generalize classes to make them reusable? *Object Mag.,* **3(4),** 73–75.

HENDERSON-SELLERS, B. and TEGARDEN, D., 1994a, Clarification concerning modularization and McCabe's cyclomatic complexity, *Comm. ACM,* **37(4),** 92–94.

HENDERSON-SELLERS, B. and TEGARDEN, D., 1994b, The theoretical extension of two versions of cyclomatic complexity to multiple entry/exit modules, *Software Quality J.,* **3,** 253–269.

HENDERSON-SELLERS, B., PANT, Y. R., and VERNER, J. M., 1993a, Cyclomatic complexity: theme and variations, *Australian J. Information Syst.,* **1(1),** 24–37.

HENDERSON-SELLERS, B., MOSER, S., SEEHUSEN, S., and WEINELT, B., 1993b, A proposed multidimensional framework for object-oriented metrics, *Measurement—for improved IT management, Procs. First Australian Conf. Software Metrics, ACOSM '93,* ed. J. M. Verner, Australian Software Metrics Association, Sydney, 24–30.

HENDERSON-SELLERS, B., GUIGNE, J.-L., KOLBE, K., and LEBRUN, V., 1994, MOSES CASE tool, Presented at *OOPSLA '94,* (October), Portland, OR (unpublished).

HENDERSON-SELLERS, B., CONSTANTINE, L. L., and GRAHAM, I. M., 1995b, Coupling and cohesion (towards a valid metrics suite for object-oriented analysis and design), submitted for publication.

HENRY, S. and KAFURA, D., 1981, Software structure metrics based on information flow, *IEEE Trans. Software Eng.,* **7(5),** 510–518.

HENRY, S. and LI, W., 1992, Metrics for object-oriented systems, presented at OOPSLA '92 Workshop on Metrics for Object-Oriented Software Development, Washington DC, October 1992 (unpublished).

HOPKINS, T. P., 1991, Do we need object-oriented design metrics? *Hotline on Obj.-Oriented Technol.,* **2(8),** 16–17.

HUMPHREY, W. S., 1989, *Managing the Software Process,* Addison-Wesley, Reading, MA.

HUMPHREY, W. S., 1994, A personal commitment to software quality, *American Programmer,* **7(12),** 2–12.

HUMPHRYS, M., 1991, The objective evidence. A real-life comparison of procedural and object-oriented programming, IISL Innovative Solutions Project, IBM Ireland Information Services Ltd (IISL), internal report.

IEEE, 1983, IEEE Standard 729–1983, *IEEE Standard Glossary of Software Engineering Terminology,* IEEE, New York, 38 pp.

IIVARI, J., 1990, Hierarchical spiral model for information systems and software development. Part 2: design process, *Inf. Software Technol.,* **32(7),** 450–458.

INCE, D., 1990, Software metrics: An introduction, *Inf. Software Technol.,* **32,** 297–303.

IPSEN, D. C., 1960, *Units, Dimensions, and Dimensionless Numbers,* McGraw-Hill, New York.

ISO, 1991, *ISO-9126—Information Technology–Software Evaluation–Quality Characteristics and Guide-Lines for Their Use,* International Standards Organization, Brussels.

IYENGAR, S. S., PARAMESWARAN, N., and FULLER, J., 1982, A measure of logical complexity of programs, *Computing Languages,* **7,** 147–160.

JACOBSON, I., CHRISTERSON, M., JØNSSON, P. and ÖVERGAARD, G., 1992, *Object-Oriented Software Engineering: A Use Case Driven Approach,* Addison-Wesley, Reading, MA, 524 pp.

JACOBSON, I., ERICSSON, M., and JACOBSON, A., 1995, *The Object Advantage. Business Process Reengineering with Object Technology,* Addison-Wesley/ACM, Reading, MA, 347 pp.

JEFFERY, D. R., 1987a, A software development productivity model for MIS environments, *J. Syst. Software,* **7(2),** 115–125.

JOHNSON, R. E. and FOOTE, B., 1988, Designing reusable classes, *J. Object-Oriented Programming,* **1(2),** 22–35.

JONES, C., 1986, *Programming Productivity,* McGraw-Hill, New York.

JONES, C., 1991, *Applied Software Measurement: Assuring Productivity and Quality,* McGraw-Hill, New York.

JONES, T. C., 1988, A short history of function points and feature points, ACI Computer Services, 45 pp.

JUDD, C. M., SMITH, E. R., and KIDDER, L. H., 1991, *Research Methods in Social Relations,* 6th ed., Holt, Rinehart and Winston, Fort Worth, TX, 573 pp.

KANDIBUR, M., 1992, Victory is the main object in war, *Object Magazine,* **2(4),** 28–30.

KEARNEY, J. K., SEDLMEYER, R. L., THOMPSON, W. B., GRAY, M. A., and ADLER, M. A., 1986, Software complexity measurement, *Comm ACM,* **29(11),** 1044–1050.

KERLINGER, F. N., 1964, *Foundations of Behavioral Research,* Holt, Rinehart, and Winston, New York.

KEYES, J., 1992, New metrics needed for new generation: lines of code, function points won't do at the dawn of the graphical, object era, *Software Mag.,* **12(6),** 42–52.

KINTSCH, W., 1977, *Memory and Cognition,* John Wiley, New York.

KITCHENHAM, B., 1993, Using function points for software cost estimation—some empirical results, in *Procs. CSR Conference,* Amsterdam, 16 pp.

KITCHENHAM, B. A. and LINKMAN, S. J., 1990, Design metrics in practice, *Inf. Soft. Technol.,* **32(4),** 304–310.

KITCHENHAM, B. A. and WALKER, J. G., 1986, The meaning of quality, *Procs. Conf. Software Eng. 86,* 393–406.

KLIR, G. J., 1985, *Architecture of Systems Problem Solving,* Plenum Press, New York, 325–353.

KOKOL, P., IVANEK, B., and ZUMER, V., 1988, Software effort metrics: how to join them, *ACM SIGSOFT Software Eng. Notes,* **13(2),** 55–57.

KOLEWE, R., 1993, Metrics in object-oriented design and programming, *Software Development,* October, 53–62.

LAI, S.-T. and YANG, C.-C., 1995, A multi-layer metrics combination model for reusable software components, Chapter 55 in *Software Quality and Productivity. Theory, Practice, Education and Training,* eds. M. Lee, B.-Z. Barta, and P. Juliff, Chapman & Hall, London, 361–366.

LAKSHMANAN, K. B., JAYAPRAKASH, S., and SINHA, P. K., 1991, Properties of control-flow complexity measures, *IEEE Trans. Software Eng.,* **17(12),** 1289–1295.

LALONDE, W. and PUGH, J., 1994, Gathering metric information using metalevel facilities, *J. Obj.-Oriented Programming,* **7(1),** 33–37.

LANGHAAR, H. L., 1951, *Dimensional Analysis and Theory of Models,* John Wiley, New York.

LARANJEIRA, L. A., 1990, Software size estimation of object-oriented systems, *IEEE Trans. Software Eng.,* **16(5),** 510–522.

LEBRUN, V. and GUIGNE, J.-L., 1995, Aaron metrics, COTAR/UTS internal report, 4 pp (unpublished).

LEDGARD, H. and MARCOTTY, M., 1975, A genealogy of control structures, *Commun. ACM,* **18(11),** pp. 629–639.

LEVITIN, A. V., 1986, How to Measure Size, and How Not to, in *Proc. Tenth COMPSAC 1986,* Chicago, Oct 8–10, 1986, IEEE Computer Society Press, Washington DC, 314–318.

LEWIS, J. and HENRY, S., 1989, A methodology for integrating maintainability using software metrics, *Procs. Conf. on Software Maintenance,* Miami, October, 16–19. IEEE, Piscataway, NJ, 32–39.

LEWIS, J. A., HENRY, S. M., KAFURA, D. G., and SCHULMAN, R. S., 1992, On the relationship between the object-oriented paradigm and software reuse: an empirical investigation, *J. Obj.-Oriented Programming,* **5(4),** 35–41.

LI, H. F. and CHEUNG, W. K., 1987, An empirical study of software metrics, *IEEE Trans. Software Eng.,* **SE–13(6),** 697–708.

LI, W. and HENRY, S., 1993, Object-oriented metrics that predict maintainability, *J. Sys. Software,* **23,** 111–122.

LIEBERHERR, K. J., HOLLAND, I. and RIEL, A., 1988, Object-oriented programming: an objective sense of style, *Procs. OOPSLA '88,* ACM Press, New York, NY, 323–334.

LISTER, A. M., 1982, Software Science—the emperor's new clothes? *Australian Computer J.,* **14(2),** 66–70.

LORENZ, M., 1993, *Object-Oriented Software Development: A Practical Guide,* Prentice Hall, NJ, 227 pp.

LORENZ, M. and KIDD, J., 1994, *Object-Oriented Software Metrics,* Prentice Hall, NJ, 200 pp.

LOW, G., HENDERSON-SELLERS, B., and HAN, D., 1995, Comparison of object-oriented and traditional systems development issues in distributed environments, *Inf. Management,* **28,** 327–340.

LYNCH, T., 1995, Measuring the value and performance of your IT department, Chapter 27 in *Software Quality and Productivity. Theory, Practice, Education and Training,* eds. M. Lee, B.-Z. Barta, and P. Juliff, Chapman & Hall, London, 183–186.

MCCABE, T. J., 1976, A complexity measure, *IEEE Trans. Software Eng.,* **2(4),** 308–320.

MCCABE, T. J., 1993, OO Tool Features New Metrics, The Outlook, Fall, 1993, McCabe and Associates, 5501 Twin Knolls Road, Columbia, MD.

MCCABE, T. J. and BUTLER, C. W., 1989, Design complexity measurement and testing, *Comm. ACM,* **32(12),** 1415–1425.

MCCALL, J. A., RICHARDS, P. G., and WALTERS, G. F., 1977, *Factors in Software Quality,* Vols. I, II, and III (NTIS AD/A–049 014/015/055), NTIS, Springfield, VA.

MCCLURE, C. L., 1978, A model for program complexity analysis, *3rd Int. Conf. Software Eng.,* Atlanta, May, IEEE Computer Society Press, Washington DC, 149–157.

MCCOLL, R. B. and MCKIM, J. C., JR., 1992, Evaluating and extending NPath as a software complexity measure, *J. Systems Software,* **17,** 275–279.

MCGREGOR, J. D. and SYKES, D. A., 1992, *Object-Oriented Software Development. Engineering Software for Reuse,* Van Nostrand Reinhold, New York, 352 pp.

MACRO, A. and BUXTON, J., 1987, *The Craft of Software Engineering,* Addison-Wesley, Reading, MA.

MAGEL, K., 1981, Regular expressions in a program complexity metric, *ACM SIGPLAN Not.,* **16(7),** 61–65.

MASOTTI, G., 1991, EC++: extended C++, *J. Object-Oriented Programming,* **4(5),** 10–20.

MAYER, R. E., 1979, A psychology of learning BASIC, *Comm. ACM,* **22(11),** 589–593.

MEHRENS, W. A. and LEHMANN, I. J., 1978, *Measurement and Evaluation in Education and Psychology,* 2nd ed., Holt, Rinehart, and Winston, New York.

MELTON, A. V., GUSTAFSON, D. A., BIEMAN, J. M., and BAKER, A. L., 1990, A mathematical perspective for software measures research, *IEE Software Eng. J.,* September, 246–254.

MENZIES, T., EDWARDS, J. M., and NG, K., 1992, The case of the mysterious missing reusable libraries, in *Technology of Object-Oriented Languages and Systems: TOOLS12&9,* eds. C. Mingins, B. Haebich, J. Potter, and B. Meyer, Prentice Hall, Sydney, Australia, 421–427.

MEYER, B., 1988, *Object-Oriented Software Construction,* Prentice Hall, Hemel Hempstead, UK, 534 pp.

MEYER, B., 1989, The new culture of software development: reflections on the practice of object-oriented design, *Procs. TOOLS '89,* Paris, November 13–15, ISE, Santa Barbara and Paris, 13–23.

MEYER, B., 1990, Tools for the new culture: lessons from the design of the Eiffel libraries, *Comms. ACM,* **33(9),** 68–88.

MEYER, B., 1992a, Design by contract, pp, 1–50 in *Advances in Object-Oriented Software Engineering,* eds. D. Mandrioli and B. Meyer, Prentice Hall, Englewood Cliffs, NJ.

MEYER, B., 1992b, Applying "design by contract," *IEEE Computer,* **25(10),** 40–51.

MEYER, B., 1992c, Public communication, presentation at the Object-Oriented Special Interest Group of the Australian Computer Society (NSW Branch), October 14, Sydney, Australia.

MEYER, B., 1992d, Software engineering: reflections on a scientific discipline and its educational requirements, seminar presented at University of Technology, October 12, Sydney, Australia.

MEYER, B., 1992e, Object-oriented technology: a management perspective, Tutorial Notes, TOOLS9, December 2, Sydney, Australia.

MEYER, B., 1995, *Object Success: A Manager's Guide to Object Orientation, Its Impact on the Corporation and Its Use for Reengineering the Software Process,* Prentice Hall, Hemel Hempstead, UK.

MILLER, G., 1956, The magical number seven, plus or minus two: some limits on our capacity for processing information, *The Psychological Review,* **63(2),** 81–97.

MILLER, J., DARROCH, G., WOOD, M., BROOKS, A., and ROPER, M., 1995, Changing programming paradigm—an empirical investigation, Chapter 8 in *Software Quality and Productivity. Theory, Practice, Education and Training,* eds. M. Lee, B.-Z. Barta, and P. Juliff, Chapman & Hall, London, 62–65.

MINGINS, C., DURNOTA, B., and SMITH, G., 1993, Collection and analysis of software metrics from the Eiffel class hierarchy, in *TOOLS11* eds. R. Ege, M. Singh, and B. Meyer, Prentice-Hall, Englewood Cliffs, NJ, 427–435.

MOHANTY, S. N., 1979, Models and measurements for quality assessment of software, *Computing Surveys,* **11(3),** 251–275.

MOHER, T. C., 1985, Estimating the distribution of software complexity *within* a program, in *Proc. CHI '85: Human Factors in Computing,* eds. B. Curtis and L. Borman, ACM, New York, 61–64.

MORI, R., 1989, What lies ahead, *Byte*, **14(1)**, 346–348.

MORI, R. and KAWAHARA, M., 1990, Superdistribution: the concept and the architecture, *Trans. IEICE*, **E–73(7)**.

MUNSON, J. and KHOSHGOFTAAR, T., 1989, The dimensionality of program complexity, *Proc. 11th Ann. Int. Conf. Software Engineering*, Pittsburgh, IEEE Computer Society Press, Washington DC, 245–253.

MUNSON, J. C. and KHOSHGOFTAAR, T. M., 1990, Applications of a relative complexity metric for software project management, *J. Systems and Software*, **12**, 283–291.

MUNSON, J. C. and KHOSHGOFTAAR, T. M., 1993, Measurement of data structure complexity, *J. Systems and Software*, **20**, 217–225.

MYERS, G. J., 1977, An extension to the cyclomatic measure of program complexity, *SIGPLAN Notices*, October 1977, 61–64.

MYERS, G. J., 1978, *Composite Structured Design*, Van Nostrand Reinhold, Wokingham, UK.

NAURENS, L., 1985, *Abstract Measurement Theory*, MIT Press, Cambridge, MA.

NEJMEH, B. A., 1988, NPATH: a measure of execution path complexity and it applications, *Comm. ACM*, **31(2)**, 188–200.

NERSON, J.-M., 1992, O-O development of a date and time management cluster, *J. Obj.-Oriented Programming*, **5(1)**, 39–46.

OVIEDO, E. I., 1980, Control flow, data flow and program complexity, *Proc. COMPSAC 80*, Chicago, Nov. 1980, IEEE Computer Society Press, Washington DC, 146–152.

PAGE-JONES, M., 1992, Comparing techniques by means of encapsulation and connascence, *Comm. ACM*, **35(10)**, 147–151.

PANT, Y. R., 1993, Generalization of object-oriented components for software reuse, M. eng. thesis, University of New South Wales, Sydney, Australia, 153 pp.

PANT, Y. R., VERNER, J. M., and HENDERSON-SELLERS, B., 1995a, S/C: a software size/complexity measure, Chapter 50 in *Software Quality and Productivity. Theory, Practice, Education and Training*, eds. M. Lee, B.-Z. Barta, and P. Juliff, Chapman & Hall, London, 320–327.

PANT, Y. R., HENDERSON-SELLERS, B., and VERNER, J. M., 1995b, Generalization of object-oriented components for reuse: measurements of effort and size change, *J. Obj.-Oriented Programming* (in press).

PFLEEGER, S. L., 1991, *Software Engineering. The Production of Quality Software*, 2nd ed., Macmillan, New York, 517 pp.

PFLEEGER, S. L., 1993, Lessons learned in building a corporate metrics program, *IEEE Software*, **10(3)**, 67–74.

PIWOWARSKI, P., 1982, A nesting level complexity measure, *SIGPLAN Notices*, **17(9)**, 44–50.

PRATAP, S., 1992, Objects and reuse, *Hotline on Obj.-Oriented Technol.*, **3(12)**, 16–18.

PRATHER, R. E., 1984, An axiomatic theory of software complexity measure, *Computer J.*, **27(4)**, 340–347.

PREE, W., 1995, *Design Patterns for Object-Oriented Software Development*, Addison-Wesley, Reading, MA.

PUTNAM, L. H., 1978, A general empirical solution to the macro software sizing and estimation problem, *IEEE Trans. Software Eng.*, **SE–4(4)**, 345–361.

RAJARAMAN, C. and LYU, M. R., 1992a, Some coupling measures for C++ programs, in *Procs. TOOLS USA '92*, Prentice Hall, Englewood Cliffs, NJ, 225–234.

RAJARAMAN, C. and LYU, M. R., 1992b, Reliability and maintainability related software coupling metrics in C++ programs, *IEEE,* 303–311.

RAMAMURTHY, B. and MELTON, A., 1988, A synthesis of software science measures and the cyclomatic number, *IEEE Trans. Soft. Eng.,* **14(8)**, 1116–1121.

RATIONAL, 1991, The C++ Booch Components Version 1.4—Quick Reference, Santa Clara, CA.

REYNOLDS, G., 1978, Two statistical heresies, *Weather,* **33(2)**, 74–76.

ROBERTS, F. S., 1979, *Measurement Theory with Applications to Decision Making, Utility, and the Social Sciences,* Addison-Wesley, Reading, MA.

ROBILLARD, R. N. and BOLOIX, G., 1989, The interconnectivity metrics, *J. Systems and Software,* **10,** 29–39.

ROMBACH, H. D., 1987, A controlled experiment on the impact of software structure on maintainability, *IEEE Trans. Software Eng.,* **13(3)**, 344–354.

ROMBACH, H. D., 1990, Design measurement: some lessons learned, *IEEE Software,* **7(3)**, 17–25.

ROWE, A. and WHITTY, R., 1993, Ami: promoting a quantitative approach to software management, *Software Quality J.,* **2,** 291–296.

RUBIN, H., 1993, Debunking metric myths, *Amer. Programmer,* **6(2)**, 24–31.

RUMBAUGH, J., 1992, An object or not an object?, *J. Obj.-Oriented Programming,* **5(3)**, 20–25.

RUMBAUGH, J., BLAHA, M., PREMERLANI, W., EDDY, F., and LORENSEN, W., 1991, *Object-oriented Modelling and Design,* Prentice Hall, Englewood Cliffs, NJ, 500 pp.

SAGRI, M., 1989, Rated and operational complexity of program—an extension to McCabe's theory of complexity measure, *ACM SIGPLAN Notices,* **24(8)**, 8–12.

SAKKINEN, M., 1989, Disciplined inheritance, *ECOOP '89: Proc. European Conf. Object-Oriented Programming,* British Computer Society Workshop Series, Cambridge University Press, Cambridge, UK, 39–56.

SCHNEIDEWIND, N. F., 1992, Methodology for validating software metrics, *IEEE Trans. Software Eng.,* **18(5)**, 410–422.

SELIC, B., GULLEKSON, G., MCGEE, J., and ENGELBERG, I., 1992, ROOM: An object-oriented methodology for developing real-time systems, in *CASE'92 Fifth Int. Workshop on Computer-Aided Software Eng.,* Montreal, Quebec.

SEVEL, V., 1994, Metric: C$^3$ and OOMT, unpublished internal COTAR/UTS report, 118 pp.

SEVEL, V. and HENDERSON-SELLERS, B., 1995, The C$^3$ metric and some empirical results, paper in preparation.

SHANNON, C. E. and WEAVER, W., 1949, *The Mathematical Theory of Communication,* University of Illinois Press, Urbana.

SHARBLE, R. C. and COHEN, S. S., 1993, The object-oriented brewery: a comparison of two object-oriented development methods, *ACM SIGSOFT Software Engineering Notes,* **18(2)**, 60–73.

SHEETZ, S. D., TEGARDEN, D. P., and MONARCHI, D. E., 1991, Measuring object-oriented system complexity, in *Proceedings of the First Workshop on Information Technologies and Systems,* 14–15 December, MIT Sloan School of Management, Cambridge, MA.

SHEN, V. Y., CONTE, S. D., and DUNSMORE, H. E., 1983, Software science revisited: a critical analysis of the theory and its empirical support, *IEEE Trans. Software Eng,* **9(2)**, 155–165.

SHEPPERD, M., 1988, A critique of cyclomatic complexity as a software metric, *Software Eng. J.,* **3**, 30–36.

SHEPPERD, M., 1990, Early life-cycle metrics and software quality modules, *Inf. Software Technol.,* **32**(4), 311–316.

SHEPPERD, M., 1992, Products, processes and metrics, *Inf. Software Technol.,* **34**(10), 674–680.

SHNEIDERMAN, B. and MAYER, R., 1979, Syntactic/semantic interactions in programmer behavior: a model and experimental results, *Int. J. Computer and Information Sciences,* **8**(3), 219–238.

SMART, P. F., WOODFIELD, S. N., EMBLEY, D. W., and SCOTT, D. T., 1988, An empirical investigation of the effect of education and tools on software reusability, in *Procs. Seventh Annual Int. Phoenix Conf. on Computers and Communications,* March 1988 IEEE Comp. Soc. Press, Washington, DC, 224–228.

SMITH, M. L. and GLASS, G. V., 1987, *Research and Evaluation in Education and the Social Sciences,* Prentice Hall, Englewood Cliffs, NJ.

SOLOWAY, E. and EHRLICH, K., 1984, Empirical studies of programming knowledge, *IEEE Trans. Software Eng.,* **10**(5), 595–609.

SOLOWAY, E., EHRLICH, K., and BLACK, J. B., 1983, Beyond numbers: don't ask "How Many" . . . ask "Why," in *Human Factors in Computing: Proc. of CHI '83 Conf.,* ed. A. Janda, Dec. 12–15, Boston, ACM, New York, 240–246.

STARK, G. and DURST, R. C., 1994, Using metrics in management decision making, *IEEE Computer,* **27**(9), 42–48.

STATHIS, J. and JEFFERY, D. R., 1993, An empirical study of Albrecht function points, in *Measurement—for improved IT management, Procs. First Australian Conference on Software Metrics, ACOSM '93,* ed. J. M. Verner, Australian Software Metrics Association, Sydney, 96–117.

STEVENS, W. P., MYERS, G. J., and CONSTANTINE, L. L., 1974, Structured design, *IBM Syst. J.,* **13**(2), 115–139.

STROUSTRUP, B., 1986, *The C++ Programming Language,* Addison-Wesley, Reading, MA, 328 pp.

STROUSTRUP, B., 1988, What is object-oriented programming? *IEEE Software,* May, 1–19.

SULLIVAN, J. E., 1975, Measuring the complexity of computer software, Mitre Corporation, P.O. Box 208, Bedford, MA 01730.

SUTCLIFFE, A., 1989, *Human-Computer Interface Design,* Springer-Verlag, New York.

SYMONS, C. R., 1988, Function point analysis: difficulties and improvements, *IEEE Trans. Software Eng.,* **SE–14**(1), 2–11.

SZENTES, J. and GRAS, J., 1986, Some practical views of software complexity metrics and a universal measurement tool, First Australian Software Engineering Conference (ASWEC), Canberra, May, 14–16.

TAN, M. and YAP, C. Y., 1995, Impact of organizational maturity on software quality, Chapter 36 in *Software Quality and Productivity. Theory, Practice, Education and Training,* eds. M. Lee, B.-Z. Barta, and P. Juliff, Chapman & Hall, London, 231–234.

TANIK, M. M., 1980, A comparison of program complexity prediction models, *ACM SIGSOFT, Software Engineering Notes,* **5**(4), 10–16.

TAYLOR, D., 1995, *Business Engineering with Object Technology,* J. Wiley, New York, 188 pp.

TEGARDEN, D. P. and SHEETZ, S. D., 1992, Object-oriented system complexity: an integrated model of structure and perceptions, presented at OOPSLA '92 Workshop on Metrics for Object-Oriented Software Development, Washington DC (unpublished).

TEGARDEN, D. P., SHEETZ, S. D., and MONARCHI, D. E., 1992, Effectiveness of traditional software metrics for object-oriented systems, HICSS-92, IEEE, San Diego, 359–368.

TEGARDEN, D. P., SHEETZ, S. D., and MONARCHI, D. E., 1995, A software complexity model of object-oriented systems, *Decision Support Systems* **13**, 241–262.

THOMAS, D., 1989, In search of an object-oriented development process, *J. Obj.-Oriented Programming,* **2(1)**, 60–63.

THOMAS, D. and JACOBSON, I., 1989, Managing object-oriented software engineering, tutorial presented at TOOLS '89, Paris, November.

THOMSETT, R., 1990, Management implications of object-oriented development, *ACS Newsletter,* October, 5–7, 10–12.

THOMSON, N., JOHNSON, R., MACLEOD, R., MILLER, G., and HANSEN, T., 1994, Project estimation using an adaptation of function points and use cases for OO projects, position paper submitted to OOPSLA 94 Workshop on metrics, Portland, OR (unpublished).

TIAN, J. and ZELKOWITZ, M. V., 1992, A formal program complexity model and its application, *J. Systems and Software,* **17,** 253–266.

TRACZ, W. J., 1979, Computer programming and the human thought process, *Software—Practice and Experience,* **9,** 127–137.

TROY, D. A. and ZWEBEN, S. H., 1981, Measuring the quality of structured designs, *J. Systems and Software,* **2,** 113–120.

TSAI, W. T., LOPEX, M. A., RODRIGUEZ, V., and VOLOVIK, D., 1986, An approach measuring data structure complexity, *COMPSAC 86,* Chicago, 8–10 October 1986, IEEE Computer Society Press, Washington DC, 240–246.

VERNER, J. M., 1991, Software Size Metrics: A Review, Technical Report No. 52, University of New South Wales, Kensington, Australia.

VERNER, J. M., 1993, The acid test: using measurement to improve the quality of the testing process, *Amer. Programmer,* **6(2),** 36–42.

VERNER, J. and TATE, G., 1988, Estimating size and effort in fourth-generation development, *IEEE Software,* **5,** 15–22.

VERNER, J. M. and TATE, G., 1992, A software size model, *IEEE Trans. Soft. Eng.,* **18(4),** 265–278.

WEGNER, P., 1990, Concepts and paradigms of object-oriented programming, *OOPS Messenger,* **1(1),** 7–87.

WEISER, M., 1981, Program slicing, *Proc. 5th Int. Conf. S. E.,* 439–449.

WELLER, E. F., 1994, Using metrics to manage software projects, *IEEE Computer,* **27(9),** 27–33.

WEYUKER, E. J., 1988, Evaluating software complexity measures, *IEEE Trans. Software Eng.,* **14(9),** 1357–1365.

WILD, F. H., III, 1991, Managing class coupling: apply the principles of structured design to object-oriented programming, *UNIX Review,* **9(10),** 44–47.

WILDE, N. and HUITT, R., 1992, Issues in the maintenance of object oriented programs, presented at Workshop on Object-Oriented Software Engineering Practice, Denver, February.

WILLIAMS, L. G., 1988, A behavioral approach to software process modeling, *Procs. 4th Int. Software Process Workshop,* ed. C. Tully, *ACM SIGSOFT Software Eng. Notes,* **14(4),** 167–170.

WINBLAD, A. L., EDWARDS, S. D., and KING, D. R., 1990, *Object-Oriented Software,* Addison-Wesley, Reading, MA, 291 pp.

WIRFS-BROCK, R. J. and JOHNSON, R. E., 1990, A survey of current research in object-oriented design, *Comm. ACM,* **33(9),** 104–124.

WIRFS-BROCK, A., and WILKERSON, B., 1989, Variables limit reusability, *J. Obj.-Oriented Programming,* **2(1),** 34–40.

WIRFS-BROCK, R. J., WILKERSON, B., and WIENER, L., 1990, *Designing Object-Oriented Software,* Prentice Hall, Englewood Cliffs, NJ, 368 pp.

WOODFIELD, S. N. 1980, Enhanced effort estimation by extending basic programming models to include modularity effects, Ph.D. thesis, Department Computer Science, Purdue University.

WOODFIELD, S. N., DUNSMORE, H. E., and SHEN, V. Y., 1981a, The effect of modularization and comments on program comprehension, *Proc. 5th Int. Conf. Software Eng., 1981,* IEEE Computer Society Press, Washington DC, 215–223.

WOODFIELD, S. N., SHEN, V. Y., and DUNSMORE, H. E., 1981b, A study of several metrics for programming effort, *J. Systems and Software,* **2,** 97–103.

WOODWARD, M., HENNELL, M., and HEDLEY, D., 1979, A measure of control flow complexity in program text, *IEEE Trans. Software Eng.,* **5(1),** 45–50.

YAP, L.-M. and HENDERSON-SELLERS, B., 1993, Centre for Information Technology Research Report No. 93/3, University of New South Wales, Sydney, Australia, 109 pp.

YAU, S. S. and COLLOFELLO, J. S., 1980, Some stability measures for software maintenance, *IEEE Trans. Software Eng.,* **6(6),** 545–552.

YOURDON, E. and CONSTANTINE, L. L., 1979, *Structured Design: Fundamentals of a Discipline of Computer Program and Systems Design,* Yourdon Press/Prentice Hall, Englewood Cliffs, NJ, 473 pp.

YU, W. D., SMITH, D. P., and HUANG, S. T., 1991, Software productivity measurements, *Proc. IEEE COMPSAC 1991,* IEEE, Los Alamitos, CA, Kogakuin University, Tokyo, Japan, 11–13 Sept. 1991, pp. 558–564.

ZUSE, H., 1990, *Software Complexity: Measures and Methods,* Walter de Gruyter, Berlin, 605 pp.

ZUSE, H., 1994, Foundations of the validation of object-oriented software measures, in *Theorie und Praxin der Softwaremessung,* eds. R. Dumke, H. Zuse, Deutscher Universitätsverlag, Wiesbaden, Germany, 136–214.

ZUSE, H. and BOLLMANN, P., 1989, Software metrics: using measurement theory to describe the properties and scales of static software complexity metrics, *ACM SIGPLAN Notices,* **24(8),** 23–33.

ZWEBEN, S. H., 1990, On the resolution of the software science anomaly, *J. Syst. Software,* **12(2),** 167–171.

# INDEX